ITALIAN HOURS

ITALIAN HOURS

BY

HENRY JAMES

GROVE PRESS, INC.   NEW YORK
EVERGREEN BOOKS INC.   LONDON

Library of Congress Catalog Card Number: 59-5420

Italian Hours is published in two editions:
An Evergreen Book (E-156)
A cloth bound edition

Distributed in Canada by McClelland & Stewart Ltd.,
25 Hollinger Road, Toronto 16

MANUFACTURED IN THE UNITED STATES OF AMERICA
.

PREFACE

THE chapters of which this volume is composed have with few exceptions already been collected, and were then associated with others commemorative of other impressions of (no very extensive) excursions and wanderings. The notes on various visits to Italy are here for the first time exclusively placed together, and as they largely refer to quite other days than these—the date affixed to each paper sufficiently indicating this—I have introduced a few passages that speak for a later and in some cases a frequently repeated vision of the places and scenes in question. I have not hesitated to amend my text, expressively, wherever it seemed urgently to ask for this, though I have not pretended to add the element of information or the weight of curious and critical insistence to a brief record of light inquiries and conclusions. The fond appeal of the observer concerned is all to aspects and appearances—above all to the interesting face of things as it mainly *used* to be.

H. J.

1909.

CONTENTS

CONTENTS

ITALIAN HOURS

VENICE

IT is a great pleasure to write the word; but I am not sure
there is not a certain impudence in pretending to add
anything to it. Venice has been painted and described
many thousands of times, and of all the cities of the
world is the easiest to visit without going there. Open the
first book and you will find a rhapsody about it; step into
the first picture-dealer's and you will find three or four high-
coloured "views" of it. There is notoriously nothing more
to be said on the subject. Every one has been there, and every
one has brought back a collection of photographs. There is
as little mystery about the Grand Canal as about our local
thoroughfare, and the name of St. Mark is as familiar as the
postman's ring. It is not forbidden, however, to speak of
familiar things, and I hold that for the true Venice-lover Venice
is always in order. There is nothing new to be said about her
certainly, but the old is better than any novelty. It would be a
sad day indeed when there should be something new to say.
I write these lines with the full consciousness of having no
information whatever to offer. I do not pretend to enlighten
the reader; I pretend only to give a fillip to his memory; and
I hold any writer sufficiently justified who is himself in love
with his theme.

A

I

Mr. Ruskin has given it up, that is very true; but only after extracting half a lifetime of pleasure and an immeasurable quantity of fame from it. We all may do the same, after it has served our turn, which it probably will not cease to do for many a year to come. Meantime it is Mr. Ruskin who beyond any one helps us to enjoy. He has indeed lately produced several aids to depression in the shape of certain little humorous —ill-humorous—pamphlets (the series of *St. Mark's Rest*) which embody his latest reflections on the subject of our city and describe the latest atrocities perpetrated there. These latter are numerous and deeply to be deplored; but to admit that they have spoiled Venice would be to admit that Venice may be spoiled—an admission pregnant, as it seems to us, with disloyalty. Fortunately one reacts against the Ruskinian contagion, and one hour of the lagoon is worth a hundred pages of demoralised prose. This queer late-coming prose of Mr. Ruskin (including the revised and condensed issue of the *Stones of Venice*, only one little volume of which has been published, or perhaps ever will be) is all to be read, though much of it appears addressed to children of tender age. It is pitched in the nursery-key, and might be supposed to emanate from an angry governess. It is, however, all suggestive, and much of it is delightfully just. There is an inconceivable want of form in it, though the author has spent his life in laying down the principles of form and scolding people for departing from them; but it throbs and flashes with the love of his subject—a love disconcerted and abjured, but which has still much of the force of inspiration. Among the many strange things that have befallen Venice, she has had the good fortune to become the object of a passion to a man of splendid genius, who has made her his own and in doing so has made her the world's. There is no better reading at Venice therefore, as I say, than Ruskin, for every true Venice-lover can separate the wheat from the chaff. The narrow theological spirit, the moralism *à tout propos*, the queer provincialities and pruderies, are mere wild weeds in a mountain of flowers. One may doubtless be very happy in Venice without reading at all—without criticising or analysing or thinking a strenuous thought. It is a city in which, I suspect, there is very little strenuous thinking, and yet it is a city in which there must be almost as much happiness as misery. The misery of Venice stands there for all the world to see; it is part of the spectacle—a thorough-going devotee of local colour might consistently say it is part of the pleasure. The Venetian people have little to call their own—little more than the bare privilege of leading their lives in the most beautiful of towns. Their habitations are decayed; their taxes heavy; their pockets light; their opportunities few. One receives an impression, however, that life presents itself to them with attractions not accounted for in this meagre train of advantages, and that they are on better terms with it than many people who have made a better bargain. They lie in the sunshine; they dabble in the sea; they wear bright rags; they fall into attitudes and harmonies; they assist at an eternal *conversazione*. It is not easy to say that one would have them other than they are, and it certainly would make an immense difference should they be better fed. The number of persons in Venice who evidently never have enough to eat is painfully large; but it would be more painful if we did not equally perceive that the rich Venetian temperament may bloom upon a dog's allowance. Nature has been kind to it, and sunshine and leisure and conversation and beautiful views form the greater part of its sustenance. It takes a great deal to make a successful American, but to make a happy Venetian takes only a handful of quick sensibility. The Italian people have at once the good and the evil fortune to be conscious of few wants; so that if the civilisation of a society is measured by the number of its needs, as seems to be the common opinion to-day, it is to be feared that the children of the lagoon would make but a poor figure in a set of comparative tables. Not their misery, doubtless, but the way they elude their misery, is what pleases the sentimental tourist, who is gratified by the sight of a beautiful race that lives by the aid of its imagination. The way to enjoy Venice is to follow the example of these people and make the most of simple pleasures. Almost all the pleasures of the place are simple; this may be maintained even under the imputation of ingenious paradox. There is no simpler pleasure than looking at a fine Titian, unless it be looking at a fine Tintoret or strolling into St. Mark's—abominable the way one falls into the habit—and resting one's light-wearied eyes upon the windowless gloom; or than floating in a gondola or than hanging over a balcony or than taking one's coffee at Florian's. It is of such superficial pastimes that a Venetian day is composed, and the pleasure of the matter is in the emotions to which they minister. These are fortunately of the finest—otherwise Venice would be insufferably dull. Reading Ruskin is good; reading the old records is perhaps better; but the best thing of all is simply staying on. The only way to care for Venice as she deserves it is to give her a chance to touch you often—to linger and remain and return.

II

The danger is that you will not linger enough—a danger of which the author of these lines had known something. It is possible to dislike Venice, and to entertain the sentiment in a responsible and intelligent manner. There are travellers who think the place odious, and those who are not of this opinion often find themselves wishing that the others were only more numerous. The sentimental tourist's sole quarrel with his Venice is that he has too many competitors there. He likes to be alone ; to be original ; to have (to himself, at least) the air of making discoveries. The Venice of to-day is a vast museum where the little wicket that admits you is perpetually turning and creaking, and you march through the institution with a herd of fellow-gazers. There is nothing left to discover or describe, and originality of attitude is completely impossible. This is often very annoying ; you can only turn your back on your impertinent playfellow and curse his want of delicacy. But this is not the fault of Venice ; it is the fault of the rest of the world. The fault of Venice is that, though she is easy to admire, she is not so easy to live with as you count living in other places. After you have stayed a week and the bloom of novelty has rubbed off you wonder if you can accommodate yourself to the peculiar conditions. Your old habits become impracticable and you find yourself obliged to form new ones of an undesirable and unprofitable character. You are tired of your gondola (or you think you are) and you have seen all the principal pictures and heard the names of the palaces announced a dozen times by your gondolier, who brings them out almost as impressively as if he were an English butler bawling titles into a drawing-room. You have walked several hundred times round the Piazza and bought several bushels of photographs. You have visited the antiquity-mongers whose horrible sign-boards dishonour some of the grandest vistas in the Grand Canal ; you have tried the opera and found it very bad ; you have bathed at the Lido and found the water flat. You have begun to have a shipboard-feeling—to regard the Piazza as an enormous saloon and the Riva degli Schiavoni as a promenade-deck. You are obstructed and encaged ; your desire for space is unsatisfied ; you miss your usual exercise. You try to take a walk and you fail, and meantime, as I say, you have come to regard your gondola as a sort of magnified baby's cradle. You have no desire to be rocked to sleep, though you are sufficiently kept awake by the irritation produced, as you gaze across the shallow lagoon, by the attitude of the perpetual gondolier, with his turned-out toes, his protruded chin, his absurdly unscientific stroke.   The canals have a horrible smell, and the everlasting Piazza, where you have looked repeatedly at every article in every shop-window and found them all rubbish, where the young Venetians who sell bead bracelets and "panoramas" are perpetually thrusting their wares at you, where the same tightly-buttoned officers are for ever sucking the same black weeds, at the same empty tables, in front of the same cafés—the Piazza, as I say, has resolved itself into a magnificent tread-mill.   This is the state of mind of those shallow inquirers who find Venice all very well for a week ; and if in such a state of mind you take your departure you act with fatal rashness.   The loss is your own, moreover ; it is not—with all deference to your personal attractions—that of your companions who remain behind ; for though there are some disagreeable things in Venice there is nothing so disagreeable as the visitors.   The conditions are peculiar, but your intolerance of them evaporates before it has had time to become a prejudice.   When you have called for the bill to go, pay it and remain, and you will find on the morrow that you are deeply attached to Venice.   It is by living there from day to day that you feel the fulness of her charm ; that you invite her exquisite influence to sink into your spirit.   The creature varies like a nervous woman, whom you know only when you know all the aspects of her beauty.   She has high spirits or low, she is pale or red, grey or pink, cold or warm, fresh or wan, according to the weather or the hour.   She is always interesting and almost always sad ; but she has a thousand occasional graces and is always liable to happy accidents.   You become extraordinarily fond of these things ; you count upon them ; they make part of your life.   Tenderly fond you become ; there is something indefinable in those depths of personal acquaintance that gradually establish themselves.   The place seems to personify itself, to become human and sentient and conscious of your affection. You desire to embrace it, to caress it, to possess it; and finally a soft sense of possession grows up and your visit becomes a perpetual love-affair. It is very true that if you go, as the author of these lines on a certain occasion went, about the middle of March, a certain amount of disappointment is possible. He had paid no visit for several years, and in the interval the beautiful and helpless city had suffered an increase of injury, The barbarians are in full possession and you tremble for what they may do. You are reminded from the moment of your arrival that Venice scarcely exists any more as a city at all; that she exists only as a battered peep-show and bazaar. There was a horde of savage Germans encamped in the Piazza, and they filled the Ducal Palace and the Academy with their uproar. The English and Americans came a little later. They came in good time, with a great many French, who were discreet enough to make very long repasts at the Caffè Quadri, during which they were out of the way. The months of April and May of the year 1881 were not, as a general thing, a favourable season for visiting the Ducal Palace and the Academy. The *valet-de-place* had marked them for his own and held triumphant possession of them. He celebrates his triumphs in a terrible brassy voice, which resounds all over the place, and has, whatever language he be speaking, the accent of some other idiom. During all the spring months in Venice these gentry abound in the great resorts, and they lead their helpless captives through churches and galleries in dense irresponsible groups. They infest the Piazza; they pursue you along the Riva; they hang about the bridges and the doors of the cafés. In saying just now that I was disappointed at first, I had chiefly in mind the impression that assails me to-day in the whole precinct of St. Mark's. The condition of this ancient sanctuary is surely a great scandal. The pedlars and com-missioners ply their trade—often a very unclean one—at the very door of the temple; they follow you across the threshold, into the sacred dusk, and pull your sleeve, and hiss into your

ear, scuffling with each other for customers. There is a great
deal of dishonour about St. Mark's altogether, and if Venice,
as I say, has become a great bazaar, this exquisite edifice is now
the biggest booth.

III

It is treated as a booth in all ways, and if it had not somehow a great spirit of solemnity within it the traveller would
soon have little warrant for regarding it as a religious affair.
The restoration of the outer walls, which has lately been so
much attacked and defended, is certainly a great shock. Of
the necessity of the work only an expert is, I suppose, in a
position to judge; but there is no doubt that, if a necessity
it be, it is one that is deeply to be regretted. To no more
distressing necessity have people of taste lately had to resign
themselves. Wherever the hand of the restorer has been laid
all semblance of beauty has vanished; which is a sad fact,
considering that the external loveliness of St. Mark's has been
for ages less impressive only than that of the still comparatively
uninjured interior. I know not what is the measure of necessity
in such a case, and it appears indeed to be a very delicate
question. To-day, at any rate, that admirable harmony of
faded mosaic and marble which, to the eye of the traveller
emerging from the narrow streets that lead to the Piazza, filled
all the further end of it with a sort of dazzling silvery presence
—to-day this lovely vision is in a way to be completely reformed
and indeed well-nigh abolished. The old softness and mellowness of colour—the work of the quiet centuries and of the
breath of the salt sea—is giving way to large crude patches
of new material which have the effect of a monstrous malady
rather than of a restoration to health. They look like blotches
of red and white paint and dishonourable smears of chalk on
the cheeks of a noble matron. The face toward the Piazzetta

is in especial the newest-looking thing conceivable—as new as a new pair of boots or as the morning's paper. We do not profess, however, to undertake a scientific quarrel with these changes; we admit that our complaint is a purely sentimental one. The march of industry in united Italy must doubtless be looked at as a whole, and one must endeavour to believe that it is through innumerable lapses of taste that this deeply interesting country is groping her way to her place among the nations. For the present, it is not to be denied, certain odd phases of the process are more visible than the result, to arrive at which it seems necessary that, as she was of old a passionate votary of the beautiful, she should to-day burn everything that she has adored. It is doubtless too soon to judge her, and there are moments when one is willing to forgive her even the restoration of St. Mark's. Inside as well there has been a considerable attempt to make the place more tidy; but the general effect, as yet, has not seriously suffered. What I chiefly remember is the straightening out of that dark and rugged old pavement—those deep undulations of primitive mosaic in which the fond spectator was thought to perceive an intended resemblance to the waves of the ocean. Whether intended or not the analogy was an image the more in a treasure-house of images; but from a considerable portion of the church it has now disappeared. Throughout the greater part indeed the pavement remains as recent generations have known it—dark, rich, cracked, uneven, spotted with porphyry and time-blackened malachite, polished by the knees of innumerable worshippers; but in other large stretches the idea imitated by the restorers is that of the ocean in a dead calm, and the model they have taken the floor of a London club-house or of a New York hotel. I think no Venetian and scarcely any Italian cares much for such differences; and when, a year ago, people in England were writing to the *Times* about the whole business and holding meetings to protest against it the dear children of the lagoon—so far as they heard

or heeded the rumour—thought them partly busy-bodies and
partly asses. Busy-bodies they doubtless were, but they took
a good deal of disinterested trouble. It never occurs to the
Venetian mind of to-day that such trouble may be worth taking;
the Venetian mind vainly endeavours to conceive a state of
existence in which personal questions are so insipid that people
have to look for grievances in the wrongs of brick and marble.
I must not, however, speak of St. Mark's as if I had the pretension of giving a description of it or as if the reader desired
one. The reader has been too well served already. It is surely
the best-described building in the world. Open the *Stones
of Venice*, open Théophile Gautier's *Italia*, and you will see.
These writers take it very seriously, and it is only because
there is another way of taking it that I venture to speak of it;
the way that offers itself after you have been in Venice a couple
of months, and the light is hot in the great Square, and you
pass in under the pictured porticoes with a feeling of habit and
friendliness and a desire for something cool and dark. There
are moments, after all, when the church is comparatively quiet
and empty, and when you may sit there with an easy consciousness of its beauty. From the moment, of course, that you go
into any Italian church for any purpose but to say your prayers
or look at the ladies, you rank yourself among the trooping
barbarians I just spoke of; you treat the place as an orifice
in the peep-show. Still, it is almost a spiritual function—
or, at the worst, an amorous one—to feed one's eyes on the
molten colour that drops from the hollow vaults and thickens
the air with its richness. It is all so quiet and sad and faded
and yet all so brilliant and living. The strange figures in the
mosaic pictures, bending with the curve of niche and vault, stare
down through the glowing dimness; the burnished gold that
stands behind them catches the light on its little uneven cubes.
St. Mark's owes nothing of its character to the beauty of proportion or perspective; there is nothing grandly balanced or

far-arching; there are no long lines nor triumphs of the perpendicular. The church arches indeed, but arches like a dusky cavern. Beauty of surface, of tone, of detail, of things near enough to touch and kneel upon and lean against—it is from this the effect proceeds. In this sort of beauty the place is incredibly rich, and you may go there every day and find afresh some lurking pictorial nook. It is a treasury of bits, as the painters say; and there are usually three or four of the fraternity with their easels set up in uncertain equilibrium on the undulating floor. It is not easy to catch the real complexion of St. Mark's, and these laudable attempts at portraiture are apt to look either lurid or livid. But if you cannot paint the old loose-looking marble slabs, the great panels of basalt and jasper, the crucifixes of which the lonely anguish looks deeper in the vertical light, the tabernacles whose open doors disclose a dark Byzantine image spotted with dull, crooked gems—if you cannot paint these things you can at least grow fond of them. You grow fond even of the old benches of red marble, partly worn away by the breeches of many generations and attached to the base of those wide pilasters of which the precious plating, delightful in its faded brownness, with a faint grey bloom upon it, bulges and yawns a little with honourable age.

IV

Even at first, when the vexatious sense of the city of the Doges reduced to earning its living as a curiosity-shop was in its keenness, there was a great deal of entertainment to be got from lodging on Riva Schiavoni and looking out at the far-shimmering lagoon. There was entertainment indeed in simply getting into the place and observing the queer incidents of a Venetian installation. A great many persons contribute indirectly to this undertaking, and it is surprising how they spring out at you during your novitiate to remind you that they are bound up in some mysterious manner with the constitution of your little establishment. It was an interesting problem for instance to trace the subtle connection existing between the niece of the landlady and the occupancy of the fourth floor. Superficially it was none too visible, as the young lady in question was a dancer at the Fenice theatre—or when that was closed at the Rossini—and might have been supposed absorbed by her professional duties. It proved necessary, however, that she should hover about the premises in a velvet jacket and a pair of black kid gloves with one little white button; as also, that she should apply a thick coating of powder to her face, which had a charming oval and a sweet weak expression, like that of most of the Venetian maidens, who, as a general thing—it was not a peculiarity of the landlady's niece—are fond of besmearing themselves with flour. You soon recognise that it is not only the many-twinkling lagoon you behold from a habitation on the Riva; you see a little of everything Venetian. Straight across, before my windows, rose the great pink mass of San Giorgio Maggiore, which has for an ugly Palladian church a success beyond all reason. It is a success of position, of colour, of the immense detached Campanile, tipped with a tall gold angel. I know not whether it is because San Giorgio is so grandly conspicuous, with a great deal of worn, faded-looking brickwork; but for many persons the whole place has a kind of suffusion of rosiness. Asked what may be the leading colour in the Venetian concert, we should inveterately say Pink, and yet without remembering after all that this elegant hue occurs very often. It is a faint, shimmering, airy, watery pink; the bright sea-light seems to flush with it and the pale whiteish-green of lagoon and canal to drink it in. There is indeed a great deal of very evident brickwork, which is never fresh or loud in colour, but always burnt out, as it were, always exquisitely mild.

Certain little mental pictures rise before the collector of memories at the simple mention, written or spoken, of the places he has loved. When I hear, when I see, the magical name I have written above these pages, it is not of the great Square that I think, with its strange basilica and its high arcades, nor of the wide mouth of the Grand Canal, with the stately steps and the well-poised dome of the Salute; it is not of the low lagoon, nor the sweet Piazzetta, nor the dark chambers of St. Mark's. I simply see a narrow canal in the heart of the city—a patch of green water and a surface of pink wall. The gondola moves slowly; it gives a great smooth swerve, passes under a bridge, and the gondolier's cry, carried over the quiet water, makes a kind of splash in the stillness. A girl crosses the little bridge, which has an arch like a camel's back, with an old shawl on her head, which makes her characteristic and charming; you see her against the sky as you float beneath. The pink of the old wall seems to fill the whole place; it sinks even into the opaque water. Behind the wall is a garden, out of which the long arm of a white June rose—the roses of Venice are splendid—has flung itself by way of spontaneous ornament. On the other side of this small water-way is a great shabby façade of Gothic windows and balconies—balconies on which dirty clothes are hung and under which a cavernous-looking doorway opens from a low flight of slimy water-steps. It is very hot and still, the canal has a queer smell, and the whole place is enchanting.

It is poor work, however, talking about the colour of things in Venice. The fond spectator is perpetually looking at it from his window, when he is not floating about with that delightful sense of being for the moment a part of it, which any gentleman in a gondola is free to entertain. Venetian windows and balconies are a dreadful lure, and while you rest your elbows on these cushioned ledges the precious hours fly away. But in truth Venice isn't in fair weather a place for concentration of mind. The effort required for sitting down to a writing-table is heroic, and the brightest page of MS. looks dull beside the brilliancy of your *milieu*. All nature beckons you forth and murmurs to you sophistically that such hours should be devoted to collecting impressions. Afterwards, in ugly places, at unprivileged times, you can convert your impressions into prose. Fortunately for the present proser the weather wasn't always fine; the first month was wet and windy, and it was better to judge of the matter from an open casement than to respond to the advances of persuasive gondoliers. Even then however there was a constant entertainment in the view. It was all cold colour, and the steel-grey floor of the lagoon was stroked the wrong way by the wind. Then there were charming cool intervals, when the churches, the houses, the anchored fishing-boats, the whole gently-curving line of the Riva, seemed to be washed with a pearly white. Later it all turned warm—warm to the eye as well as to other senses. After the middle of May the whole place was in a glow. The sea took on a thousand shades, but they were only infinite variations of blue, and those rosy walls I just spoke of began to flush in the thick sunshine. Every patch of colour, every yard of weather-stained stucco, every glimpse of nestling garden or daub of sky above a *calle*, began to shine and sparkle—began, as the painters say, to " compose." The lagoon was streaked with odd currents, which played across it like huge smooth finger-marks. The gondolas multiplied and spotted it all over; every gondola and gondolier looking, at a distance, precisely like every other.

There is something strange and fascinating in this mysterious impersonality of the gondola. It has an identity when you are in it, but, thanks to their all being of the same size, shape and colour, and of the same deportment and gait, it has none, or as little as possible, as you see it pass before you. From my windows on the Riva there was always the same silhouette—the long, black, slender skiff, lifting its head and throwing it back a little, moving yet seeming not to move, with the grotesquely-graceful figure on the poop. This figure inclines, as may be, more to the graceful or to the grotesque—standing in the " second position " of the dancing-master, but indulging from

the waist upward in a freedom of movement which that functionary would deprecate. One may say as a general thing that
there is something rather awkward in the movement even of the
most graceful gondolier, and something graceful in the movement
of the most awkward. In the graceful men of course the grace
predominates, and nothing can be finer than the large, firm way
in which, from their point of vantage, they throw themselves
over their tremendous oar. It has the boldness of a plunging
bird and the regularity of a pendulum. Sometimes, as you see
this movement in profile, in a gondola that passes you—see, as
you recline on your own low cushions, the arching body of the
gondolier lifted up against the sky—it has a kind of nobleness
which suggests an image on a Greek frieze. The gondolier at
Venice is your very good friend—if you choose him happily—
and on the quality of the personage depends a good deal that of
your impressions. He is a part of your daily life, your double,
your shadow, your complement. Most people, I think, either
like their gondolier or hate him ; and if they like him, like him
very much. In this case they take an interest in him after his
departure ; wish him to be sure of employment, speak of him as
the gem of gondoliers and tell their friends to be certain to
" secure " him. There is usually no difficulty in securing him ;
there is nothing elusive or reluctant about a gondolier. Nothing
would induce me not to believe them for the most part excellent
fellows, and the sentimental tourist must always have a kindness
for them. More than the rest of the population, of course, they
are the children of Venice ; they are associated with its idiosyn-
crasy, with its essence, with its silence, with its melancholy.

When I say they are associated with its silence I should
immediately add that they are associated also with its sound.
Among themselves they are an extraordinarily talkative company. They chatter at the *traghetti*, where they always have
some sharp point under discussion ; they bawl across the canals ;
they bespeak your commands as you approach ; they defy each

other from afar.   If you happen to have a *traghetto* under your window, you are well aware that they are a vocal race.   I should go even further than I went just now, and say that the voice of the gondolier is in fact for audibility the dominant or rather the only note of Venice.   There is scarcely another heard sound, and that indeed is part of the interest of the place.   There is no noise there save distinctly human noise ; no rumbling, no vague uproar, nor rattle of wheels and hoofs.   It is all articulate and vocal and personal.   One may say indeed that Venice is emphatically the city of conversation ; people talk all over the place because there is nothing to interfere with its being caught by the ear.   Among the populace it is a general family party. The still water carries the voice, and good Venetians exchange confidences at a distance of half a mile.   It saves a world of trouble, and they don't like trouble.   Their delightful garrulous language helps them to make Venetian life a long *conversazione*. This language, with its soft elisions, its odd transpositions, its kindly contempt for consonants and other disagreeables, has in it something peculiarly human and accommodating.   If your gondolier had no other merit he would have the merit that he speaks Venetian.   This may rank as a merit even—some people perhaps would say especially—when you don't understand what he says.   But he adds to it other graces which make him an agreeable feature in your life.   The price he sets on his services is touchingly small, and he has a happy art of being obsequious without being, or at least without seeming, abject.   For occasional liberalities he evinces an almost lyrical gratitude.   In short he has delightfully good manners, a merit which he shares for the most part with the Venetians at large.   One grows very fond of these people, and the reason of one's fondness is the frankness and sweetness of their address.   That of the Italian family at large has much to recommend it ; but in the Venetian manner there is something peculiarly ingratiating. One feels that the race is old, that it has a long and rich civilisa-

tion in its blood, and that if it hasn't been blessed by fortune it
has at least been polished by time. It hasn't a genius for stiff
morality, and indeed makes few pretensions in that direction.
It scruples but scantly to represent the false as the true, and
has been accused of cultivating the occasion to grasp and to
overreach, and of steering a crooked course—not to your and
my advantage—amid the sanctities of property. It has been
accused further of loving if not too well at least too often, of
being in fine as little austere as possible. I am not sure it is
very brave, nor struck with its being very industrious. But it
has an unfailing sense of the amenities of life; the poorest
Venetian is a natural man of the world. He is better company
than persons of his class are apt to be among the nations of
industry and virtue—where people are also sometimes perceived
to lie and steal and otherwise misconduct themselves. He has a
great desire to please and to be pleased.

V

In that matter at least the cold-blooded stranger begins at
last to imitate him; begins to lead a life that shall be before
all things easy; unless indeed he allow himself, like Mr. Ruskin,
to be put out of humour by Titian and Tiepolo. The hours
he spends among the pictures are his best hours in Venice, and I
am ashamed to have written so much of common things when
I might have been making festoons of the names of the masters.
Only, when we have covered our page with such festoons what
more is left to say? When one has said Carpaccio and Bellini,
the Tintoret and the Veronese, one has struck a note that must
be left to resound at will. Everything has been said about the
mighty painters, and it is of little importance that a pilgrim the
more has found them to his taste. "Went this morning to the
Academy; was very much pleased with Titian's 'Assumption.'"
That honest phrase has doubtless been written in many a

traveller's diary, and was not indiscreet on the part of its author. But it appeals little to the general reader, and we must moreover notoriously not expose our deepest feelings. Since I have mentioned Titian's "Assumption" I must say that there are some people who have been less pleased with it than the observer we have just imagined. It is one of the possible disappointments of Venice, and you may if you like take advantage of your privilege of not caring for it. It imparts a look of great richness to the side of the beautiful room of the Academy on which it hangs ; but the same room contains two or three works less known to fame which are equally capable of inspiring a passion. " The ' Annunciation ' struck me as coarse and superficial " : that note was once made in a simple-minded tourist's book. At Venice, strange to say, Titian is altogether a disappointment ; the city of his adoption is far from containing the best of him. Madrid, Paris, London, Florence, Dresden, Munich—these are the homes of his greatness.

There are other painters who have but a single home, and the greatest of these is the Tintoret. Close beside him sit Carpaccio and Bellini, who make with him the dazzling Venetian trio. The Veronese may be seen and measured in other places ; he is most splendid in Venice, but he shines in Paris and in Dresden. You may walk out of the noon-day dusk of Trafalgar Square in November, and in one of the chambers of the National Gallery see the family of Darius rustling and pleading and weeping at the feet of Alexander. Alexander is a beautiful young Venetian in crimson pantaloons, and the picture sends a glow into the cold London twilight. You may sit before it for an hour and dream you are floating to the water-gate of the Ducal Palace, where a certain old beggar who has one of the handsomest heads in the world—he has sat to a hundred painters for Doges and for personages more sacred—has a prescriptive right to pretend to pull your gondola to the steps and to hold out a greasy immemorial cap. But you must go to Venice in very fact to see the other masters, who form part of your life while you are there, who illuminate your view of the universe. It is difficult to express one's relation to them; the whole Venetian art-world is so near, so familiar, so much an extension and adjunct of the spreading actual, that it seems almost invidious to say one owes more to one of them than to the other. Nowhere, not even in Holland, where the correspondence between the real aspects and the little polished canvases is so constant and so exquisite, do art and life seem so interfused and, as it were, so consanguineous. All the splendour of light and colour, all the Venetian air and the Venetian history are on the walls and ceilings of the palaces; and all the genius of the masters, all the images and visions they have left upon canvas, seem to tremble in the sunbeams and dance upon the waves. That is the perpetual interest of the place—that you live in a certain sort of knowledge as in a rosy cloud. You don't go into the churches and galleries by way of a change from the streets; you go into them because they offer you an exquisite reproduction of the things that surround you. All Venice was both model and painter, and life was so pictorial that art couldn't help becoming so. With all diminutions life is pictorial still, and this fact gives an extraordinary freshness to one's perception of the great Venetian works. You judge of them not as a connoisseur, but as a man of the world, and you enjoy them because they are so social and so true. Perhaps of all works of art that are equally great they demand least reflection on the part of the spectator—they make least of a mystery of being enjoyed. Reflection only confirms your admiration, yet is almost ashamed to show its head. These things speak so frankly and benignantly to the sense that even when they arrive at the highest style—as in the Tintoret's " Presentation of the little Virgin at the Temple "—they are still more familiar.

But it is hard, as I say, to express all this, and it is painful as well to attempt it—painful because in the memory of vanished hours so filled with beauty the consciousness of present loss oppresses. Exquisite hours, enveloped in light and silence, to have known them once is to have always a terrible standard of enjoyment. Certain lovely mornings of May and June come back with an ineffaceable fairness. Venice isn't smothered in flowers at this season, in the manner of Florence and Rome; but the sea and sky themselves seem to blossom and rustle. The gondola waits at the wave-washed steps, and if you are wise you will take your place beside a discriminating companion. Such a companion in Venice should of course be of the sex that discriminates most finely. An intelligent woman who knows her Venice seems doubly intelligent, and it makes no woman's perceptions less keen to be aware that she can't help looking graceful as she is borne over the waves. The handsome Pasquale, with uplifted oar, awaits your command, knowing, in a general way, from observation of your habits, that your intention is to go to see a picture or two. It perhaps doesn't immensely matter what picture you choose : the whole affair is so charming. It is charming to wander through the light and shade of intricate canals, with perpetual architecture above you and perpetual fluidity beneath. It is charming to disembark at the polished steps of a little empty *campo*—a sunny shabby square with an old well in the middle, an old church on one side and tall Venetian windows looking down. Sometimes the windows are tenantless; sometimes a lady in a faded dressing-gown leans vaguely on the sill. There is always an old man holding out his hat for coppers; there are always three or four small boys dodging possible umbrella-pokes while they precede you, in the manner of custodians, to the door of the church.

VI

The churches of Venice are rich in pictures, and many a masterpiece lurks in the unaccommodating gloom of side-chapels and sacristies. Many a noble work is perched behind the dusty candles and muslin roses of a scantily-visited altar; some of them indeed, hidden behind the altar, suffer in a darkness that can never be explored. The facilities offered you for approaching the picture in such cases are a mockery of your irritated wish. You stand at tip-toe on a three-legged stool, you climb a rickety ladder, you almost mount upon the shoulders of the *custode*. You do everything but see the picture. You see just enough to be sure it's beautiful. You catch a glimpse of a divine head, of a fig-tree against a mellow sky, but the rest is impenetrable mystery. You renounce all hope, for instance, of approaching the magnificent Cima da Conegliano in San Giovanni in Bragora; and bethinking yourself of the immaculate purity that shines in the spirit of this master, you renounce it with chagrin and pain. Behind the high altar in that church hangs a Baptism of Christ by Cima which I believe has been more or less repainted. You make the thing out in spots, you see it has a fulness of perfection. But you turn away from it with a stiff neck and promise yourself consolation in the Academy and at the Madonna dell' Orto, where two noble works by the same hand—pictures as clear as a summer twilight—present themselves in better circumstances. It may be said as a general thing that you never see the Tintoret. You admire him, you adore him, you think him the greatest of painters, but in the great majority of cases your eyes fail to deal with him. This is partly his own fault; so many of his works have turned to blackness and are positively rotting in their frames. At the Scuola di San Rocco, where there are acres of him, there is scarcely anything at all adequately visible save the immense "Crucifixion" in the upper story. It is true that in looking at this huge composition you look at many pictures; it has not only a multitude of figures but a wealth of episodes; and you pass from one of these to the other as if you were "doing" a gallery. Surely no single picture in the world contains more of human life; there is everything in it, including the most exquisite beauty. It is one of the greatest things of art; it is always interesting. There are works of the artist which contain touches more exquisite, revelations of beauty more radiant, but there is no other vision of so intense a reality, an execution so splendid. The interest, the impressiveness, of that whole corner of Venice, however melancholy the effect of its gorgeous and ill-lighted chambers, gives a strange importance to a visit to the Scuola. Nothing that all travellers go to see appears to suffer less from the incursions of travellers. It is one of the loneliest booths of the bazaar, and the author of these lines has always had the good fortune, which he wishes to every other traveller, of having it to himself. I think most visitors find the place rather alarming and wicked-looking. They walk about a while among the fitful figures that gleam here and there out of the great tapestry (as it were) with which the painter has hung all the walls, and then, depressed and bewildered by the portentous solemnity of these objects, by strange glimpses of unnatural scenes, by the echo of their lonely footsteps on the vast stone floors, they take a hasty departure, finding themselves again, with a sense of release from danger, a sense that the *genius loci* was a sort of mad white-washer who worked with a bad mixture, in the bright light of the *campo*, among the beggars, the orange-vendors and the passing gondolas. Solemn indeed is the place, solemn and strangely suggestive, for the simple reason that we shall scarcely find four walls elsewhere that inclose within a like area an equal quantity of genius. The air is thick with it and dense and difficult to breathe; for it was genius that was not happy, inasmuch as it lacked the art to fix itself for ever. It is not immortality that we breathe at the Scuola di San Rocco, but conscious, reluctant mortality.

Fortunately, however, we can turn to the Ducal Palace, where everything is so brilliant and splendid that the poor dusky Tintoret is lifted in spite of himself into the concert. This deeply original building is of course the loveliest thing in Venice, and a morning's stroll there is a wonderful illumination. Cunningly select your hour—half the enjoyment of Venice is a question of dodging—and enter at about one o'clock, when the tourists have flocked off to lunch and the echoes of the charming chambers have gone to sleep among the sunbeams. There is no brighter place in Venice—by which I mean that on the whole there is none half so bright. The reflected sunshine plays up through the great windows from the glittering lagoon and shimmers and twinkles over gilded walls and ceilings. All the history of Venice, all its splendid stately past, glows around you in a strong sea-light. Every one here is magnificent, but the great Veronese is the most magnificent of all. He swims before you in a silver cloud; he thrones in an eternal morning. The deep blue sky burns behind him, streaked across with milky bars; the white colonnades sustain the richest canopies, under which the first gentlemen and ladies in the world both render homage and receive it. Their glorious garments rustle in the air of the sea and their sun-lighted faces are the very complexion of Venice. The mixture of pride and piety, of politics and religion, of art and patriotism, gives a splendid dignity to every scene. Never was a painter more nobly joyous, never did an artist take a greater delight in life, seeing it all as a kind of breezy festival and feeling it through the medium of perpetual success. He revels in the gold-framed ovals of the ceilings, multiplies himself there with the fluttering movement of an embroidered banner that tosses itself into the blue. He was the happiest of painters and produced the happiest picture in the world. "The Rape of Europa" surely deserves this title; it is impossible to look at it without aching with envy. Nowhere else in art is such a temperament revealed; never did inclination and opportunity combine to express such enjoyment. The mixture of flowers and gems and brocade, of blooming flesh and shining sea and waving groves, of youth,

health, movement, desire—all this is the brightest vision that
ever descended upon the soul of a painter. Happy the artist
who could entertain such a vision ; happy the artist who could
paint it as the masterpiece I here recall is painted.

The Tintoret's visions were not so bright as that; but he
had several that were radiant enough. In the room that contains the work just cited are several smaller canvases by the
greatly more complex genius of the Scuola di San Rocco, which
are almost simple in their loveliness, almost happy in their
simplicity. They have kept their brightness through the centuries, and they shine with their neighbours in those golden
rooms. There is a piece of painting in one of them which
is one of the sweetest things in Venice and which reminds
one afresh of those wild flowers of execution that bloom so
profusely and so unheeded in the dark corners of all of the
Tintoret's work. "Pallas chasing away Mars" is, I believe,
the name that is given to the picture ; and it represents in
fact a young woman of noble appearance administering a gentle
push to a fine young man in armour, as if to tell him to keep
his distance. It is of the gentleness of this push that I speak,
the charming way in which she puts out her arm, with a single
bracelet on it, and rests her young hand, its rosy fingers parted,
on his dark breastplate. She bends her enchanting head with
the effort—a head which has all the strange fairness that the
Tintoret always sees in women—and the soft, living, flesh-like
glow of all these members, over which the brush has scarcely
paused in its course, is as pretty an example of genius as all
Venice can show. But why speak of the Tintoret when I can
say nothing of the great "Paradise," which unfolds its somewhat smoky splendour and the wonder of its multitudinous
circles in one of the other chambers ? If it were not one of
the first pictures in the world it would be about the biggest,
and we must confess that the spectator gets from it at first
chiefly an impression of quantity. Then he sees that this

quantity is really wealth; that the dim confusion of faces is a magnificent composition, and that some of the details of this composition are extremely beautiful. It is impossible however in a retrospect of Venice to specify one's happiest hours, though as one looks backward certain ineffaceable moments start here and there into vividness. How is it possible to forget one's visits to the sacristy of the Frari, however frequent they may have been, and the great work of John Bellini which forms the treasure of that apartment?

VII

Nothing in Venice is more perfect than this, and we know of no work of art more complete. The picture is in three compartments: the Virgin sits in the central division with her child; two venerable saints, standing close together, occupy each of the others. It is impossible to imagine anything more finished or more ripe. It is one of those things that sum up the genius of a painter, the experience of a life, the teaching of a school. It seems painted with molten gems, which have only been clarified by time, and it is as solemn as it is gorgeous and as simple as it is deep. Giovanni Bellini is more or less everywhere in Venice, and, wherever he is, almost certain to be first—first, I mean, in his own line: he paints little else than the Madonna and the saints; he has not Carpaccio's care for human life at large, nor the Tintoret's nor that of the Veronese. Some of his greater pictures, however, where several figures are clustered together, have a richness of sanctity that is almost profane. There is one of them on the dark side of the room at the Academy that contains Titian's " Assumption," which if we could only see it—its position is an inconceivable scandal—would evidently be one of the mightiest of so-called sacred pictures. So too is the Madonna of San Zaccaria, hung in a cold, dim, dreary place, ever so much too high, but so mild and serene, and so grandly disposed and accompanied, that the proper attitude for even the most critical amateur, as he looks at it, strikes one as the bended knee. There is another noble John Bellini, one of the very few in which there is no Virgin, at San Giovanni Crisostomo—a St. Jerome, in a red dress, sitting aloft upon the rocks and with a landscape of extraordinary purity behind him. The absence of the peculiarly erect Madonna makes it an interesting surprise among the works of the painter and gives it a somewhat less strenuous air. But it has brilliant beauty and the St. Jerome is a delightful old personage.

The same church contains another great picture for which the haunter of these places must find a shrine apart in his memory; one of the most interesting things he will have seen, if not the most brilliant. Nothing appeals more to him than three figures of Venetian ladies which occupy the foreground of a smallish canvas of Sebastian del Piombo, placed above the high altar of San Giovanni Crisostomo. Sebastian was a Venetian by birth, but few of his productions are to be seen in his native place; few indeed are to be seen anywhere. The picture represents the patron-saint of the church, accompanied by other saints and by the worldly votaries I have mentioned. These ladies stand together on the left, holding in their hands little white caskets; two of them are in profile, but the foremost turns her face to the spectator. This face and figure are almost unique among the beautiful things of Venice, and they leave the susceptible observer with the impression of having made, or rather having missed, a strange, a dangerous, but a most valuable, acquaintance. The lady, who is superbly handsome, is the typical Venetian of the sixteenth century, and she remains for the mind the perfect flower of that society. Never was there a greater air of breeding, a deeper expression of tranquil superiority. She walks a goddess—as if she trod without sinking the waves of the Adriatic. It is impossible to conceive a more perfect expression of the aristocratic spirit either in its pride or in its benignity. This magnificent creature is so strong and secure that she is gentle, and so quiet that in comparison all minor assumptions of calmness suggest only a vulgar alarm. But for all this there are depths of possible disorder in her light-coloured eye.

I had meant however to say nothing about her, for it's not right to speak of Sebastian when one hasn't found room for Carpaccio. These visions come to one, and one can neither hold them nor brush them aside. Memories of Carpaccio, the magnificent, the delightful—it's not for want of such visitations, but only for want of space, that I haven't said of him what I would. There is little enough need of it for Carpaccio's sake, his fame being brighter to-day—thanks to the generous lamp Mr. Ruskin has held up to it—than it has ever been. Yet there is something ridiculous in talking of Venice without making him almost the refrain. He and the Tintoret are the two great realists, and it is hard to say which is the more human, the more various. The Tintoret had the mightier temperament, but Carpaccio, who had the advantage of more newness and more responsibility, sailed nearer to perfection. Here and there he quite touches it, as in the enchanting picture, at the Academy, of St. Ursula asleep in her little white bed, in her high clean room, where the angel visits her at dawn; or in the noble St. Jerome in his study at S. Giorgio Schiavoni. This latter work is a pearl of sentiment, and I may add without being fantastic a ruby of colour. It unites the most masterly finish with a kind of universal largeness of feeling, and he who has it well in his memory will never hear the name of Carpaccio without a throb of almost personal affection. Such indeed is the feeling that descends upon you in that wonderful little chapel of St. George of the Slaves, where this most personal and sociable of artists has expressed all the sweetness of his imagination. The place is small and incommodious, the pictures are out of sight and ill-lighted, the custodian is rapacious, the visitors are mutually intolerable, but the shabby little chapel is a palace of art. Mr. Ruskin has written a pamphlet about it which is a real aid to enjoyment, though I can't but think the generous artist, with his keen senses and his just feeling, would have suffered to hear his eulogist declare that one of his other productions—in the Museo Civico of Palazzo Correr, a delightful portrait of two Venetian ladies with pet animals— is the "finest picture in the world." It has no need of that to be thought admirable; and what more can a painter desire?

VIII

May in Venice is better than April, but June is best of all. Then the days are hot, but not too hot, and the nights are more beautiful than the days. Then Venice is rosier than ever in the morning and more golden than ever as the day descends. She seems to expand and evaporate, to multiply all her reflections and iridescences. Then the life of her people and the strangeness of her constitution become a perpetual comedy, or at least a perpetual drama. Then the gondola is your sole habitation, and you spend days between sea and sky. You go to the Lido, though the Lido has been spoiled. When I first saw it, in 1869, it was a very natural place, and there was but a rough lane across the little island from the landing-place to the beach. There was a bathing-place in those days, and a restaurant, which was very bad, but where in the warm evenings your dinner didn't much matter as you sat letting it cool on the wooden terrace that stretched out into the sea. To-day the Lido is a part of united Italy and has been made the victim of villainous improvements. A little cockney village has sprung up on its rural bosom and a third-rate boulevard leads from Santa Elisabetta to the Adriatic. There are bitumen walks and gas-lamps, lodging-houses, shops and a *teatro diurno*. The bathing-establishment is bigger than before, and the restaurant as well; but it is a compensation perhaps that the cuisine is no better. Such as it is, however, you won't scorn occasionally to partake of it on the breezy platform under which bathers dart and splash, and which looks out to where the fishing-boats, with sails of orange and crimson, wander along the darkening horizon. The beach at the Lido is still lonely and beautiful, and you can easily walk away from the cockney village. The return to Venice in the sunset is classical and indispensable, and those who at that glowing hour have floated toward the towers that rise out of the lagoon will not easily part with the impression. But you indulge in larger excursions—you go to Burano and Torcello, to Malamocco and Chioggia. Torcello, like the Lido, has been improved; the deeply interesting little cathedral of the eighth century, which stood there on the edge of the sea, as touching in its ruin, with its grassy threshold and its primitive mosaics, as the bleached bones of a human skeleton washed ashore by the tide, has now been restored and made cheerful, and the charm of the place, its strange and suggestive desolation, has well-nigh departed.

It will still serve you as a pretext, however, for a day on the lagoon, especially as you will disembark at Burano and admire the wonderful fisher-folk, whose good looks—and bad manners, I am sorry to say—can scarcely be exaggerated. Burano is celebrated for the beauty of its women and the rapacity of its children, and it is a fact that though some of the ladies are rather bold about it every one of them shows you a handsome face. The children assail you for coppers, and in their desire to be satisfied pursue your gondola into the sea. Chioggia is a larger Burano, and you carry away from either place a half-sad, half-cynical, but altogether pic-torial impression; the impression of bright-coloured hovels, of bathing in stagnant canals, of young girls with faces of a delicate shape and a susceptible expression, with splendid heads of hair and complexions smeared with powder, faded yellow shawls that hang like old Greek draperies, and little wooden shoes that click as they go up and down the steps of the convex bridges; of brown-cheeked matrons with lustrous tresses and high tempers, massive throats encased with gold beads, and eyes that meet your own with a certain traditional defiance. The men throughout the islands of Venice are almost as handsome as the women; I have never seen so many good-looking rascals. At Burano and Chioggia they sit mending their nets, or lounge at the street corners, where conversation is always high-pitched, or clamour to you to take a boat; and everywhere they decorate the scene with their splendid colour— cheeks and throats as richly brown as the sails of their fishing-smacks—their sea-faded tatters which are always a "costume," their soft Venetian jargon, and the gallantry with which they wear their hats, an article that nowhere sits so well as on a mass of dense Venetian curls. If you are happy you will find yourself, after a June day in Venice (about ten o'clock), on a balcony that overhangs the Grand Canal, with your elbows on the broad ledge, a cigarette in your teeth and a little good company beside you. The gondolas pass beneath, the watery surface gleams here and there from their lamps, some of which are coloured lanterns that move mysteriously in the darkness. There are some evenings in June when there are too many gondolas, too many lanterns, too many serenades in front of the hotels. The serenading in particular is overdone; but on such a balcony as I speak of you needn't suffer from it, for in the apartment behind you—an accessible refuge—there is more good company, there are more cigarettes. If you are wise you will step back there presently.

1882.

THE GRAND CANAL

THE honour of representing the plan and the place at their best might perhaps appear, in the City of St. Mark, properly to belong to the splendid square which bears the patron's name and which is the centre of Venetian life so far (this is pretty well all the way indeed) as Venetian life is a matter of strolling and chaffering, of gossiping and gaping, of circulating without a purpose, and of staring—too often with a foolish one—through the shop-windows of dealers whose hospitality makes their doorsteps dramatic, at the very vulgarest rubbish in all the modern market. If the Grand Canal, however, is not quite technically a "street," the perverted Piazza is perhaps even less normal; and I hasten to add that I am glad not to find myself studying my subject under the international arcades, or yet (I will go the length of saying) in the solemn presence of the church. For indeed in that case I foresee I should become still more confound-ingly conscious of the stumbling-block that inevitably, even with his first few words, crops up in the path of the lover of Venice who rashly addresses himself to expression. "Venetian life" is a mere literary convention, though it be an indispensable figure. The words have played an effective part in the literature of sensibility; they constituted thirty years ago the title of Mr. Howells's delightful volume of impressions; but in using them to-day one owes some frank amends to one's own lucidity. Let me carefully premise therefore that so often as they shall again drop from my pen, so often shall I beg to be regarded as syste-matically superficial.

Venetian life, in the large old sense, has long since come to an end, and the essential present character of the most melancholy of cities resides simply in its being the most beautiful of tombs. Nowhere else has the past been laid to rest with such tenderness, such a sadness of resignation and remembrance. Nowhere else is the present so alien, so discontinuous, so like a crowd in a cemetery without garlands for the graves. It has no flowers in its hands, but, as a compensation perhaps—and the thing is doubtless more to the point—it has money and little red books. The everlasting shuffle of these irresponsible visitors in the Piazza is contemporary Venetian life. Everything else is only a reverberation of that. The vast mausoleum has a turnstile at the door, and a functionary in a shabby uniform lets you in, as per tariff, to see how dead it is. From this *constatation*, this cold curiosity, proceed all the industry, the prosperity, the vitality of the place. The shopkeepers and gondoliers, the beggars and the models, depend upon it for a living; they are the custodians and the ushers of the great museum—they are even themselves to a certain extent the objects of exhibition. It is in the wide vestibule of the square that the polyglot pilgrims gather most densely; Piazza San Marco is the lobby of the opera in the intervals of the performance. The present fortune of Venice, the lamentable difference, is most easily measured there, and that is why, in the effort to resist our pessimism, we must turn away both from the purchasers and from the vendors of *ricordi*. The *ricordi* that we prefer are gathered best where the gondola glides —best of all on the noble waterway that begins in its glory at the Salute and ends in its abasement at the railway station. It is, however, the cockneyfied Piazzetta (forgive me, shade of St. Theodore—has not a brand new café begun to glare there, electrically, this very year?) that introduces us most directly to the great picture by which the Grand Canal works its first spell, and to which a thousand artists, not always with a talent apiece, have paid their tribute. We pass into the Piazzetta to look down the great throat, as it were, of Venice, and the vision must console us for turning our back on St. Mark's.

We have been treated to it again and again, of course, even if we have never stirred from home ; but that is only a reason the more for catching at any freshness that may be left in the world of photography. It is in Venice above all that we hear the small buzz of this vulgarising voice of the familiar ; yet perhaps it is in Venice too that the picturesque fact has best mastered the pious secret of how to wait for us. Even the classic Salute waits like some great lady on the threshold of her saloon. She is more ample and serene, more seated at her door, than all the copyists have told us, with her domes and scrolls, her scolloped buttresses and statues forming a pompous crown, and her wide steps disposed on the ground like the train of a robe. This fine air of the woman of the world is carried out by the well-bred assurance with which she looks in the direction of her old-fashioned Byzantine neighbour ; and the juxtaposition of two churches so distinguished and so different, each splendid in its sort, is a sufficient mark of the scale and range of Venice. However, we ourselves are looking away from St. Mark's—we must blind our eyes to that dazzle ; without it indeed there are brightnesses and fascinations enough. We see them in abundance even while we look away from the shady steps of the Salute. These steps are cool in the morning, yet I don't know that I can justify my excessive fondness for them any better than I can explain a hundred of the other vague infatuations with which Venice sophisticates the spirit. Under such an influence fortunately one needn't explain—it keeps account of nothing but perceptions and affections. It is from the Salute steps perhaps, of a summer morning, that this view of the open mouth of the city is most brilliantly amusing. The whole thing composes as if composition were the chief end of human institutions. The charming architectural promontory of the Dogana stretches out the most graceful of arms, balancing in its hand the gilded globe on which

c

revolves the delightful satirical figure of a little weathercock of a woman. This Fortune, this Navigation, or whatever she is called—she surely needs no name—catches the wind in the bit of drapery of which she has divested her rotary bronze loveliness. On the other side of the Canal twinkles and glitters the long row of the happy palaces which are mainly expensive hotels. There is a little of everything everywhere, in the bright Venetian air, but to these houses belongs especially the appearance of sitting, across the water, at the receipt of custom, of watching in their hypocritical loveliness for the stranger and the victim. I call them happy, because even their sordid uses and their vulgar signs melt somehow, with their vague sea-stained pinks and drabs, into that strange gaiety of light and colour which is made up of the reflection of superannuated things. The atmosphere plays over them like a laugh, they are of the essence of the sad old joke. They are almost as charming from other places as they are from their own balconies, and share fully in that universal privilege of Venetian objects which consists of being both the picture and the point of view.

This double character, which is particularly strong in the Grand Canal, adds a difficulty to any control of one's notes. The Grand Canal may be practically, as an impression, the cushioned balcony of a high and well-loved palace—the memory of irresistible evenings, of the sociable elbow, of endless lingering and looking; or it may evoke the restlessness of a fresh curiosity, of methodical inquiry, in a gondola piled with references. There are no references, I ought to mention, in the present remarks, which sacrifice to accident, not to completeness. A rhapsody on Venice is always in order, but I think the catalogues are finished. I should not attempt to write here the names of all the palaces, even if the number of those I find myself able to remember in the immense array were less insignificant. There are many I delight in that I don't know, or at least don't keep, apart. Then there are the bad reasons for prefer-

ence that are better than the good, and all the sweet bribery of
association and recollection.   These things, as one stands on
the Salute steps, are so many delicate fingers to pick straight
out of the row a dear little featureless house which, with its
pale green shutters, looks straight across at the great door and
through the very keyhole, as it were, of the church, and which
I needn't call by a name—a pleasant American name—that
every one in Venice, these many years, has had on grateful lips.
It is the very friendliest house in all the wide world, and it has,
as it deserves to have, the most beautiful position.   It is a real
porto di mare, as the gondoliers say—a port within a port; it
sees everything that comes and goes, and takes it all in with
practised eyes.   Not a tint or a hint of the immense iridescence
is lost upon it, and there are days of exquisite colour on which
it may fancy itself the heart of the wonderful prism.   We wave
to it from the Salute steps, which we must decidedly leave if
we wish to get on, a grateful hand across the water, and turn
into the big white church of Longhena—an empty shaft beneath
a perfunctory dome—where an American family and a German
party, huddled in a corner upon a pair of benches, are gazing,
with a conscientiousness worthy of a better cause, at nothing in
particular.

For there is nothing particular in this cold and conventional
temple to gaze at save the great Tintoretto of the sacristy, to
which we quickly pay our respects, and which we are glad to
have for ten minutes to ourselves.   The picture, though full
of beauty, is not the finest of the master's ; but it serves again
as well as another to transport—there is no other word—those
of his lovers for whom, in far-away days when Venice was an
early rapture, this strange and mystifying painter was almost
the supreme revelation.   The plastic arts may have less to say
to us than in the hungry years of youth, and the celebrated
picture in general be more of a blank ; but more than the others
any fine Tintoret still carries us back, calling up not only the

rich particular vision but the freshness of the old wonder. Many things come and go, but this great artist remains for us in Venice a part of the company of the mind. The others are there in their obvious glory, but he is the only one for whom the imagination, in our expressive modern phrase, sits up. "The Marriage in Cana," at the Salute, has all his characteristic and fascinating unexpectedness—the sacrifice of the figure of our Lord, who is reduced to the mere final point of a clever perspective, and the free, joyous presentation of all the other elements of the feast. Why, in spite of this queer one-sidedness, does the picture give us no impression of a lack of what the critics call reverence? For no other reason that I can think of than because it happens to be the work of its author, in whose very mistakes there is a singular wisdom. Mr. Ruskin has spoken with sufficient eloquence of the serious loveliness of the row of heads of the women on the right, who talk to each other as they sit at the foreshortened banquet. There could be no better example of the roving independence of the painter's vision, a real spirit of adventure for which his subject was always a cluster of accidents; not an obvious order, but a sort of peopled and agitated chapter of life, in which the figures are submissive pictorial notes. These notes are all there in their beauty and heterogeneity, and if the abundance is of a kind to make the principle of selection seem in comparison timid, yet the sense of "composition" in the spectator—if it happen to exist—reaches out to the painter in peculiar sympathy. Dull must be the spirit of the worker tormented in any field of art with that particular question who is not moved to recognise in the eternal problem the high fellowship of Tintoretto.

If the long reach from this point to the deplorable iron bridge which discharges the pedestrian at the Academy—or, more comprehensively, to the painted and gilded Gothic of the noble Palazzo Foscari—is too much of a curve to be seen at any one point as a whole, it represents the better the arched

neck, as it were, of the undulating serpent of which the Canalazzo has the likeness. We pass a dozen historic houses, we
note in our passage a hundred component "bits," with the
baffled sketcher's sense, and with what would doubtless be,
save for our intensely Venetian fatalism, the baffled sketcher's
temper. It is the early palaces, of course, and also, to be fair,
some of the late, if we could take them one by one, that give
the Canal the best of its grand air. The fairest are often
cheek-by-jowl with the foulest, and there are few, alas, so fair
as to have been completely protected by their beauty. The
ages and the generations have worked their will on them, and
the wind and the weather have had much to say; but dis-
figured and dishonoured as they are, with the bruises of their
marbles and the patience of their ruin, there is nothing like
them in the world, and the long succession of their faded,
conscious faces makes of the quiet water-way they overhang a
promenade historique of which the lesson, however often we read
it, gives, in the depth of its interest, an incomparable dignity
to Venice. We read it in the Romanesque arches, crooked
to-day in their very curves, of the early middle-age, in the
exquisite individual Gothic of the splendid time, and in the
cornices and columns of a decadence almost as proud. These
things at present are almost equally touching in their good
faith; they have each in their degree so effectually parted with
their pride. They have lived on as they could and lasted as
they might, and we hold them to no account of their infirmities,
for even those of them whose blank eyes to-day meet criticism
with most submission are far less vulgar than the uses we have
mainly managed to put them to. We have botched them and
patched them and covered them with sordid signs; we have
restored and improved them with a merciless taste, and the best
of them we have made over to the pedlars. Some of the most
striking objects in the finest vistas at present are the huge
advertisements of the curiosity-shops.

The antiquity-mongers in Venice have all the courage of their opinion, and it is easy to see how well they know they can confound you with an unanswerable question. What is the whole place but a curiosity-shop, and what are you here for yourself but to pick up odds and ends? " We pick them up *for* you," say these honest Jews, whose prices are marked in dollars, "and who shall blame us if, the flowers being pretty well plucked, we add an artificial rose or two to the composition of the bouquet?" They take care in a word that there be plenty of relics, and their establishments are huge and active. They administer the antidote to pedantry, and you can complain of them only if you never cross their thresholds. If you take this step you are lost, for you have parted with the correctness of your attitude. Venice becomes frankly from such a moment the big depressing dazzling joke in which after all our sense of her contradictions sinks to rest—the grimace of an over-strained philosophy. It's rather a comfort, for the curiosity-shops are amusing. You have bad moments indeed as you stand in their halls of humbug and, in the intervals of haggling, hear through the high windows the soft plash of the sea on the old water-steps, for you think with anger of the noble homes that are laid waste in such scenes, of the delicate lives that must have been, that might still be, led there. You reconstruct the admirable house according to your own needs; leaning on a back balcony, you drop your eyes into one of the little green gardens with which, for the most part, such establishments are exasperatingly blessed, and end by feeling it a shame that you yourself are not in possession. (I take for granted, of course, that as you go and come you are, in imagination, perpetually lodging yourself and setting up your gods; for if this innocent pastime, this borrowing of the mind, be not your favourite sport there is a flaw in the appeal that Venice makes to you.) There may be happy cases in which your envy is tempered, or perhaps I should rather say intensified, by real participation. If you have had the good fortune to enjoy the hospitality of an old Venetian home and to lead your life a little in the painted chambers that still echo with one of the historic names, you have entered by the shortest step into the inner spirit of the place. If it didn't savour of treachery to private kindness I should like to speak frankly of one of these delightful, even though alienated, structures, to refer to it as a splendid example of the old palatial type. But I can only do so in passing, with a hundred precautions, and, lifting the curtain at the edge, drop a commemorative word on the success with which, in this particularly happy instance, the cosmopolite habit, the modern sympathy, the intelligent, flexible attitude, the latest fruit of time, adjust themselves to the great gilded, relinquished shell and try to fill it out. A Venetian palace that has not too grossly suffered and that is not overwhelming by its mass makes almost any life graceful that may be led in it. With cultivated and generous contemporary ways it reveals a pre-established harmony. As you live in it day after day its beauty and its interest sink more deeply into your spirit; it has its moods and its hours and its mystic voices and its shifting expressions. If in the absence of its masters you have happened to have it to yourself for twenty-four hours you will never forget the charm of its haunted stillness, late on the summer afternoon for instance, when the call of playing children comes in behind from the campo, nor the way the old ghosts seemed to pass on tip-toe on the marble floors. It gives you practically the essence of the matter that we are considering, for beneath the high balconies Venice comes and goes, and the particular stretch you command contains all the characteristics. Everything has its turn, from the heavy barges of merchandise, pushed by long poles and the patient shoulder, to the floating pavilions of the great serenades, and you may study at your leisure the admirable Venetian arts of managing a boat and organising a spectacle. Of the beautiful free stroke with which the gondola, especially when there are two oars, is impelled, you never, in the Venetian scene, grow weary; it is always in the picture, and the large profiled action that lets the standing rowers throw themselves forward to a constant recovery has the double value of being, at the fag-end of greatness, the only energetic note. The people from the hotels are always afloat, and, at the hotel pace, the solitary gondolier (like the solitary horseman of the old-fashioned novel) is, I confess, a somewhat melancholy figure. Perched on his poop without a mate, he re-enacts perpetually, in high relief, with his toes turned out, the comedy of his odd and charming movement. He always has a little the look of an absent-minded nursery-maid pushing her small charges in a perambulator.

But why should I risk too free a comparison, where this picturesque and amiable class are concerned? I delight in their sun-burnt complexions and their childish dialect; I know them only by their merits, and I am grossly prejudiced in their favour. They are interesting and touching, and alike in their virtues and their defects human nature is simplified as with a big effective brush. Affecting above all is their dependence on the stranger, the whimsical stranger who swims out of their ken, yet whom Providence sometimes restores. The best of them at any rate are in their line great artists. On the swarming feast-days, on the strange feast-night of the Redentore, their steering is a miracle of ease. The master-hands, the celebrities and winners of prizes—you may see them on the private gondolas in spotless white, with brilliant sashes and ribbons, and often with very handsome persons—take the right of way with a pardonable insolence. They penetrate the crush of boats with an authority of their own. The crush of boats, the universal sociable bumping and squeezing, is great when, on the summer nights, the ladies shriek with alarm, the city pays the fiddlers and the illuminated barges, scattering music and song, lead a long train down the Canal. The barges used to be rowed in rhythmic strokes, but now they are towed by the steamer. The coloured lamps, the vocalists before the hotels, are not to my sense the greatest seduction of Venice; but it would be an uncandid sketch of the Canalazzo that shouldn't touch them with indulgence. Taking one nuisance with another, they are probably the prettiest in the world, and if they have in general more magic for the new arrival than for the old Venice-lover, they in any case, at their best, keep up the immemorial tradition. The Venetians have had from the beginning of time the pride of their processions and spectacles, and it's a wonder how with empty pockets they still make a clever show. The Carnival is dead, but these are the scraps of its inheritance. Vauxhall on the water is of course more Vauxhall than ever, with the good fortune of home-made music and of a mirror that reduplicates and multiplies. The feast of the Redeemer—the great popular feast of the year—is a wonderful Venetian Vauxhall. All Venice on this occasion takes to the boats for the night and loads them with lamps and provisions. Wedged together in a mass it sups and sings; every boat is a floating arbour, a private *café-concert*. Of all Christian commemorations it is the most ingenuously and harmlessly pagan. Toward morning the passengers repair to the Lido, where, as the sun rises, they plunge, still sociably, into the sea. The night of the Redentore has been described, but it would be interesting to have an account, from the domestic point of view, of its usual morrow. It is mainly an affair of the Giudecca, however, which is bridged over from the Zattere to the great church. The pontoons are laid together during the day—it is all done with extraordinary celerity and art—and the bridge is prolonged across the Canalazzo (to Santa Maria Zobenigo), which is my only warrant for glancing at the occasion. We glance at it from our palace windows; lengthening our necks a little, as we look up toward the Salute, we see all Venice, on the July afternoon, so serried as to move slowly, pour across the temporary footway. It is a flock of very good children, and the bridged Canal is their toy. All Venice on such occasions is gentle and friendly ; not even all Venice pushes any one into the water.

But from the same high windows we catch without any stretching of the neck a still more indispensable note in the picture, a famous pretender eating the bread of bitterness. This repast is served in the open air, on a neat little terrace, by attendants in livery, and there is no indiscretion in our seeing that the pretender dines. Ever since the table d'hôte in "Candide" Venice has been the refuge of monarchs in want of thrones—she wouldn't know herself without her *rois en exil.* The exile is agreeable and soothing, the gondola lets them down gently. Its movement is an anodyne, its silence a philtre, and little by little it rocks all ambitions to sleep. The proscript has plenty of leisure to write his proclamations and even his memoirs, and I believe he has organs in which they are published ; but the only noise he makes in the world is the harmless splash of his oars. He comes and goes along the Canalazzo, and he might be much worse employed. He is but one of the interesting objects it presents, however, and I am by no means sure that he is the most striking. He has a rival, if not in the iron bridge, which, alas, is within our range, at least—to take an immediate example—in the Montecuculi Palace. Far-descended and weary, but beautiful in its crooked old age, with its lovely proportions, its delicate round arches, its carvings and its disks of marble, is the haunted Montecuculi. Those who have a kindness for Venetian gossip like to remember that it was once for a few months the property of Robert Browning, who, however, never lived in it, and who died in the splendid Rezzonico, the residence of his son and a wonderful cosmopolite "document," which, as it presents itself, in an admirable position, but a short way further down the Canal, we can almost see, in spite of the curve, from the window at which we stand. This great seventeenth-century pile, throwing itself upon the water with a peculiar florid assurance, a certain upward toss of its cornice

which gives it the air of a rearing sea-horse, decorates immensely
—and within, as well as without—the wide angle that it
commands.

There is a more formal greatness in the high square Gothic
Foscari, just below it, one of the noblest creations of the fifteenth
century, a masterpiece of symmetry and majesty. Dedicated
to-day to official uses—it is the property of the State—it looks
conscious of the consideration it enjoys, and is one of the few
great houses within our range whose old age strikes us as robust
and painless. It is visibly "kept up"; perhaps it is kept up
too much; perhaps I am wrong in thinking so well of it.
These doubts and fears course rapidly through my mind—I am
easily their victim when it is a question of architecture—as they
are apt to do to-day, in Italy, almost anywhere, in the presence
of the beautiful, of the desecrated or the neglected. We feel
at such moments as if the eye of Mr. Ruskin were upon us;
we grow nervous and lose our confidence. This makes me
inevitably, in talking of Venice, seek a pusillanimous safety in
the trivial and the obvious. I am on firm ground in rejoicing
in the little garden directly opposite our windows—it is another
proof that they really show us everything—and in feeling that
the gardens of Venice would deserve a page to themselves.
They are infinitely more numerous than the arriving stranger
can suppose; they nestle with a charm all their own in the
complications of most back-views. Some of them are exquisite,
many are large, and even the scrappiest have an artful understanding, in the interest of colour, with the waterways that edge
their foundations. On the small canals, in the hunt for amusement, they are the prettiest surprises of all. The tangle of
plants and flowers crowds over the battered walls, the greenness
makes an arrangement with the rosy sordid brick. Of all the
reflected and liquefied things in Venice, and the number of these
is countless, I think the lapping water loves them most. They
are numerous on the Canalazzo, but wherever they occur they

give a brush to the picture and in particular, it is easy to guess, give a sweetness to the house. Then the elements are complete —the trio of air and water and of things that grow. Venice without them would be too much a matter of the tides and the stones. Even the little trellises of the *traghetti* count charmingly as reminders, amid so much artifice, of the woodland nature of man. The vine-leaves, trained on horizontal poles, make a roof of chequered shade for the gondoliers and ferrymen, who doze there according to opportunity, or chatter or hail the approaching "fare." There is no "hum" in Venice, so that their voices travel far; they enter your windows and mingle even with your dreams. I beg the reader to believe that if I had time to go into everything, I would go into the *traghetti*, which have their manners and their morals, and which used to have their piety. This piety was always a *madonnina*, the protectress of the passage—a quaint figure of the Virgin with the red spark of a lamp at her feet. The lamps appear for the most part to have gone out, and the images doubtless have been sold for *bric-a-brac*. The ferrymen, for aught I know, are converted to Nihilism—a faith consistent happily with a good stroke of business. One of the figures has been left, however—the Madonnetta which gives its name to a *traghetto* near the Rialto. But this sweet survivor is a carven stone inserted ages ago in the corner of an old palace and doubtless difficult of removal. *Pazienza*, the day will come when so marketable a relic will also be extracted from its socket and purchased by the devouring American. I leave that expression, on second thought, standing; but I repent of it when I remember that it is a devouring American—a lady long resident in Venice and whose kindnesses all Venetians, as well as her country-people, know, who has rekindled some of the extinguished tapers, setting up especially the big brave Gothic shrine, of painted and gilded wood, which, on the top of its stout *palo*, sheds its influence on the place of passage opposite the Salute.

If I may not go into those of the palaces this devious discourse has left behind, much less may I enter the great galleries of the Academy, which rears its blank wall, surmounted by the lion of St. Mark, well within sight of the windows at which we are still lingering. This wondrous temple of Venetian art—for all it promises little from without—overhangs, in a manner, the Grand Canal, but if we were so much as to cross its threshold we should wander beyond recall. It contains, in some of the most magnificent halls—where the ceilings have all the glory with which the imagination of Venice alone could over-arch a room—some of the noblest pictures in the world; and whether or not we go back to them on any particular occasion for another look, it is always a comfort to know that they are there, as the sense of them on the spot is a part of the furniture of the mind—the sense of them close at hand, behind every wall and under every cover, like the inevitable reverse of a medal, of the side exposed to the air that reflects, intensifies, completes the scene. In other words, as it was the inevitable destiny of Venice to be painted, and painted with passion, so the wide world of picture becomes, as we live there, and however much we go about our affairs, the constant habitation of our thoughts. The truth is, we are in it so uninterruptedly, at home and abroad, that there is scarcely a pressure upon us to seek it in one place more than in another. Choose your standpoint at random and trust the picture to come to you. This is manifestly why I have not, I find myself conscious, said more about the features of the Canalazzo which occupy the reach between the Salute and the position we have so obstinately taken up. It is still there before us, however, and the delightful little Palazzo Dario, intimately familiar to English and American travellers, picks itself out in the foreshortened brightness. The Dario is covered with the loveliest little marble plates and sculptured circles; it is made up of exquisite pieces—as if there had been only enough to make it small—so that it looks, in its extreme antiquity, a good deal like a house of cards that hold together by a tenure it would be fatal to touch. An old Venetian house dies hard indeed, and I should add that this delicate thing, with submission in every feature, continues to resist the contact of generations of lodgers. It is let out in floors (it used to be let as a whole) and in how many eager hands—for it is in great requisition—under how many fleeting dispensations have we not known and loved it? People are always writing in advance to secure it, as they are to secure the Jenkins's gondolier, and as the gondola passes we see strange faces at the windows—though it's ten to one we recognise them—and the millionth artist coming forth with his traps at the water-gate. The poor little patient Dario is one of the most flourishing booths at the fair.

The faces at the window look out at the great Sansovino— the splendid pile that is now occupied by the Prefect. I feel decidedly that I don't object as I ought to the palaces of the sixteenth and seventeenth centuries. Their pretensions impose upon me, and the imagination peoples them more freely than it can people the interiors of the prime. Was not moreover this masterpiece of Sansovino once occupied by the Venetian post-office, and thereby intimately connected with an ineffaceable first impression of the author of these remarks? He had arrived, wondering, palpitating, twenty-three years ago, after nightfall, and, the first thing on the morrow, had repaired to the post-office for his letters. They had been waiting a long time and were full of delayed interest, and he returned with them to the gondola and floated slowly down the Canal. The mixture, the rapture, the wonderful temple of the *poste restante*, the beautiful strangeness, all humanised by good news—the memory of this abides with him still, so that there always proceeds from the splendid water-front I speak of a certain secret appeal, something that seems to have been uttered first in the sonorous chambers of youth. Of course this association falls to the ground—or

rather splashes into the water—if I am the victim of a confusion. *Was* the edifice in question twenty-three years ago the
post-office, which has occupied since, for many a day, very much
humbler quarters? I am afraid to take the proper steps for
finding out, lest I should learn that during these years I have
misdirected my emotion. A better reason for the sentiment,
at any rate, is that such a great house has surely, in the high
beauty of its tiers, a refinement of its own. They make one
think of colosseums and aqueducts and bridges, and they constitute doubtless, in Venice, the most pardonable specimen of
the imitative. I have even a timid kindness for the huge
Pesaro, far down the Canal, whose main reproach, more even
than the coarseness of its forms, is its swaggering size, its want
of consideration for the general picture, which the early examples
so reverently respect. The Pesaro is as far out of the frame as
a modern hotel, and the Cornaro, close to it, oversteps almost
equally the modesty of art. One more thing they and their
kindred do, I must add, for which, unfortunately, we can
patronise them less. They make even the most elaborate
material civilisation of the present day seem woefully shrunken
and *bourgeois*, for they simply—I allude to the biggest palaces—
can't be lived in as they were intended to be. The modern
tenant may take in all the magazines, but he bends not the bow
of Achilles. He occupies the place, but he doesn't fill it, and
he has guests from the neighbouring inns with ulsters and
Baedekers. We are far at the Pesaro, by the way, from our
attaching window, and we take advantage of it to go in rather
a melancholy mood to the end. The long straight vista from
the Foscari to the Rialto, the great middle stretch of the Canal,
contains, as the phrase is, a hundred objects of interest, but it
contains most the bright oddity of its general Deluge air. In
all these centuries it has never got over its resemblance to a
flooded city; for some reason or other it is the only part of
Venice in which the houses look as if the waters had overtaken

them. Everywhere else they reckon with them—have chosen them; here alone the lapping seaway seems to confess itself an accident.

There are persons who hold this long, gay, shabby, spotty perspective, in which, with its immense field of confused reflection, the houses have infinite variety, the dullest expanse in Venice. It was not dull, we imagine, for Lord Byron, who lived in the midmost of the three Mocenigo palaces, where the writing-table is still shown at which he gave the rein to his passions. For other observers it is sufficiently enlivened by so delightful a creation as the Palazzo Loredan, once a masterpiece and at present the Municipio, not to speak of a variety of other immemorial bits whose beauty still has a degree of freshness. Some of the most touching relics of early Venice are here— for it was here she precariously clustered—peeping out of a submersion more pitiless than the sea. As we approach the Rialto indeed the picture falls off and a comparative commonness suffuses it. There is a wide paved walk on either side of the Canal, on which the waterman—and who in Venice is not a waterman?—is prone to seek repose. I speak of the summer days—it is the summer Venice that is the visible Venice. The big tarry barges are drawn up at the *fondamenta*, and the barelegged boatmen, in faded blue cotton, lie asleep on the hot stones. If there were no colour anywhere else there would be enough in their tanned personalities. Half the low doorways open into the warm interior of waterside drinking-shops, and here and there, on the quay, beneath the bush that overhangs the door, there are rickety tables and chairs. Where in Venice is there not the amusement of character and of detail? The tone in this part is very vivid, and is largely that of the brown plebeian faces looking out of the patchy miscellaneous houses— the faces of fat undressed women and of other simple folk who are not aware that they enjoy, from balconies once doubtless patrician, a view the knowing ones of the earth come thousands of miles to envy them. The effect is enhanced by the tattered clothes hung to dry in the windows, by the sun-faded rags that flutter from the polished balustrades—these are ivory-smooth with time; and the whole scene profits by the general law that renders decadence and ruin in Venice more brilliant than any prosperity. Decay is in this extraordinary place golden in tint and misery *couleur de rose*. The gondolas of the correct people are unmitigated sable, but the poor market-boats from the islands are kaleidoscopic.

The Bridge of the Rialto is a name to conjure with, but, honestly speaking, it is scarcely the gem of the composition. There are of course two ways of taking it—from the water or from the upper passage, where its small shops and booths abound in Venetian character; but it mainly counts as a feature of the Canal when seen from the gondola or even from the awful *vaporetto*. The great curve of its single arch is much to be commended, especially when, coming from the direction of the railway-station, you see it frame with its sharp compass-line the perfect picture, the reach of the Canal on the other side. But the backs of the little shops make from the water a graceless collective hump, and the inside view is the diverting one. The big arch of the bridge—like the arches of all the bridges—is the waterman's friend in wet weather. The gondolas, when it rains, huddle beside the peopled barges, and the young ladies from the hotels, vaguely fidgeting, complain of the communication of insect life. Here indeed is a little of everything, and the jewellers of this celebrated precinct—they have their immemorial row—make almost as fine a show as the fruiterers. It is a universal market, and a fine place to study Venetian types. The produce of the islands is discharged there, and the fishmongers announce their presence. All one's senses indeed are vigorously attacked; the whole place is violently hot and bright, all odorous and noisy. The churning of the screw of the *vaporetto* mingles with the other sounds—not indeed that this

D

offensive note is confined to one part of the Canal. But just
here the little piers of the resented steamer are particularly near
together, and it seems somehow to be always kicking up the
water. As we go further down we see it stopping exactly
beneath the glorious windows of the Ca' d' Oro. It has chosen
its position well, and who shall gainsay it for having put itself
under the protection of the most romantic façade in Europe ?
The companionship of these objects is a symbol ; it expresses
supremely the present and the future of Venice. Perfect, in its
prime, was the marble Ca' d' Oro, with the noble recesses of its
loggie, but even then it probably never " met a want," like the
successful *vaporetto*. If, however, we are not to go into the
Museo Civico—the old Museo Correr, which rears a staring
renovated front far down on the left, near the station, so also
we must keep out of the great vexed question of steam on the
Canalazzo, just as a while since we prudently kept out of the
Accademia. These are expensive and complicated excursions.
It is obvious that if the *vaporetti* have contributed to the ruin of
the gondoliers, already hard pressed by fate, and to that of the
palaces, whose foundations their waves undermine, and that if
they have robbed the Grand Canal of the supreme distinction of
its tranquillity, so on the other hand they have placed "rapid
transit," in the New York phrase, in everybody's reach, and
enabled everybody—save indeed those who wouldn't for the
world—to rush about Venice as furiously as people rush about
New York. The suitability of this consummation needn't be
pointed out.

Even we ourselves, in the irresistible contagion, are going so
fast now that we have only time to note in how clever and costly
a fashion the Museo Civico, the old Fondaco dei Turchi, has
been reconstructed and restored. It is a glare of white marble
without, and a series of showy majestic halls within, where a
thousand curious mementos and relics of old Venice are gathered
and classified. Of its miscellaneous treasures I fear I may

perhaps frivolously prefer the series of its remarkable living
Longhis, an illustration of manners more copious than the
celebrated Carpaccio, the two ladies with their little animals and
their long sticks. Wonderful indeed to-day are the museums of
Italy, where the renovations and the *belle ordonnance* speak of funds
apparently unlimited, in spite of the fact that the numerous custodians frankly look starved. What is the pecuniary source of all
this civic magnificence—it is shown in a hundred other ways—and
how do the Italian cities manage to acquit themselves of expenses
that would be formidable to communities richer and doubtless
less æsthetic? Who pays the bills for the expressive statues
alone, the general exuberance of sculpture, with which every
piazzetta of almost every village is patriotically decorated? Let
us not seek an answer to the puzzling question, but observe
instead that we are passing the mouth of the populous Cana-
reggio, next widest of the water-ways, where the race of Shylock
abides, and at the corner of which the big colourless church of
San Geremia stands gracefully enough on guard. The Cana-
reggio, with its wide lateral footways and humpbacked bridges,
makes on the feast of St. John an admirable noisy, tawdry theatre
for one of the prettiest and the most infantile of the Venetian
processions.

The rest of the course is a reduced magnificence, in spite of
interesting bits, of the battered pomp of the Pesaro and the
Cornaro, of the recurrent memories of royalty in exile which
cluster about the Palazzo Vendramin Calergi, once the residence
of the Comte de Chambord and still that of his half-brother, in
spite too of the big Papadopoli gardens, opposite the station, the
largest private grounds in Venice, but of which Venice in general
mainly gets the benefit in the usual form of irrepressible greenery
climbing over walls and nodding at water. The rococo church
of the Scalzi is here, all marble and malachite, all a cold, hard
glitter and a costly, curly ugliness, and here too, opposite, on the
top of its high steps, is San Simeone Profeta, I won't say im-

mortalised, but unblushingly misrepresented, by the perfidious Canaletto. I shall not stay to unravel the mystery of this prosaic painter's malpractices ; he falsified without fancy, and as he apparently transposed at will the objects he reproduced, one is never sure of the particular view that may have constituted his subject. It would look exactly like such and such a place if almost everything were not different. San Simeone Profeta appears to hang there upon the wall ; but it is on the wrong side of the Canal and the other elements quite fail to correspond. One's confusion is the greater because one doesn't know that everything may not really have changed, even beyond all probability—though it's only in America that churches cross the street or the river—and the mixture of the recognisable and the different makes the ambiguity maddening, all the more that the painter is almost as attaching as he is bad. Thanks at any rate to the white church, domed and porticoed, on the top of its steps, the traveller emerging for the first time upon the terrace of the railway-station seems to have a Canaletto before him. He speedily discovers indeed even in the presence of this scene of the final accents of the Canalazzo—there is a charm in the old pink warehouses on the hot *fondamenta*—that he has something much better. He looks up and down at the gathered gondolas ; he has his surprise after all, his little first Venetian thrill ; and as the terrace of the station ushers in these things we shall say no harm of it, though it is not lovely. It is the beginning of his experience, but it is the end of the Grand Canal.

1892.

VENICE: AN EARLY IMPRESSION

THERE would be much to say about that golden chain of historic cities which stretches from Milan to Venice, in which the very names—Brescia, Verona, Mantua, Padua—are an ornament to one's phrase; but I should have to draw upon recollections now three years old and to make my short story a long one. Of Verona and Venice only have I recent impressions, and even to these I must do hasty justice. I came into Venice, just as I had done before, toward the end of a summer's day, when the shadows begin to lengthen and the light to glow, and found that the attendant sensations bore repetition remarkably well. There was the same last intolerable delay at Mestre, just before your first glimpse of the lagoon confirms the already distinct sea-smell which has added speed to the precursive flight of your imagination; then the liquid level, edged afar off by its band of undiscriminated domes and spires, soon distinguished and proclaimed, however, as excited and contentious heads multiply at the windows of the train; then your long rumble on the immense white railway-bridge, which, in spite of the invidious contrast drawn, and very properly, by Mr. Ruskin between the old and the new approach, does truly, in a manner, shine across the green lap of the lagoon like a mighty causeway of marble; then the plunge into the station, which would be exactly similar to every other plunge save for one little fact —that the keynote of the great medley of voices borne back from the exit is not "Cab, sir!" but "Barca, signore!"

I do not mean, however, to follow the traveller through every phase of his initiation, at the risk of stamping poor Venice beyond repair as the supreme bugbear of literature; though for my own part I hold that to a fine healthy romantic appetite the subject can't be too diffusely treated. Meeting in the Piazza on the evening of my arrival a young American painter who told me that he had been spending the summer just where I found him, I could have assaulted him for very envy. He was painting forsooth the interior of St. Mark's. To be a young American painter unperplexed by the mocking, elusive soul of things and satisfied with their wholesome light-bathed surface and shape; keen of eye; fond of colour, of sea and sky and anything that may chance between them; of old lace and old brocade and old furniture (even when made to order); of time-mellowed harmonies on nameless canvases and happy contours in cheap old engravings; to spend one's mornings in still, productive analysis of the clustered shadows of the Basilica, one's afternoons anywhere, in church or campo, on canal or lagoon, and one's evenings in starlight gossip at Florian's, feeling the sea-breeze throb languidly between the two great pillars of the Piazzetta and over the low black domes of the church—this, I consider, is to be as happy as is consistent with the preservation of reason.

The mere use of one's eyes in Venice is happiness enough, and generous observers find it hard to keep an account of their profits in this line. Everything the attention touches holds it, keeps playing with it—thanks to some inscrutable flattery of the atmosphere. Your brown-skinned, white-shirted gondolier, twisting himself in the light, seems to you, as you lie at contemplation beneath your awning, a perpetual symbol of Venetian "effect." The light here is in fact a mighty magician and, with all respect to Titian, Veronese and Tintoret, the greatest artist of them all. You should see in places the material with which it deals—slimy brick, marble battered and befouled, rags, dirt, decay. Sea and sky seem to meet half-way, to blend their tones into a soft iridescence, a lustrous compound of wave and cloud and a hundred nameless local reflections, and then to fling the clear tissue against every object of vision. You may see these elements at work everywhere, but to see them in their intensity you should choose the finest day in the month and have yourself rowed far away across the lagoon to Torcello. Without making this excursion you can hardly pretend to know Venice or to sympathise with that longing for pure radiance which animated her great colourists. It is a perfect bath of light, and I couldn't get rid of a fancy that we were cleaving the upper atmosphere on some hurrying cloud-skiff. At Torcello there is nothing but the light to see—nothing at least but a sort of blooming sand-bar intersected by a single narrow creek which does duty as a canal and occupied by a meagre cluster of huts the dwellings apparently of market-gardeners and fishermen, and by a ruinous church of the eleventh century. It is impossible to imagine a more penetrating case of unheeded collapse. Torcello was the mother-city of Venice, and she lies there now, a mere mouldering vestige, like a group of weather-bleached parental bones left impiously unburied. I stopped my gondola at the mouth of the shallow inlet and walked along the grass beside a hedge to the low-browed, crumbling cathedral. The charm of certain vacant grassy spaces, in Italy, overfrowned by masses of brickwork that are honeycombed by the suns of centuries, is something that I hereby renounce once for all the attempt to express; but you may be sure that whenever I mention such a spot enchantment lurks in it.

A delicious stillness covered the little campo at Torcello; I remember none so subtly audible save that of the Roman Campagna. There was no life but the visible tremor of the brilliant air and the cries of half-a-dozen young children who dogged our steps and clamoured for coppers. These children, by the way, were the handsomest little brats in the world, and each was furnished with a pair of eyes that could only have signified the protest of nature against the meanness of fortune. They were very nearly as naked as savages, and their little bellies protruded like those of infant cannibals in the illustrations of books of travel; but as they scampered and sprawled in the soft, thick grass, grinning like suddenly-translated cherubs and showing their hungry little teeth, they suggested forcibly that the best assurance of happiness in this world is to be found in the maximum of innocence and the minimum of wealth. One small urchin—framed, if ever a child was, to be the joy of an aristocratic mamma—was the most expressively beautiful creature I had ever looked upon. He had a smile to make Correggio sigh in his grave; and yet here he was running wild among the sea-stunted bushes, on the lonely margin of a decaying world, in prelude to how blank or to how dark a destiny? Verily nature is still at odds with propriety; though indeed if they ever really pull together I fear nature will quite lose her distinction. An infant citizen of our own republic, straight-haired, pale-eyed and freckled, duly darned and catechised, marching into a New England schoolhouse, is an object often seen and soon forgotten; but I think I shall always remember with infinite tender conjecture, as the years roll by, this little unlettered Eros of the Adriatic strand. Yet all youthful things at Torcello were not cheerful, for the poor lad who brought us the key of the cathedral was shaking with an ague, and his melancholy presence seemed to point the moral of forsaken nave and choir. The church, admirably primitive and curious, reminded me of the two or three oldest churches of Rome— St. Clement and St. Agnes. The interior is rich in grimly mystical mosaics of the twelfth century and the patchwork of precious fragments in the pavement not inferior to that of St. Mark's. But the terribly distinct Apostles are ranged against their dead gold backgrounds as stiffly as grenadiers presenting arms—intensely personal sentinels of a personal Deity. Their stony stare seems to wait forever vainly for some visible revival of primitive orthodoxy, and one may well wonder whether it finds much beguilement in idly-gazing troops of Western heretics —passionless even in their heresy.

I had been curious to see whether in the galleries and temples of Venice I should be disposed to transpose my old estimates— to burn what I had adored and adore what I had burned. It is a sad truth that one can stand in the Ducal Palace for the first time but once, with the deliciously ponderous sense of that particular half-hour's being an era in one's mental history ; but I had the satisfaction of finding at least—a great comfort in a short stay — that none of my early memories were likely to change places and that I could take up my admirations where I had left them. I still found Carpaccio delightful, Veronese magnificent, Titian supremely beautiful and Tintoret scarce to be appraised. I repaired immediately to the little church of San Cassano, which contains the smaller of Tintoret's two great Crucifixions ; and when I had looked at it awhile I drew a long breath and felt I could now face any other picture in Venice with proper self-possession. It seemed to me I had advanced to the uttermost limit of painting ; that beyond this another art— inspired poetry—begins, and that Bellini, Veronese, Giorgione, and Titian, all joining hands and straining every muscle of their genius, reach forward not so far but that they leave a visible space in which Tintoret alone is master. I well remember the exaltations to which he lifted me when first I learned to know him ; but the glow of that comparatively youthful amazement is dead, and with it, I fear, that confident vivacity of phrase of which, in trying to utter my impressions, I felt less the magnilo- quence than the impotence. In his power there are many weak spots, mysterious lapses and fitful intermissions ; but when the list of his faults is complete he still remains to me the most *interesting* of painters. His reputation rests chiefly on a more superficial sort of merit—his energy, his unsurpassed produc- tivity, his being, as Théophile Gautier says, *le roi des fougueux.*

These qualities are immense, but the great source of his impressiveness is that his indefatigable hand never drew a line that was not, as one may say, a moral line. No painter ever had such breadth and such depth ; and even Titian, beside him, scarce figures as more than a great decorative artist. Mr. Ruskin, whose eloquence in dealing with the great Venetians sometimes outruns his discretion, is fond of speaking even of Veronese as a painter of deep spiritual intentions. This, it seems to me, is pushing matters too far, and the author of "The Rape of Europa" is, pictorially speaking, no greater casuist than any other genius of supreme good taste. Titian was assuredly a mighty poet, but Tintoret — well, Tintoret was almost a prophet. Before his greatest works you are conscious of a sudden evaporation of old doubts and dilemmas, and the eternal problem of the conflict between idealism and realism dies the most natural of deaths. In his genius the problem is practically solved ; the alternatives are so harmoniously interfused that I defy the keenest critic to say where one begins and the other ends. The homeliest prose melts into the most ethereal poetry—the literal and the imaginative fairly confound their identity.

This, however, is vague praise. Tintoret's great merit, to my mind, was his unequalled distinctness of vision. When once he had conceived the germ of a scene it defined itself to his imagination with an intensity, an amplitude, an individuality of expression, which make one's observation of his pictures seem less an operation of the mind than a kind of supplementary experience of life. Veronese and Titian are content with a much looser specification, as their treatment of any subject that the author of the Crucifixion at San Cassano has also treated abundantly proves. There are few more suggestive contrasts than that between the absence of a total character at all commensurate with its scattered variety and brilliancy in Veronese's "Marriage of Cana," at the Louvre, and the poignant, almost startling, completeness of Tintoret's illustration of the theme

at the Salute church. To compare his " Presentation of the
Virgin," at the Madonna dell' Orto, with Titian's at the Academy, or his " Annunciation " with Titian's close at hand, is
to measure the essential difference between observation and
imagination. One has certainly not said all that there is to say
for Titian when one has called him an observer. *Il y mettait
du sien*, and I use the term to designate roughly the artist whose
apprehension, infinitely deep and strong when applied to the
single figure or to easily balanced groups, spends itself vainly
on great dramatic combinations—or rather leaves them ungauged.
It was the whole scene that Tintoret seemed to have beheld in a
flash of inspiration intense enough to stamp it ineffaceably on
his perception ; and it was the whole scene, complete, peculiar,
individual, unprecedented, that he committed to canvas with all
the vehemence of his talent. Compare his " Last Supper," at
San Giorgio—its long, diagonally placed table, its dusky spaciousness, its scattered lamp-light and halo-light, its startled, gesticulating figures, its richly realistic foreground—with the customary
formal, almost mathematical rendering of the subject, in which
impressiveness seems to have been sought in elimination rather
than comprehension. You get from Tintoret's work the impression that he *felt*, pictorially, the great, beautiful, terrible
spectacle of human life very much as Shakespeare felt it poeti-
cally—with a heart that never ceased to beat a passionate accompaniment to every stroke of his brush. Thanks to this fact
his works are signally grave, and their almost universal and
rapidly increasing decay doesn't relieve their gloom. Nothing
indeed can well be sadder than the great collection of Tintorets
at San Rocco. Incurable blackness is settling fast upon all of
them, and they frown at you across the sombre splendour of
their great chambers like gaunt twilight phantoms of pictures.
To our children's children Tintoret, as things are going, can be
hardly more than a name ; and such of them as shall miss the
tragic beauty, already so dimmed and stained, of the great

" Bearing of the Cross " in that temple of his spirit will live and die without knowing the largest eloquence of art. If you wish to add the last touch of solemnity to the place recall as vividly as possible while you linger at San Rocco the painter's singularly interesting portrait of himself, at the Louvre. The old man looks out of the canvas from beneath a brow as sad as a sunless twilight, with just such a stoical hopelessness as you might fancy him to wear if he stood at your side gazing at his rotting canvases. It isn't whimsical to read it as the face of a man who felt that he had given the world more than the world was likely to repay. Indeed before every picture of Tintoret you may remember this tremendous portrait with profit. On one side the power, the passion, the illusion of his art ; on the other the mortal fatigue of his spirit. The world's knowledge of him is so small that the portrait throws a doubly precious light on his personality ; and when we wonder vainly what manner of man he was, and what were his purpose, his faith and his method, we may find forcible assurance there that they were at any rate his life—one of the most intellectually passionate ever led.

Verona, which was my last Italian stopping-place, is in any conditions a delightfully interesting city; but the kindness of my own memory of it is deepened by a subsequent ten days' experience of Germany. I rose one morning at Verona, and went to bed at night at Botzen! The statement needs no comment, and the two places, though but fifty miles apart, are as painfully dissimilar as their names. I had prepared myself for your delectation with a copious tirade on German manners, German scenery, German art and the German stage—on the lights and shadows of Innsbrück, Munich, Nüremberg and Heidelberg; but just as I was about to put pen to paper I glanced into a little volume on these very topics lately published by that famous novelist and moralist, M. Ernest Feydeau, the fruit of a summer's observation at Homburg. This work produced a reaction; and if I chose to follow M. Feydeau's own example when he wishes to qualify his approbation I might call his treatise by any vile name known to the speech of man. But I content myself with pronouncing it superficial. I then reflect that my own opportunities for seeing and judging were extremely limited, and I suppress my tirade, lest some more enlightened critic should come and hang me with the same rope. Its sum and substance was to have been that—superficially— Germany is ugly; that Munich is a nightmare, Heidelberg a disappointment (in spite of its charming castle) and even Nüremberg not a joy for ever. But comparisons are odious, and if Munich is ugly Verona is beautiful enough. You may laugh at my logic, but will probably assent to my meaning. I carried away from Verona a precious mental picture upon which I cast an introspective glance whenever between Botzen and Strassburg the oppression of external circumstance became painful. It was a lovely August afternoon in the Roman arena—a ruin in which repair and restoration have been so watchfully and plausibly practised that it seems all of one harmonious antiquity. The vast stony oval rose high against the sky in a single clear, continuous line, broken here and there only by strolling and reclining loungers. The massive tiers inclined in solid monotony to the central circle, in which a small open-air theatre was in active operation. A small quarter of the great slope of masonry facing the stage was roped off into an auditorium, in which the narrow level space between the foot-lights and the lowest step figured as the pit. Foot-lights are a figure of speech, for the performance was going on in the broad glow of the afternoon, with a delightful and apparently by no means misplaced confidence in the good-will of the spectators. What the piece was that was deemed so superbly able to shift for itself I know not—very possibly the same drama that I remember seeing advertised during my former visit to Verona; nothing less than *La Tremenda Giustizia di Dio.* If titles are worth anything this product of the melodramatist's art might surely stand upon its own legs. Along the tiers above the little group of regular spectators was gathered a free-list of unauthorised observers, who, although beyond ear-shot, must have been enabled by the generous breadth of Italian gesture to follow the tangled thread of the piece. It was all deliciously Italian— the mixture of old life and new, the mountebank's booth (it was hardly more) grafted on the antique circus, the dominant presence of a mighty architecture, the loungers and idlers beneath the kindly sky and upon the sun-warmed stones. I never felt more keenly the difference between the background to life in very old and very new civilisations. There are other things in Verona to make it a liberal education to be born there, though that it *is* one for the contemporary Veronese I don't pretend to say. The Tombs of the Scaligers, with their soaring pinnacles, their high-poised canopies, their exquisite refinement and concentration of the Gothic idea, I can't profess, even after much worshipful gazing, to have fully comprehended and enjoyed. They seemed to me full of deep architectural meanings, such as must drop gently into the mind one by one, after infinite tranquil contemplation. But even to the hurried and preoccupied traveller the solemn little chapel-yard in the city's heart, in which they stand girdled by their great swaying curtain of linked and twisted iron, is one of the most impressive spots in Italy. Nowhere else is such a wealth of artistic achievement crowded into so narrow a space; nowhere else are the daily comings and goings of men blessed by the presence of *manlier* art. Verona is rich furthermore in beautiful churches—several with beautiful names: San Fermo, Santa Anastasia, San Zenone. This last is a structure of high antiquity and of the most impressive loveliness. The nave terminates in a double choir, that is a sub-choir or crypt into which you descend and where you wander among primitive columns whose variously grotesque capitals rise hardly higher than your head, and an upper choral plane reached by broad stairways of the bravest effect. I shall never forget the impression of majestic chastity that I received from the great nave of the building on my former visit. I then decided to my satisfaction that every church is from the devotional point of view a solecism that has not something of a similar absolute felicity of proportion ; for strictly formal beauty seems best to express our conception of spiritual beauty. The nobly serious character of San Zenone is deepened by its single picture—a masterpiece of the most serious of painters, the severe and exquisite Mantegna.

1872.

TWO OLD HOUSES AND THREE
YOUNG WOMEN

THERE are times and places that come back yet again, but that, when the brooding tourist puts out his hand to them, meet it a little slowly, or even seem to recede a step, as if in slight fear of some liberty he may take. Surely they should know by this time that he is capable of taking none. He has his own way—he makes it all right. It now becomes just a part of the charming solicitation that it presents precisely a problem—that of *giving* the particular thing as much as possible without at the same time giving it, as we say, away. There are considerations, proprieties, a necessary indirectness—he must use, in short, a little art. No necessity, however, more than this, makes him warm to his work, and thus it is that, after all, he hangs his three pictures.

I

The evening that was to give me the first of them was by no means the first occasion of my asking myself if that inveterate "style" of which we talk so much be absolutely conditioned— in dear old Venice and elsewhere—on decrepitude. Is it the style that has brought about the decrepitude, or the decrepitude that has, as it were, intensified and consecrated the style? There is an ambiguity about it all that constantly haunts and beguiles. Dear old Venice has lost her complexion, her figure, her reputation, her self-respect; and yet, with it all, has so puzzlingly not lost a shred of her distinction. Perhaps indeed the case is simpler than it seems, for the poetry of misfortune is familiar to us all, whereas, in spite of a stroke here and there of some happy justice that charms, we scarce find ourselves anywhere arrested by the poetry of a run of luck. The misfortune of Venice being, accordingly, at every point, what we most touch, feel and see, we end by assuming it to be of the essence of her dignity ; a consequence, we become aware, by the way, sufficiently discouraging to the general application or pretension of style, and all the more that, to make the final felicity deep, the original greatness must have been something tremendous. If it be the ruins that are noble we have known plenty that were not, and moreover there are degrees and varieties : certain monuments, solid survivals, hold up their heads and decline to ask for a grain of your pity. Well, one knows of course when to keep one's pity to oneself ; yet one clings, even in the face of the colder stare, to one's prized Venetian privilege of making the sense of doom and decay a part of every impression. Cheerful work, it may be said of course ; and it is doubtless only in Venice that you gain more by such a trick than you lose. What was most beautiful is gone ; what was next most beautiful is, thank goodness, going—that, I think, is the monstrous description of the better part of your thought. Is it really your fault if the place makes you want so desperately to read history into everything ?

You do that wherever you turn and wherever you look, and you do it, I should say, most of all at night. It comes to you there with longer knowledge, and with all deference to what flushes and shimmers, that the night is the real time. It perhaps even wouldn't take much to make you award the palm to the nights of winter. This is certainly true for the form of progression that is most characteristic, for every question of departure and arrival by gondola. The little closed cabin of this perfect vehicle, the movement, the darkness and the plash, the indistinguishable swerves and twists, all the things you don't see and all the things you do feel—each dim recognition and obscure

E

arrest is a possible throb of your sense of being floated to your doom, even when the truth is simply and sociably that you are going out to tea. Nowhere else is anything as innocent so mysterious, nor anything as mysterious so pleasantly deterrent to protest. These are the moments when you are most daringly Venetian, most content to leave cheap trippers and other aliens the high light of the mid-lagoon and the pursuit of pink and gold. The splendid day is good enough for *them*; what is best for you is to stop at last, as you are now stopping, among clustered *pali* and softly-shifting poops and prows, at a great flight of water-steps that play their admirable part in the general effect of a great entrance. The high doors stand open from them to the paved chamber of a basement tremendously tall and not vulgarly lighted, from which, in turn, mounts the slow stone staircase that draws you further on. The great point is, that if you are worthy of this impression at all, there isn't a single item of it of which the association isn't noble. Hold to it fast that there is no other such dignity of arrival as arrival by water. Hold to it that to float and slacken and gently bump, to creep out of the low, dark *felze* and make the few guided movements and find the strong crooked and offered arm, and then, beneath lighted palace-windows, pass up the few damp steps on the precautionary carpet—hold to it that these things constitute a preparation of which the only defect is that it may sometimes perhaps really prepare too much. It's so stately that what can come after?—it's so good in itself that what, upstairs, as we comparative vulgarians say, can be better? Hold to it, at any rate, that if a lady, in especial, scrambles out of a carriage, tumbles out of a cab, flops out of a tram-car, and hurtles, projectile-like, out of a "lightning-elevator," she alights from the Venetian conveyance as Cleopatra may have stepped from her barge. Upstairs—whatever may be yet in store for her— her entrance shall still advantageously enjoy the support most opposed to the "momentum" acquired. The beauty of the matter has been in the absence of all momentum—elsewhere so scientifically applied to us, from behind, by the terrible life of our day—and in the fact that, as the elements of slowness, the felicities of deliberation, doubtless thus all hang together, the last of calculable dangers is to enter a great Venetian room with a rush.

Not the least happy note, therefore, of the picture I am trying to frame is that there was absolutely no rushing ; not only in the sense of a scramble over marble floors, but, by reason of something dissuasive and distributive in the very air of the place, a suggestion, under the fine old ceilings and among types of face and figure abounding in the unexpected, that here were many things to consider. Perhaps the simplest rendering of a scene into the depths of which there are good grounds of discretion for not sinking would be just this emphasis on the value of the unexpected for such occasions—with due qualification, naturally, of its degree. Unexpectedness pure and simple, it is needless to say, may easily endanger any social gathering, and I hasten to add moreover that the figures and faces I speak of were probably not in the least unexpected to each other. The stage they occupied was a stage of variety—Venice has ever been a garden of strange social flowers. It is only as reflected in the consciousness of the visitor from afar—brooding tourist even call him, or sharp-eyed bird on the branch—that I attempt to give you the little drama ; beginning with the felicity that most appealed to him, the visible, unmistakable fact that he was the only representative of his class. The whole of the rest of the business was but what he saw and felt and fancied—what he was to remember and what he was to forget. Through it all, I may say distinctly, he clung to his great Venetian clue—the explanation of everything by the historic idea. It was a high historic house, with such a quantity of recorded past twinkling in the multitudinous candles that one grasped at the idea of something waning and displaced, and might even fondly and secretly nurse the conceit

that what one was having was just the very last. Wasn't it
certainly, for instance, no mere illusion that there is no appreciable future left for such manners—an urbanity so comprehensive, a form so transmitted, as those of such a hostess and
such a host? The future is for a different conception of the
graceful altogether—so far as it's for a conception of the graceful at all. Into that computation I shall not attempt to enter ;
but these representative products of an antique culture, at least,
and one of which the secret seems more likely than not to be
lost, were not common, nor indeed was any one else—in the
circle to which the picture most insisted on restricting itself.

Neither, on the other hand, was any one either very beautiful
or very fresh : which was again, exactly, a precious " value "
on an occasion that was to shine most, to the imagination, by
the complexity of its references. Such old, old women with
such old, old jewels ; such ugly, ugly ones with such handsome,
becoming names ; such battered, fatigued gentlemen with such
inscrutable decorations ; such an absence of youth, for the most
part, in either sex—of the pink and white, the " bud " of new
worlds ; such a general personal air, in fine, of being the worse
for a good deal of wear in various old ones. It was not a society
—that was clear—in which little girls and boys set the tune ;
and there was that about it all that might well have cast a
shadow on the path of even the most successful little girl. Yet
also—let me not be rudely inexact—it was in honour of youth
and freshness that we had all been convened. The fiançailles
of the last—unless it were the last but one—unmarried daughter
of the house had just been brought to a proper climax ; the
contract had been signed, the betrothal rounded off—I'm not
sure that the civil marriage hadn't, that day, taken place.
The occasion then had in fact the most charming of
heroines and the most ingenuous of heroes, a young man, the
latter, all happily suffused with a fair Austrian blush. The
young lady had had, besides other more or less shining recent

ancestors, a very famous paternal grandmother, who had played a great part in the political history of her time and whose portrait, in the taste and dress of 1830, was conspicuous in one of the rooms. The granddaughter of this celebrity, of royal race, was strikingly like her and, by a fortunate stroke, had been habited, combed, curled in a manner exactly to reproduce the portrait. These things were charming and amusing, as indeed were several other things besides. The great Venetian beauty of our period was there, and nature had equipped the great Venetian beauty for her part with the properest sense of the suitable, or in any case with a splendid generosity—since on the ideally suitable *character* of so brave a human symbol who shall have the last word? This responsible agent was at all events the beauty in the world about whom probably, most, the absence of question (an absence never wholly propitious) would a little smugly and monotonously flourish: the one thing wanting to the interest she inspired was thus the possibility of ever discussing it. There were plenty of suggestive subjects round about, on the other hand, as to which the exchange of ideas would by no means necessarily have dropped. You profit to the full at such times by all the old voices, echoes, images—by that element of the history of Venice which represents all Europe as having at one time and another revelled or rested, asked for pleasure or for patience there; which gives you the place supremely as the refuge of endless strange secrets, broken fortunes and wounded hearts.

II

There had been, on lines of further or different speculation, a young Englishman to luncheon, and the young Englishman had proved "sympathetic"; so that when it was a question afterwards of some of the more hidden treasures, the browner depths of the old churches, the case became one for mutual guidance and gratitude—for a small afternoon tour and the wait of a pair of friends in the warm little *campi*, at locked doors for which the nearest urchin had scurried off to fetch the keeper of the key. There are few brown depths to-day into which the light of the hotels doesn't shine, and few hidden treasures about which pages enough, doubtless, haven't already been printed : my business, accordingly, let me hasten to say, is not now with the fond renewal of any discovery—at least in the order of impressions most usual. Your discovery may be, for that matter, renewed every week ; the only essential is the good luck—which a fair amount of practice has taught you to count upon—of not finding, for the particular occasion, other discoverers in the field. Then, in the quiet corner, with the closed door—then in the presence of the picture and of your companion's sensible emotion—not only the original happy moment, but everything else, is renewed. Yet once again it can all come back. The old custode, shuffling about in the dimness, jerks away, to make sure of his tip, the old curtain that isn't much more modern than the wonderful work itself. He does his best to create light where light can never be ; but you have your practised groping gaze, and in guiding the young eyes of your less confident associate, moreover, you feel you possess the treasure. These are the most refined pleasures that Venice has still to give, these odd happy passages of communication and response.

But the point of my reminiscence is that there were other communications that day, as there were certainly other responses. I have forgotten exactly what it was we were looking for—without much success—when we met the three Sisters. Nothing requires more care, as a long knowledge of Venice works in, than not to lose the useful faculty of getting lost. I had so successfully done my best to preserve it that I could at that moment conscientiously profess an absence of any suspicion of where we might be. It proved enough that, wherever we were, we were where the three sisters found us. This was on a little bridge near a big campo, and a part of the charm of the matter was the theory that it was very much out of the way. They took us promptly in hand—they were only walking over to San Marco to match some coloured wool for the manufacture of such belated cushions as still bloom with purple and green in the long leisures of old palaces; and that mild errand could easily open a parenthesis. The obscure church we had feebly imagined we were looking for proved, if I am not mistaken, that of the sisters' parish; as to which I have but a confused recollection of a large grey void and of admiring for the first time a fine work of art of which I have now quite lost the identity. This was the effect of the charming beneficence of the three sisters, who presently were to give our adventure a turn in the emotion of which everything that had preceded seemed as nothing. It actually strikes me even as a little dim to have been told by them, as we all fared together, that a certain low, wide house, in a small square as to which I found myself without particular association, had been in the far-off time the residence of George Sand. And yet this was a fact that, though I could then only feel it must be for another day, would in a different connection have set me richly reconstructing.

Madame Sand's famous Venetian year has been of late immensely in the air—a tub of soiled linen which the muse of history, rolling her sleeves well up, has not even yet quite ceased energetically and publicly to wash. The house in question must have been the house to which the wonderful lady betook herself when, in 1834, after the dramatic exit of Alfred de Musset, she enjoyed that remarkable period of rest and refreshment with the so long silent, the but recently rediscovered, reported, extinguished, Doctor Pagello. As an old Sandist—not exactly indeed of the *première heure*, but of the fine high noon and golden afternoon of the great career—I had been, though I confess too inactively, curious as to a few points in the topography of the eminent adventure to which I here allude; but had never got beyond the little public fact, in itself always a bit of a thrill to the Sandist, that the present Hotel Danieli had been the scene of its first remarkable stages. I am not sure indeed that the curiosity I speak of has not at last, in my breast, yielded to another form of wonderment—truly to the rather rueful question of why we have so continued to concern ourselves, and why the fond observer of the footprints of genius is likely so to continue attentive to an altercation neither in itself and in its day, nor in its preserved and attested records, at all positively edifying. The answer to such an inquiry would doubtless reward patience, but I fear we can now glance at its possibilities only long enough to say that interesting persons— so they be of a sufficiently approved and established interest —render in some degree interesting whatever happens to them, and give it an importance even when very little else (as in the case I refer to) may have operated to give it a dignity. Which is where I leave the issue of further identifications.

For the three sisters, in the kindest way in the world, had asked us if we already knew their sequestered home and whether, in case we didn't, we should be at all amused to see it. My own acquaintance with them, though not of recent origin, had hitherto lacked this enhancement, at which we both now grasped with the full instinct, indescribable enough, of what it was likely to give. But how, for that matter, either, can I find the right expression of what was to remain with us of this episode? It is the fault of the sad-eyed old witch of Venice that she so easily puts more into things that can pass under the common names that do for them elsewhere. Too much for a rough sketch was to be seen and felt in the home of the three sisters, and in the delightful and slightly pathetic deviation of their doing us so simply and freely the honours of it. What was most immediately marked was their resigned cosmopolite state, the effacement of old conventional lines by foreign contact and example; by the action, too, of causes full of a special interest, but not to be emphasised perhaps—granted indeed they be named at all—without a certain sadness of sympathy. If "style," in Venice, sits among ruins, let us always lighten our tread when we pay her a visit.

Our steps were in fact, I am happy to think, almost soft enough for a death-chamber as we stood in the big, vague *sala* of the three sisters, spectators of their simplified state and their beautiful blighted rooms, the memories, the portraits, the shrunken relics of nine Doges. If I wanted a first chapter it was here made to my hand ; the painter of life and manners, as he glanced about, could only sigh—as he so frequently has to—over the vision of so much more truth than he can use. What on earth is the need to "invent," in the midst of tragedy and comedy that never cease? Why, with the subject itself, all round, so inimitable, condemn the picture to the silliness of trying not to be aware of it? The charming lonely girls, carrying so simply their great name and fallen fortunes, the despoiled *decaduta* house, the unfailing Italian grace, the space so out of scale with actual needs, the absence of books, the presence of ennui, the sense of the length of the hours and the shortness of everything else—all this was a matter not only for a second chapter and a third, but for a whole volume, a *dénoûment* and a sequel.

This time, unmistakably, it *was* the last—Wordsworth's stately "shade of that which once was great"; and it was almost as if our distinguished young friends had consented to pass away slowly in order to treat us to the vision. Ends are only ends in truth, for the painter of pictures, when they are more or less conscious and prolonged. One of the sisters had been to London, whence she had brought back the impression of having seen at the British Museum a room exclusively filled with books and documents devoted to the commemoration of her family. She must also then have encountered at the National Gallery the exquisite specimen of an early Venetian master in which one of her ancestors, then head of the State, kneels with so sweet a dignity before the Virgin and Child. She was perhaps old enough, none the less, to have seen this precious work taken down from the wall of the room in which we sat and—on terms so far too easy—carried away for ever ; and not too young, at all events, to have been present, now and then, when her candid elders, enlightened too late as to what their sacrifice might really have done for them, looked at each other with the pale hush of the irreparable. We let ourselves note that these were matters to put a great deal of old, old history into sweet young Venetian faces.

III

In Italy, if we come to that, this particular appearance is far from being only in the streets, where we are apt most to observe it—in countenances caught as we pass and in the objects marked by the guide-books with their respective stellar allowances.   It is behind the walls of the houses that old, old history is thick and that the multiplied stars of Baedeker might often best find their application.   The feast of St. John the Baptist is the feast of the year in Florence, and it seemed to me on that night that I could have scattered about me a handful of these signs.   I had the pleasure of spending a couple of hours on a signal high terrace that overlooks the Arno, as well as in the galleries that open out to it, where I met more than ever the pleasant curious question of the disparity between the old conditions and the new manners.   Make our manners, we moderns, as good as we can, there is still no getting over it that they are not good enough for many of the great places.   This was one of those scenes, and its greatness came out to the full into the hot Florentine evening, in which the pink and golden fires of the pyrotechnics arranged on Ponte Carraja—the occasion of our assembly—lighted up the large issue.   The "good people" beneath were a huge, hot, gentle, happy family ; the fireworks on the bridge, kindling river as well as sky, were delicate and charming ; the terrace connected the two wings that give bravery to the front of the palace, and the close-hung pictures in the rooms, open in a long series, offered to a lover of quiet perambulation an alternative hard to resist.

Wherever he stood—on the broad loggia, in the cluster of company, among bland ejaculations and liquefied ices, or in the presence of the mixed masters that led him from wall to wall —such a seeker for the spirit of each occasion could only turn it over that in the first place this was an intenser, finer little Florence than ever, and that in the second the testimony was again wonderful to former fashions and ideas. What did they do, in the other time, the time of so much smaller a society, smaller and fewer fortunes, more taste perhaps as to some particulars, but fewer tastes, at any rate, and fewer habits and wants—what did they do with chambers so multitudinous and so vast? Put their "state" at its highest—and we know of many ways in which it must have broken down—how did they live in them without the aid of variety? How did they, in minor communities in which every one knew every one, and every one's impression and effect had been long, as we say, discounted, find representation and emulation sufficiently amusing? Much of the charm of thinking of it, however, is doubtless that we are not able to say. This leaves us with the conviction that does them most honour: the old generations built and arranged greatly for the simple reason that they liked it, and they could bore themselves—to say nothing of each other, when it came to that—better in noble conditions than in mean ones.

It was not, I must add, of the far-away Florentine age that I most thought, but of periods more recent and of which the sound and beautiful house more directly spoke. If one had always been homesick for the Arno-side of the seventeenth and eighteenth centuries, here was a chance, and a better one than ever, to taste again of the cup. Many of the pictures—there was a charming quarter of an hour when I had them to myself —were bad enough to have passed for good in those delightful years. Shades of Grand-Dukes encompassed me—Dukes of the pleasant later sort who weren't really grand. There was still the sense of having come too late—yet not too late, after all, for this glimpse and this dream. My business was to people the place—its own business had never been to save us the trouble of understanding it. And then the deepest spell of all was perhaps that just here I was supremely out of the way of the so terribly actual Florentine question. This, as all the world knows, is a battle-ground, to-day, in many journals, with all Italy practically pulling on one side and all England, America and Germany pulling on the other : I speak of course of the more or less articulate opinion. The "improvement," the rectification of Florence is in the air, and the problem of the particular ways in which, given such desperately delicate cases, these matters should be understood. The little treasure-city is, if there ever was one, a delicate case—more delicate perhaps than any other in the world save that of our taking on ourselves to persuade the Italians that they mayn't do as they like with their own. They so absolutely may that I profess I see no happy issue from the fight. It will take more tact than our combined tactful genius may at all probably muster to convince them that their own is, by an ingenious logic, much rather *ours*. It will take more subtlety still to muster for them that truly dazzling show of examples from which they may learn that what in general is "ours" shall appear to them as a rule a sacrifice to beauty and a triumph of taste. The situation, to the truly analytic mind, offers in short, to perfection, all the elements of despair ; and I am afraid that if I hung back, at the Corsini palace, to woo illusions and invoke the irrelevant, it was because I could think, in the conditions, of no better way to meet the acute responsibility of the critic than just to shirk it.

1899.

CASA ALVISI

INVITED to "introduce" certain pages of cordial and faithful reminiscence from another hand,[1] in which a frankly predominant presence seems to live again, I undertook that office with an interest inevitably somewhat sad—so passed and gone to-day is so much of the life suggested. Those who fortunately knew Mrs. Bronson will read into her notes still more of it—more of her subject, more of herself too, and of many things—than she gives, and some may well even feel tempted to do for her what she has done here for her distinguished friend. In Venice, during a long period, for many pilgrims, Mrs. Arthur Bronson, originally of New York, was, so far as society, hospitality, a charming personal welcome were concerned, almost in sole possession; she had become there, with time, quite the prime representative of those private amenities which the Anglo-Saxon abroad is apt to miss just in proportion as the place visited is publicly wonderful, and in which he therefore finds a value twice as great as at home. Mrs. Bronson really earned in this way the gratitude of mingled generations and races. She sat for twenty years at the wide mouth, as it were, of the Grand Canal, holding out her hand, with endless good-nature, patience, charity, to all decently accredited petitioners, the incessant troop of those either bewilderedly making or fondly renewing acquaintance with the dazzling city.

Casa Alvisi is directly opposite the high, broad-based florid

[1] "Browning in Venice," being Recollections of the late Katharine De Kay Bronson, with a Prefatory Note by H. J. (*Cornhill Magazine*, February 1902).

church of S. Maria della Salute—so directly that from the balcony over the water-entrance your eye, crossing the canal, seems to find the key-hole of the great door right in a line with it; and there was something in this position that for the time made all Venice-lovers think of the genial *padrona* as thus levying in the most convenient way the toll of curiosity and sympathy. Every one passed, every one was seen to pass, and few were those not seen to stop and to return. The most generous of hostesses died a year ago at Florence; her house knows her no more—it had ceased to do so for some time before her death; and the long, pleased procession—the charmed arrivals, the happy sojourns at anchor, the reluctant departures that made Ca' Alvisi, as was currently said, a social *porto di mare*—is, for remembrance and regret, already a possession of ghosts; so that, on the spot, at present, the attention ruefully averts itself from the dear little old faded but once familiarly bright façade, overtaken at last by the comparatively vulgar uses that are doing their best to "paint out" in Venice, right and left, by staring signs and other vulgarities, the immemorial note of distinction. The house, in a city of palaces, was small, but the tenant clung to her perfect, her inclusive position—the one right place that gave her a better command, as it were, than a better house obtained by a harder compromise; not being fond, moreover, of spacious halls and massive treasures, but of compact and familiar rooms, in which her remarkable accumulation of minute and delicate Venetian objects could show. She adored—in the way of the Venetian, to which all her taste addressed itself—the small, the domestic and the exquisite; so that she would have given a Tintoretto or two, I think, without difficulty, for a cabinet of tiny gilded glasses or a dinner-service of the right old silver.

The general receptacle of these multiplied treasures played at any rate, through the years, the part of a friendly private-box at the constant operatic show, a box at the best point of the best tier, with the cushioned ledge of its front raking the whole scene

and with its withdrawing rooms behind for more detached conversation ; for easy—when not indeed slightly difficult—polyglot
talk, artful *bibite*, artful cigarettes too, straight from the hand of
the hostess, who could do all that belonged to a hostess, place
people in relation and keep them so, take up and put down the
topic, cause delicate tobacco and little gilded glasses to circulate,
without ever leaving her sofa-cushions or intermitting her good-
nature. She exercised in these conditions, with never a block, as
we say in London, in the traffic, with never an admission, an
acceptance of the least social complication, her positive genius
for easy interest, easy sympathy, easy friendship. It was as if,
at last, she had taken the human race at large, quite irrespective
of geography, for her neighbours, with neighbourly relations as
a matter of course. These things, on her part, had at all events
the greater appearance of ease from their having found to their
purpose—and as if the very air of Venice produced them—a
cluster of forms so light and immediate, so pre-established by
picturesque custom. The old bright tradition, the wonderful
Venetian legend had appealed to her from the first, closing
round her house and her well-plashed water-steps, where the
waiting gondolas were thick, quite as if, actually, the ghost of
the defunct Carnival—since I have spoken of ghosts—still
played some haunting part.

Let me add, at the same time, that Mrs. Bronson's social
facility, which was really her great refuge from importunity, a
defence with serious thought and serious feeling quietly cherished
behind it, had its discriminations as well as its inveteracies, and
that the most marked of all these, perhaps, was her attachment
to Robert Browning. Nothing in all her beneficent life had probably made her happier than to have found herself able to
minister, each year, with the returning autumn, to his pleasure
and comfort. Attached to Ca' Alvisi, on the land side, is a
somewhat melancholy old section of a Giustiniani palace, which
she had annexed to her own premises mainly for the purpose of

placing it, in comfortable guise, at the service of her friends. She liked, as she professed, when they were the real thing, to have them under her hand; and here succeeded each other, through the years, the company of the privileged and the more closely domesticated, who liked, harmlessly, to distinguish between themselves and outsiders. Among visitors partaking of this pleasant provision Mr. Browning was of course easily first. But I must leave her own pen to show him as her best years knew him. The point was, meanwhile, that if her charity was great even for the outsider, this was by reason of the inner essence of it—her perfect tenderness for Venice, which she always recognised as a link. That was the true principle of fusion, the key to communication. She communicated in proportion—little or much, measuring it as she felt people more responsive or less so; and she expressed herself, or in other words her full affection for the place, only to those who had most of the same sentiment. The rich and interesting form in which she found it in Browning may well be imagined—together with the quite independent quantity of the genial at large that she also found; but I am not sure that his favour was not primarily based on his paid tribute of such things as "Two in a Gondola" and "A Toccata of Galuppi." He had more ineffaceably than any one recorded his initiation from of old.

She was thus, all round, supremely faithful; yet it was perhaps after all with the very small folk, those to the manner born, that she made the easiest terms. She loved, she had from the first enthusiastically adopted, the engaging Venetian people, whose virtues she found touching and their infirmities but such as appeal mainly to the sense of humour and the love of anecdote; and she befriended and admired, she studied and spoiled them. There must have been a multitude of whom it would scarce be too much to say that her long residence among them was their settled golden age. When I consider that they have lost her now I fairly wonder to what shifts they have been put and how long they may not have to wait for such another messenger of Providence. She cultivated their dialect, she renewed their boats, she piously relighted—at the top of the tide-washed *pali* of traghetto or lagoon—the neglected lamp of the tutelary Madonnetta ; she took cognisance of the wives, the children, the accidents, the troubles, as to which she became, perceptibly, the most prompt, the established remedy. On lines where the amusement was happily less one-sided she put together in dialect many short comedies, dramatic proverbs, which, with one of her drawing-rooms permanently arranged as a charming diminutive theatre, she caused to be performed by the young persons of her circle—often, when the case lent itself, by the wonderful small offspring of humbler friends, children of the Venetian lower class, whose aptitude, teachability, drollery, were her constant delight. It was certainly true that an impression of Venice as humanly sweet might easily found itself on the frankness and quickness and amiability of these little people. They were at least so much to the good ; for the philosophy of their patroness was as Venetian as everything else ; helping her to accept experience without bitterness and to remain fresh, even in the fatigue which finally overtook her, for pleasant surprises and proved sincerities. She was herself sincere to the last for the place of her predilection ; inasmuch as though she had arranged herself, in the later time—and largely for the love of "Pippa Passes"—an alternative refuge at Asolo, she absented herself from Venice with continuity only under coercion of illness.

At Asolo, periodically, the link with Browning was more confirmed than weakened, and there, in old Venetian territory, and with the invasion of visitors comparatively checked, her preferentially small house became again a setting for the pleasure of talk and the sense of Italy. It contained again its own small treasures, all in the pleasant key of the homelier Venetian spirit. The plain beneath it stretched away like a purple sea from the lower cliffs of the hills, and the white *campanili* of the villages, as one was perpetually saying, showed on the expanse like scattered sails of ships. The rumbling carriage, the old-time, rattling, red-velveted carriage of provincial, rural Italy, delightful and quaint, did the office of the gondola; to Bassano, to Treviso, to high-walled Castelfranco, all pink and gold, the home of the great Giorgione. Here also memories cluster; but it is in Venice again that her vanished presence is most felt, for there, in the real, or certainly the finer, the more sifted Cosmopolis, it falls into its place among the others evoked, those of the past seekers of poetry and dispensers of romance. It is a fact that almost every one interesting, appealing, melancholy, memorable, odd, seems at one time or another, after many days and much life, to have gravitated to Venice by a happy instinct, settling in it and treating it, cherishing it, as a sort of repository of consolations; all of which to-day, for the conscious mind, is mixed with its air and constitutes its unwritten history. The deposed, the defeated, the disenchanted, the wounded, or even only the bored, have seemed to find there something that no other place could give. But such people came for themselves, as we seem to see them—only with the egotism of their grievances and the vanity of their hopes. Mrs. Bronson's case was beautifully different—she had come altogether for others.

FROM CHAMBÉRY TO MILAN

YOUR truly sentimental tourist will never take it from any occasion that there is absolutely nothing for him, and it was at Chambéry—but four hours from Geneva—that I accepted the situation and decided there might be mysterious delights in entering Italy by a whizz through an eight-mile tunnel, even as a bullet through the bore of a gun. I found my reward in the Savoyard landscape, which greets you betimes with the smile of anticipation. If it is not so Italian as Italy it is at least more Italian than anything *but* Italy—more Italian, too, I should think, than can seem natural and proper to the swarming red-legged soldiery who so publicly proclaim it of the empire of M. Thiers. The light and the complexion of things had to my eyes not a little of that mollified depth last loved by them rather further on. It was simply perhaps that the weather was hot and the mountains drowsing in that iridescent haze that I have seen nearer home than at Chambéry. But the vegetation, assuredly, had an all but Transalpine twist and curl, and the classic wayside tangle of corn and vines left nothing to be desired in the line of careless grace. Chambéry as a town, however, constitutes no foretaste of the monumental cities. There is shabbiness and shabbiness, the fond critic of such things will tell you ; and that of the ancient capital of Savoy lacks style. I found a better pastime, however, than strolling through the dark dull streets in quest of effects that were not forthcoming. The first urchin you meet will show you the way to Les Charmettes and the Maison Jean-Jacques. A very pleasant way it becomes as soon as it leaves the town—a winding, climbing by-road, bordered with such a tall and sturdy hedge as to give it the air of an English lane—if you can fancy an English lane introducing you to the haunts of a Madame de Warens.

The house that formerly sheltered this lady's singular ménage stands on a hillside above the road, which a rapid path connects with the little grass-grown terrace before it. It is a small shabby, homely dwelling, with a certain reputable solidity, however, and more of internal spaciousness than of outside promise. The place is shown by an elderly competent dame who points out the very few surviving objects which you may touch with the reflection—complacent in whatsoever degree suits you—that they have known the familiarity of Rousseau's hand. It was presumably a meagrely-appointed house, and I wondered that on such scanty features so much expression should linger. But the structure has an ancient ponderosity, and the dust of the eighteenth century seems to lie on its worm-eaten floors, to cling to the faded old *papiers à ramages* on the walls and to lodge in the crevices of the brown wooden ceilings. Madame de Warens's bed remains, with the narrow couch of Jean-Jacques as well, his little warped and cracked yellow spinet, and a battered, turnip-shaped silver timepiece, engraved with its master's name—its primitive tick as extinct as his passionate heart-beats. It cost me, I confess, a somewhat pitying acceleration of my own to see this intimately personal relic of the *genius loci*—for it had dwelt in his waistcoat-pocket, than which there is hardly a material point in space nearer to a man's consciousness—tossed so irreverently upon the table on which you deposit your fee, beside the dog's-eared visitors' record or *livre de cuisine* recently denounced by Madame George Sand. In fact the place generally, in so far as some faint ghostly presence of its famous inmates seems to linger there, is by no means exhilarating. Coppet and Ferney tell, if not of pure happiness, at least of prosperity and honour, wealth and success. But Les

Charmettes is haunted by ghosts unclean and forlorn. The place tells of poverty, perversity, distress. A good deal of clever modern talent in France has been employed in touching up the episode of which it was the scene and tricking it out in idyllic love-knots. But as I stood on the charming terrace I have mentioned—a little jewel of a terrace, with grassy flags and a mossy parapet, and an admirable view of great swelling violet hills—stood there reminded how much sweeter Nature is than man, the story looked rather wan and unlovely beneath these literary decorations, and I could pay it no livelier homage than is implied in perfect pity. Hero and heroine have become too much creatures of history to take up attitudes as part of any poetry. But, not to moralise too sternly for a tourist between trains, I should add that, as an illustration, to be inserted mentally in the text of the " Confessions," a glimpse of Les Charmettes is pleasant enough. It completes the rare charm of good autobiography to behold with one's eyes the faded and battered background of the story ; and Rousseau's narrative is so incomparably vivid and forcible that the sordid little house at Chambéry seems of a hardly deeper shade of reality than so many other passages of his projected truth.

If I spent an hour at Les Charmettes, fumbling thus help-lessly with the past, I recognised on the morrow how strongly the Mont Cenis Tunnel smells of the time to come. As I passed along the Saint-Gothard highway a couple of months since, I perceived, half up the Swiss ascent, a group of navvies at work in a gorge beneath the road. They had laid bare a broad surface of granite and had punched in the centre of it a round black cavity, of about the dimensions, as it seemed to me, of a soup-plate. This was to attain its perfect develop-ment some eight years hence. The Mont Cenis may therefore be held to have set a fashion which will be followed till the highest Himalaya is but the ornamental apex or snow-capped gable-tip of some resounding fuliginous corridor. The tunnel differs but in length from other tunnels; you spend half an hour in it. But you whirl out into the blest peninsula, and as you look back seem to see the mighty mass shrug its shoulders over the line, the mere turn of a dreaming giant in his sleep. The tunnel is certainly not a poetic object, but there is no perfection without its beauty; and as you measure the long rugged outline of the pyramid of which it forms the base you accept it as the perfection of a short cut. Twenty-four hours from Paris to Turin is speed for the times—speed which may content us, at any rate, until expansive Berlin has succeeded in placing itself at thirty-six from Milan.

To enter Turin then of a lovely August afternoon was to find a city of arcades, of pink and yellow stucco, of innumerable cafés, of blue-legged officers, of ladies draped in the North-Italian mantilla. An old friend of Italy coming back to her finds an easy waking for dormant memories. Every object is a reminder and every reminder a thrill. Half an hour after my arrival, as I stood at my window, which overhung the great square, I found the scene, within and without, a rough epitome of every pleasure and every impression I had formerly gathered from Italy: the balcony and the Venetian-blind, the cool floor of speckled concrete, the lavish delusions of frescoed wall and ceiling, the broad divan framed for the noonday siesta, the massive mediæval Castello in mid-piazza, with its shabby rear and its pompous Palladian front, the brick campaniles beyond, the milder, yellower light, the range of colour, the suggestion of sound. Later, beneath the arcades, I found many an old acquaintance: beautiful officers, resplendent, slow-strolling, contemplative of female beauty; civil and peaceful dandies, hardly less gorgeous, with that religious faith in moustache and shirt-front which distinguishes the *belle jeunesse* of Italy; ladies with heads artfully shawled in Spanish-looking lace, but with too little art—or too much nature at least—in the region of the bodice; well-conditioned young *abbati* with neatly drawn stockings. These indeed are not objects of first-rate interest, and with such Turin is rather meagrely furnished. It has no architecture, no churches, no monuments, no romantic street-scenery. It has the great votive temple of the Superga, which stands on a high hilltop above the city, gazing across at Monte Rosa and lifting its own fine dome against the sky with no contemptible art. But when you have seen the Superga from the quay beside the Po, a skein of a few yellow threads in August, despite its frequent habit of rising high and running wild, and said to yourself that in architecture position is half the battle, you have nothing left to visit but the Museum of pictures. The Turin Gallery, which is large and well arranged, is the fortunate owner of three or four masterpieces ; a couple of magnificent Vandycks and a couple of Paul Veroneses ; the latter a Queen of Sheba and a Feast at the House of Levi— the usual splendid combination of brocades, grandees and marble colonnades dividing those skies *de turquoise malade* to which Théophile Gautier is fond of alluding. The Veroneses are fine, but with Venice in prospect the traveller feels at liberty to keep his best attention in reserve. If, however, he has the proper relish for Vandyck, let him linger long and fondly here ; for that admiration will never be more potently stirred than by the adorable group of the three little royal highnesses, sons and the daughter of Charles I. All the purity of childhood is here, and all its soft solidity of structure, rounded tenderly beneath the spangled satin and contrasted charmingly with the pompous rigidity. Clad respectively in crimson, white and blue, these small scions stand up in their ruffs and fardingales in dimpled serenity, squaring their infantine stomachers at the spectator with an innocence, a dignity, a delightful grotesqueness, which make the picture a thing of close truth as well as of fine decorum. You might kiss their hands, but you certainly would think twice before pinching their cheeks—provocative as they are of this tribute of admiration—and would altogether lack presumption to lift them off the ground or the higher level or dais on which they stand so sturdily planted by right of birth.   There is something inimitable in the paternal gallantry with which the painter has touched off the young lady.   She was a princess, yet she was a baby, and he has contrived, we let ourselves fancy, to interweave an intimation that she was a creature whom, in her teens, the lucklessly smitten—even as he was prematurely—must vainly sigh for.   Though the work is a masterpiece of execution its merits under this head may be emulated, at a distance;   the lovely modulations of colour in the three contrasted and harmonised little satin petticoats, the solidity of the little heads, in spite of all their prettiness, the happy, unexaggerated squareness and maturity of *pose*, are, severally, points to study, to imitate, and to reproduce with profit.   But the taste of such a consummate thing is its great secret as well as its great merit—a taste which seems one of the lost instincts of mankind.   Go and enjoy this supreme expression of Vandyck's fine sense, and admit that never was a politer production.

Milan speaks to us of a burden of felt life of which Turin is innocent, but in its general aspect still lingers a northern reserve which makes the place rather perhaps the last of the prose capitals than the first of the poetic.   The long Austrian occupation perhaps did something to Germanise its physiognomy;   though indeed this is an indifferent explanation when one remembers how well, temperamentally speaking, Italy held her own in Venetia.   Milan, at any rate, if not bristling with the æsthetic impulse, opens to us frankly enough the thick volume of her past.   Of that volume the Cathedral is the fairest and fullest page—a structure not supremely interesting, not logical, not even, to some minds, commandingly beautiful, but grandly curious and superbly rich.   I hope, for my own part, never to grow too particular to admire it.   If it had no other distinction it would still have that of impressive, immeasurable achievement. As I strolled beside its vast indented base one evening, and felt it, above me, rear its grey mysteries into the starlight while the restless human tide on which I floated rose no higher than the first few layers of street-soiled marble, I was tempted to believe that beauty in great architecture is almost a secondary merit, and that the main point is mass—such mass as may make it a supreme embodiment of vigorous effort. Viewed in this way a great building is the greatest conceivable work of art. More than any other it represents difficulties mastered, resources combined, labour, courage and patience. And there are people who tell us that art has nothing to do with morality! Little enough, doubtless, when it is concerned, even ever so little, in painting the roof of Milan Cathedral within to represent carved stone-work. Of this famous roof every one has heard—how good it is, how bad, how perfect a delusion, how transparent an artifice. It is the first thing your cicerone shows you on entering the church. The occasionally accommodating art-lover may accept it philosophically, I think; for the interior, though admirably effective as a whole, has no great sublimity, nor even purity, of pitch. It is splendidly vast and dim; the altar-lamps twinkle afar through the incense-thickened air like fog-lights at sea, and the great columns rise straight to the roof, which hardly curves to meet them, with the girth and altitude of oaks of a thousand years; but there is little refinement of design—few of those felicities of proportion which the eye caresses, when it finds them, very much as the memory retains and repeats some happy line of poetry or some haunting musical phrase. Consistently brave, none the less, is the result produced, and nothing braver than a certain exhibition that I privately enjoyed of the relics of St. Charles Borromeus. This holy man lies at his eternal rest in a small but gorgeous sepulchral chapel, beneath the boundless pavement and before the high altar; and for the modest sum of five francs you may have his shrivelled mortality unveiled and gaze at it with whatever reserves occur to you. The Catholic Church never renounces a chance of the sublime for fear of a chance of the ridiculous—especially when the chance of the sublime may be the very excellent chance of five francs. The performance in question, of which the good San Carlo paid in the first instance the cost, was impressive certainly, but as a monstrous matter or a grim comedy may still be. The little sacristan, having secured his audience, whipped on a white tunic over his frock, lighted a couple of extra candles and proceeded to remove from above the altar, by means of a crank, a sort of sliding shutter, just as you may see a shop-boy do of a morning at his master's window. In this case too a large sheet of plate-glass was uncovered, and to form an idea of the *étalage* you must imagine that a jeweller, for reasons of his own, has struck an unnatural partnership with an undertaker. The black mummified corpse of the saint is stretched out in a glass coffin, clad in his mouldering canonicals, mitred, crosiered and gloved, glittering with votive jewels. It is an extraordinary mixture of death and life; the desiccated clay, the ashen rags, the hideous little black mask and skull, and the living, glowing, twinkling splendour of diamonds, emeralds and sapphires. The collection is really fine, and many great historic names are attached to the different offerings. Whatever may be the better opinion as to the future of the Church, I can't help thinking she will make a figure in the world so long as she retains this great fund of precious "properties," this prodigious capital decoratively invested and scintillating throughout Christendom at effectively-scattered points. You see I am forced to agree after all, in spite of the sliding shutter and the profane swagger of the sacristan, that a certain pastoral majesty saved the situation, or at least made irony gape. Yet it was from a natural desire to breathe a sweeter air that I immediately afterwards undertook the interminable climb to the roof of the cathedral. This is another world of wonders, and one which enjoys due

renown, every square inch of wall on the winding stairways being
bescribbled with a traveller's name. There is a great glare from
the far-stretching slopes of marble, a confusion (like the masts
of a navy or the spears of an army) of image-capped pinnacles,
biting the impalpable blue, and, better than either, the goodliest
view of level Lombardy sleeping in its rich transalpine light
and resembling, with its white-walled dwellings and the spires
on its horizon, a vast green sea spotted with ships. After two
months of Switzerland the Lombard plain is a rich rest to the
eye, and the yellow, liquid, free-flowing light—as if on favoured
Italy the vessels of heaven were more widely opened—had for
mine a charm which made me think of a great opaque mountain
as a blasphemous invasion of the atmospheric spaces.

I have mentioned the cathedral first, but the prime treasure
of Milan at the present hour is the beautiful, tragical Leonardo.
The cathedral is good for another thousand years, but we ask
whether our children will find in the most majestic and most
luckless of frescoes much more than the shadow of a shadow.
Its fame has been for a century or two that, as one may say, of
an illustrious invalid whom people visit to see how he lasts, with
leave-taking sighs and almost death-bed or tiptoe precautions.
The picture needs not another scar or stain, now, to be the
saddest work of art in the world ; and battered, defaced, ruined
as it is, it remains one of the greatest. We may really compare
its anguish of decay to the slow conscious ebb of life in a human
organism. The production of the prodigy was a breath from
the infinite, and the painter's conception not immeasurably less
complex than the scheme, say, of his own mortal constitution.
There has been much talk lately of the irony of fate, but I
suspect fate was never more ironical than when she led the most
scientific, the most calculating of all painters to spend fifteen
long years in building his goodly house upon the sand. And
yet, after all, may not the playing of that trick represent but a
deeper wisdom, since if the thing enjoyed the immortal health

and bloom of a first-rate Titian we should have lost one of the most pertinent lessons in the history of art? We know it as hearsay, but here is the plain proof, that there is no limit to the amount of "stuff" an artist may put into his work. Every painter ought once in his life to stand before the Cenacolo and decipher its moral. Mix with your colours and mess on your palette every particle of the very substance of your soul, and this lest perchance your "prepared surface" shall play you a trick! Then, and then only, it will fight to the last—it will resist even in death. Raphael was a happier genius; you look at his lovely "Marriage of the Virgin" at the Brera, beautiful as some first deep smile of conscious inspiration, but to feel that he foresaw no complaint against fate, and that he knew the world he wanted to know and charmed it into never giving him away. But I have left no space to speak of the Brera, nor of that paradise of bookworms with an eye for their background—if such creatures exist—the Ambrosian Library; nor of that mighty basilica of Saint Ambrose, with its spacious atrium and its crudely solemn mosaics, in which it is surely your own fault if you don't forget Dr. Strauss and M. Renan and worship as grimly as a Christian of the ninth century.

It is part of the sordid prose of the Mont Cenis road that, unlike those fine old unimproved passes, the Simplon, the Splügen and—yet awhile longer—the Saint-Gothard, it denies you a glimpse of that paradise adorned by the four lakes even that of uncommented Scripture by the rivers of Eden. I made, however, an excursion to the Lake of Como, which, though brief, lasted long enough to suggest to me that I too was a hero of romance with leisure for a love-affair, and not a hurrying tourist with a Bradshaw in his pocket. The Lake of Como has figured largely in novels of "immoral" tendency—being commonly the spot to which inflamed young gentlemen invite the wives of other gentlemen to fly with them and ignore the restrictions of public opinion. But even the Lake of Como has been revised and improved ; the fondest prejudices yield to time ; it gives one somehow a sense of an aspiringly high tone. I should pay a poor compliment at least to the swarming inmates of the hotels which now alternate attractively by the water-side with villas old and new were I to read the appearances more cynically. But if it is lost to florid fiction it still presents its blue bosom to most other refined uses, and the unsophisticated tourist, the American at least, may do any amount of private romancing there. The pretty hotel at Cadenabbia offers him, for instance, in the most elegant and assured form, the so often precarious adventure of what he calls at home summer board. It is all so unreal, so fictitious, so elegant and idle, so framed to undermine a rigid sense of the chief end of man not being to float forever in an ornamental boat, beneath an awning tasselled like a circus-horse, impelled by an affable Giovanni or Antonio from one stately stretch of lake-laved villa steps to another, that departure seems as harsh and unnatural as the dream-dispelling note of some punctual voice at your bedside on a dusky winter morning. Yet I wondered, for my own part, where I had seen it all before — the pink-walled villas gleaming through their shrubberies of orange and oleander, the mountains shimmering in the hazy light like so many breasts of doves, the constant presence of the melodious Italian voice. Where indeed but at the Opera when the manager has been more than usually regardless of expense ? Here in the foreground was the palace of the nefarious barytone, with its banqueting-hall opening as freely on the stage as a railway buffet on the platform ; beyond, the delightful back scene, with its operatic gamut of colouring ; in the middle the scarlet-sashed *barcaiuoli*, grouped like a chorus, hat in hand, awaiting the conductor's signal. It was better even than being in a novel—this being, this fairly wallowing, in a libretto.

THE OLD SAINT-GOTHARD

LEAVES FROM A NOTE-BOOK

BERNE, *September*, 1873.—In Berne again, some eleven weeks after having left it in July. I have never been in Switzerland so late, and I came hither innocently supposing the last Cook's tourist to have paid out his last coupon and departed. But I was lucky, it seems, to discover an empty cot in an attic and a very tight place at a table d'hôte. People are all flocking out of Switzerland, as in July they were flocking in, and the main channels of egress are terribly choked. I have been here several days, watching them come and go; it is like the march-past of an army. It gives one, for an occasional change from darker thoughts, a lively impression of the numbers of people now living, and above all now moving, at extreme ease in the world. Here is little Switzerland disgorging its tens of thousands of honest folk, chiefly English, and rarely, to judge by their faces and talk, children of light in any eminent degree; for whom snow-peaks and glaciers and passes and lakes and chalets and sunsets and a *café complet*, "including honey," as the coupon says, have become prime necessities for six weeks every year. It's not so long ago that lords and nabobs monopolised these pleasures; but nowadays a month's tour in Switzerland is no more a *jeu de prince* than a Sunday excursion. To watch this huge Anglo-Saxon wave ebbing through Berne suggests, no doubt most fallaciously, that the common lot of mankind isn't after all so very hard and that the masses have reached a high standard of comfort. The view of the Oberland chain, as you see it from the garden of the hotel, really butters one's bread most handsomely; and here are I don't know how many hundred Cook's tourists a day looking at it through the smoke of their pipes. Is it really the "masses," however, that I see every day at the table d'hôte? They have rather too few h's to the dozen, but their good-nature is great. Some people complain that they "vulgarise" Switzerland; but as far as I am concerned I freely give it up to them and offer them a personal welcome and take a peculiar satisfaction in seeing them here. Switzerland is a "show country"—I am more and more struck with the bearings of that truth; and its use in the world is to reassure persons of a benevolent imagination when they begin to wish for the drudging millions a greater supply of elevating amusement. Here is amusement for a thousand years, and as elevating certainly as mountains five miles high can make it. I expect to live to see the summit of Monte Rosa heated by steam-tubes and adorned with a hotel setting three tables d'hôte a day.

I have been walking about the arcades, which used to bestow a grateful shade in July, but which seem rather dusky and chilly in these shortening autumn days. I am struck with the way the English always speak of them—with a shudder, as gloomy, as dirty, as evil-smelling, as suffocating, as freezing, as anything and everything but admirably picturesque. I take us Americans for the only people who, in travelling, judge things on the first impulse—when we do judge them at all—not from the standpoint of simple comfort. Most of us, strolling forth into these bustling basements, are, I imagine, too much amused, too much diverted from the sense of an alienable right to public ease, to be conscious of heat or cold, of thick air, or even of the universal smell of strong *charcuterie*. If the visible romantic were banished from the face of the earth I am sure the idea of it would still survive in some typical American heart. . . .

Lucerne, September.—Berne, I find, has been filling with tourists at the expense of Lucerne, which I have been having almost to myself. There are six people at the table d'hôte; the excellent dinner denotes on the part of the *chef* the easy leisure in which true artists love to work. The waiters have nothing to do but lounge about the hall and chink in their pockets the fees of the past season. The day has been lovely in itself, and pervaded, to my sense, by the gentle glow of a natural satisfaction at my finding myself again on the threshold of Italy. I am lodged *en prince*, in a room with a balcony hanging over the lake—a balcony on which I spent a long time this morning at dawn, thanking the mountain-tops, from the depths of a landscape-lover's heart, for their promise of superbly fair weather. There were a great many mountain-tops to thank, for the crags and peaks and pinnacles tumbled away through the morning mist in an endless confusion of grandeur. I have been all day in better humour with Lucerne than ever before— a forecast reflection of Italian moods. If Switzerland, as I wrote the other day, is so furiously a show-place, Lucerne is certainly one of the biggest booths at the fair. The little quay, under the trees, squeezed in between the decks of the steamboats and the doors of the hotels, is a terrible medley of Saxon dialects —a jumble of pilgrims in all the phases of devotion, equipped with book and staff, alpenstock and Baedeker. There are so many hotels and trinket-shops, so many omnibuses and steamers, so many Saint-Gothard *vetturini*, so many ragged urchins poking photographs, minerals and Lucernese English at you, that you feel as if lake and mountains themselves, in all their loveliness, were but a part of the "enterprise" of landlords and pedlars, and half expect to see the Righi and Pilatus and the fine weather figure as items on your hotel-bill between the *bougie* and the *siphon*. Nature herself assists you to this conceit; there is something so operatic and suggestive of footlights and scene-shifters in the view on which Lucerne looks out. You are one of five thousand—fifty thousand—"accommodated" spectators; you have taken your season-ticket and there is a responsible impresario somewhere behind the scenes. There is such a luxury of beauty in the prospect—such a redundancy of composition and effect—so many more peaks and pinnacles than are needed to make one heart happy or regale the vision of one quiet observer, that you finally accept the little Babel on the quay and the looming masses in the clouds as equal parts of a perfect system, and feel as if the mountains had been waiting so many ages for the hotels to come and balance the colossal group, that they show a right, after all, to have them big and numerous. The scene-shifters have been at work all day long, composing and discomposing the beautiful background of the prospect—massing the clouds and scattering the light, effacing and reviving, making play with their wonderful machinery of mist and haze. The mountains rise, one behind the other, in an enchanting gradation of distances and of melting blues and greys; you think each successive tone the loveliest and haziest possible till you see another loom dimly behind it. I couldn't enjoy even *The Swiss Times*, over my breakfast, till I had marched forth to the office of the Saint-Gothard service of coaches and demanded the banquette for to-morrow. The one place at the disposal of the office was taken, but I might possibly *m'entendre* with the conductor for his own seat—the conductor being generally visible, in the intervals of business, at the post-office. To the post-office, after breakfast, I repaired, over the fine new bridge which now spans the green Reuss and gives such a woeful air of country-cousinship to the crooked old wooden structure which did sole service when I was here four years ago. The old bridge is covered with a running hood of shingles and adorned with a series of very quaint and vivid little paintings of the "Dance of Death," quite in the Holbein manner; the new sends up a painful glare from its white limestone, and is ornamented

G

with candelabra in a meretricious imitation of platinum. As an almost professional cherisher of the quaint I ought to have chosen to return at least by the dark and narrow way; but mark how luxury unmans us. I was already demoralised. I crossed the threshold of the timbered portal, took a few steps, and retreated. It *smelt badly!* So I marched back, counting the lamps in their fine falsity. But the other, the crooked and covered way, smelt very badly indeed; and no good American is without a fund of accumulated sensibility to the odour of stale timber.

Meanwhile I had spent an hour in the great yard of the post-office, waiting for my conductor to turn up and seeing the yellow malles-postes pushed to and fro. At last, being told my man was at my service, I was brought to speech of a huge, jovial, bearded, delightful Italian, clad in the blue coat and waistcoat, with close, round silver buttons, which are a heritage of the old postilions. No, it was not he; it was a friend of his; and finally the friend was produced, *en costume de ville*, but equally jovial, and Italian enough—a brave Lucernese, who had spent half of his life between Bellinzona and Camerlata. For ten francs this worthy man's perch behind the luggage was made mine as far Bellinzona, and we separated with reciprocal wishes for good weather on the morrow. To-morrow is so manifestly determined to be as fine as any other 30th of September since the weather became on this planet a topic of conversation that I have had nothing to do but stroll about Lucerne, staring, loafing and vaguely intent on regarding the fact that, whatever happens, my place is paid to Milan. I loafed into the immense new Hôtel National and read the *New York Tribune* on a blue satin divan; after which I was rather surprised, on coming out, to find myself staring at a green Swiss lake and not at the Broadway omnibuses. The Hôtel National is adorned with a perfectly appointed Broadway bar—one of the " prohibited " ones seeking hospitality in foreign lands after the manner of an old-fashioned French or Italian refugee.

Milan, October.—My journey hither was such a pleasant piece of traveller's luck that I feel a delicacy for taking it to pieces to see what it was made of. Do what we will, however, there remains in all deeply agreeable impressions a charming something we can't analyse. I found it agreeable even, given the rest of my case, to turn out of bed, at Lucerne, by four o'clock, into the chilly autumn darkness. The thick-starred sky was cloudless, and there was as yet no flush of dawn; but the lake was wrapped in a ghostly white mist which crept halfway up the mountains and made them look as if they too had been lying down for the night and were casting away the vaporous tissues of their bedclothes. Into this fantastic fog the little steamer went creaking away, and I hung about the deck with the two or three travellers who had known better than to believe it would save them francs or midnight sighs—over those debts you "pay with your person"—to go and wait for the diligence at the Poste at Flüelen, or yet at the Guillaume Tell. The dawn came sailing up over the mountain-tops, flushed but unperturbed, and blew out the little stars and then the big ones, as a thrifty matron after a party blows out her candles and lamps; the mist went melting and wandering away into the duskier hollows and recesses of the mountains, and the summits defined their profiles against the cool soft light.

At Flüelen, before the landing, the big yellow coaches were actively making themselves bigger, and piling up boxes and bags on their roofs in a way to turn nervous people's thoughts to the sharp corners of the downward twists of the great road. I climbed into my own banquette, and stood eating peaches—half-a-dozen women were hawking them about under the horses' legs—with an air of security that might have been offensive to the people scrambling and protesting below between coupé and intérieur.   They were all English and all had false alarms about the claim of somebody else to their place, the place for which they produced their ticket, with a declaration in three or four different tongues of the inalienable right to it given them by the expenditure of British gold.   They were all serenely confuted by the stout, purple-faced, many-buttoned conductors, patted on the backs, assured that their bath-tubs had every advantage of position on the top, and stowed away according to their dues. When once one has fairly started on a journey and has but to go and go by the impetus received, it is surprising what entertainment one finds in very small things.   We surrender to the gaping traveller's mood, which surely isn't the unwisest the heart knows.   I don't envy people, at any rate, who have outlived or outworn the simple sweetness of feeling settled to go somewhere with bag and umbrella.   If we are settled on the top of a coach, and the "somewhere" contains an element of the new and strange, the case is at its best.   In this matter wise people are content to become children again.   We don't turn about on our knees to look out of the omnibus-window, but we indulge in very much the same round-eyed contemplation of accessible objects.   Responsibility is left at home or at the worst packed away in the valise, relegated to quite another part of the diligence with the clean shirts and the writing-case.   I sucked in the gladness of gaping, for this occasion, with the somewhat acrid juice of my indifferent peaches ; it made me think them very good.   This was the first of a series of kindly services it rendered me.   It made me agree next, as we started, that the gentleman at the booking-office at Lucerne had but played a harmless joke when he told me the regular seat in the banquette was taken. No one appeared to claim it ; so the conductor and I reversed positions, and I found him quite as conversible as the usual Anglo-Saxon.

He was trolling snatches of melody and showing his great yellow teeth in a jovial grin all the way to Bellinzona—and this in face of the sombre fact that the Saint-Gothard tunnel is scraping away into the mountain, all the while, under his nose, and numbering the days of the many-buttoned brotherhood. But he hopes, for long service's sake, to be taken into the employ of the railway ; *he* at least is no cherisher of quaintness and has no romantic perversity.   I found the railway coming on, however, in a manner very shocking to mine.   About an hour short of Andermatt they have pierced a huge black cavity in the mountain, around which has grown up a swarming, digging, hammering, smoke-compelling colony.   There are great barracks, with tall chimneys, down in the gorge that bristled the other day but with natural graces, and a wonderful increase of wine-shops in the little village of Göschenen above.   Along the breast of the mountain, beside the road, come wandering several miles of very handsome iron pipes, of a stupendous girth—a conduit for the water-power with which some of the machinery is worked. It lies at its mighty length among the rocks like an immense black serpent, and serves, as a mere detail, to give one the measure of the central enterprise.   When at the end of our long day's journey, well down in warm Italy, we came upon the other aperture of the tunnel, I could but uncap with a grim reverence. Truly Nature is great, but she seems to me to stand in very much the shoes of my poor friend the conductor.   She is being superseded at her strongest points, successively, and nothing remains but for her to take humble service with her master.   If she can hear herself think amid that din of blasting and hammering she must be reckoning up the years to elapse before the cleverest of Ober-Ingénieurs decides that mountains are mere obstructive matter and has the Jungfrau melted down and the residuum carried away in balloons and dumped upon another planet.

The Devil's Bridge, with the same failing apparently as the good Homer, was decidedly nodding.   The volume of water in the torrent was shrunken, and I missed the thunderous uproar and far-leaping spray that have kept up a miniature tempest in the neighbourhood on my other passages. It suddenly occurs to me that the fault is not in the good Homer's inspiration, but simply in the big black pipes above-mentioned. They dip into the rushing stream higher up, presumably, and pervert its fine frenzy to their prosaic uses. There could hardly be a more vivid reminder of the standing quarrel between use and beauty, and of the hard time poor beauty is having. I looked wistfully, as we rattled into dreary Andermatt, at the great white zigzags of the Oberalp road, which climbed away to the left. Even on one's way to Italy one may spare a throb of desire for the beautiful vision of the castled Grisons. Dear to me the memory of my day's drive last summer through that long blue avenue of mountains, to queer little mouldering Ilanz, visited before supper in the ghostly dusk. At Andermatt a sign over a little black doorway flanked by two dunghills seemed to me tolerably comical : *Minéraux, Quadrupèdes, Oiseaux, Œufs, Tableaux Antiques*. We bundled in to dinner and the American gentleman in the banquette made the acquaintance of the Irish lady in the coupé, who talked of the weather as *foine* and wore a Persian scarf twisted about her head. At the other end of the table sat an Englishman, out of the intérieur, who bore an extraordinary resemblance to the portraits of Edward VI.'s and Mary's reigns. He was a walking, a convincing Holbein. The impression was of value to a cherisher of quaintness, and he must have wondered —not knowing me for such a character—why I stared at him. It wasn't him I was staring at, but some handsome Seymour or Dudley or Digby with a ruff and a round cap and plume.

From Andermatt, through its high, cold, sunny valley, we passed into rugged little Hospenthal, and then up the last stages of the ascent. From here the road was all new to me. Among the summits of the various Alpine passes there is little to choose. You wind and double slowly into keener cold and deeper stillness ; you put on your overcoat and turn up the collar ; you count the nestling snow-patches and then you cease to count them; you pause, as you trudge before the lumbering coach, and listen to the last-heard cow-bell tinkling away below you in kindlier herbage. The sky was tremendously blue, and the little stunted bushes on the snow-streaked slopes were all dyed with autumnal purples and crimsons. It was a great display of colour. Purple and crimson too, though not so fine, were the faces thrust out at us from the greasy little double casements of a barrack beside the road, where the horses paused before the last pull. There was one little girl in particular, beginning to *lisser* her hair, as civilisation approached, in a manner not to be described, with her poor little blue-black hands. At the summit are the two usual grim little stone taverns, the steel-blue tarn, the snow-white peaks, the pause in the cold sunshine. Then we begin to rattle down with two horses. In five minutes we are swinging along the famous zigzags. Engineer, driver, horses— it's very handsomely done by all of them. The road curves and curls and twists and plunges like the tail of a kite; sitting perched in the banquette, you see it making below you and in mid-air certain bold gyrations which bring you as near as possible, short of the actual experience, to the philosophy of that immortal Irishman who wished that his fall from the house-top would only last. But the zigzags last no more than Paddy's fall, and in due time we were all coming to our senses over café au lait in the little inn at Faido. After Faido the valley, plunging deeper, began to take thick afternoon shadows from the hills, and at Airolo we were fairly in the twilight. But the pink and yellow houses shimmered through the gentle gloom, and Italy began in broken syllables to whisper that she was at hand. For the rest of the way to Bellinzona her voice was muffled in the grey of evening, and I was half vexed to lose the charming sight of the changing vegetation. But only half vexed, for the moon was climbing all the while nearer the edge of the crags that over-shadowed us, and a thin magical light came trickling down into the winding, murmuring gorges. It was a most enchanting business. The chestnut-trees loomed up with double their daylight stature; the vines began to swing their low festoons like nets to trip up the fairies. At last the ruined towers of Bellinzona stood gleaming in the moonshine, and we rattled into the great post-yard. It was eleven o'clock and I had risen at four; moonshine apart I wasn't sorry.

All that was very well; but the drive next day from Bellinzona to Como is to my mind what gives its supreme beauty to this great pass. One can't describe the beauty of the Italian lakes, nor would one try if one could; the floweriest rhetoric can recall it only as a picture on a fireboard recalls a Claude. But it lay spread before me for a whole perfect day: in the long gleam of the Major, from whose head the diligence swerves away and begins to climb the bosky hills that divide it from Lugano; in the shimmering, melting azure of the southern slopes and masses; in the luxurious tangle of nature and the familiar amenity of man; in the lawn-like inclinations, where the great grouped chestnuts make so cool a shadow in so warm a light; in the rusty vineyards, the littered cornfields and the tawdry wayside shrines. But most of all it's the deep yellow light that enchants you and tells you where you are. See it come filtering down through a vine-covered trellis on the red handkerchief with which a ragged contadina has bound her hair, and all the magic of Italy, to the eye, makes an aureole about the poor girl's head. Look at a brown-breasted reaper eating his chunk of black bread under a spreading chestnut; nowhere is shadow so charming, nowhere is colour so charged, nowhere has accident such grace. The whole drive to Lugano was one long loveliness, and the town itself is admirably Italian. There was a great unlading of the coach, during which I wandered under certain brown old arcades and bought for six sous, from a young woman in a gold necklace, a hatful of peaches and figs. When I came back I found the young man holding open the door of the second diligence, which had lately come up, and beckoning to me with a despairing smile. The young man, I must note, was the most amiable of Ticinese ; though he wore no buttons he was attached to the diligence in some amateurish capacity, and had an eye to the mail-bags and other valuables in the boot. I grumbled at Berne over the want of soft curves in the Swiss temperament ; but the children of the tangled Tessin are cast in the Italian mould. My friend had as many quips and cranks as a Neapolitan ; we walked together for an hour under the chestnuts, while the coach was plodding up from Bellinzona, and he never stopped singing till we reached a little wine-house where he got his mouth full of bread and cheese. I looked into his open door, à la Sterne, and saw the young woman sitting rigid and grim, staring over his head and with a great pile of bread and butter in her lap. He had only informed her most politely that she was to be transferred to another diligence and must do him the favour to descend ; but she evidently knew of but one way for a respectable young insulary of her sex to receive the politeness of a foreign adventurer guilty of an eye betraying latent pleasantry. Heaven only knew what he was saying ! I told her, and she gathered up her parcels and emerged. A part of the day's great pleasure perhaps was my grave sense of being an instrument in the hands of the powers toward the safe consignment of this young woman and her boxes. When once you have really bent to the helpless you are caught ; there is no such steel trap, and it holds you fast. My rather grim Abigail was a neophyte in foreign travel, though doubtless cunning enough at her trade, which I inferred to be that of making up those prodigious chignons worn mainly by English ladies. Her mistress had gone on a mule over the mountains to Cadenabbia, and she herself was coming up with the wardrobe, two big boxes and a bath-tub. I had played my part, under the powers, at Bellinzona, and had interposed between the poor girl's frightened English and the dreadful Ticinese French of the functionaries in the post-yard. At the custom-house on the Italian frontier I was of peculiar service; there was a kind of fateful fascination in it. The wardrobe was voluminous; I exchanged a paternal glance with my charge as the *douanier* plunged his brown fists into it. Who was the lady at Cadenabbia? What was she to me or I to her? She wouldn't know, when she rustled down to dinner next day, that it was I who had guided the frail skiff of her public basis of vanity to port. So unseen but not unfelt do we cross each other's orbits. The skiff however may have foundered that evening in sight of land. I disengaged the young woman from among her fellow-travellers and placed her boxes on a hand-cart in the picturesque streets of Como, within a stone's-throw of that lovely striped and toned cathedral which has the façade of cameo medallions. I could only make the *facchino* swear to take her to the steamboat. He too was a jovial dog, but I hope he was polite with precautions.

1873.

ITALY REVISITED

I

I WAITED in Paris until after the elections for the new Chamber (they took place on the 14th of October); as only after one had learned that the famous attempt of Marshal MacMahon and his ministers to drive the French nation to the polls like a flock of huddling sheep, each with the white ticket of an official candidate round his neck, had not achieved the success which the energy of the process might have promised—only then it was possible to draw a long breath and deprive the republican party of such support as might have been conveyed in one's sympathetic presence. Seriously speaking too, the weather had been enchanting—there were Italian fancies to be gathered without leaving the banks of the Seine. Day after day the air was filled with golden light, and even those chalkish vistas of the Parisian *beaux quartiers* assumed the iridescent tints of autumn. Autumn-weather in Europe is often such a very sorry affair that a fair-minded American will have it on his conscience to call attention to a rainless and radiant October.

The echoes of the electoral strife kept me company for a while after starting upon that abbreviated journey to Turin which, as you leave Paris at night, in a train unprovided with encouragements to slumber, is a singular mixture of the odious and the charming. The charming indeed I think prevails ; for the dark half of the journey is the least interesting. The morning light ushers you into the romantic gorges of the Jura, and after a big bowl of *café au lait* at Culoz you may compose yourself comfortably for the climax of your spectacle. The day before leaving Paris I met a French friend who had just returned from a visit to a Tuscan country-seat where he had been watching the vintage. " Italy," he said, "is more lovely than words can tell, and France, steeped in this electoral turmoil, seems no better than a bear-garden." The part of the bear-garden through which you travel as you approach the Mont-Cenis seemed to me that day very beautiful. The autumn colouring, thanks to the absence of rain, had been vivid and crisp, and the vines that swung their low garlands between the mulberries round about Chambéry looked like long festoons of coral and amber. The frontier station of Modane, on the further side of the Mont-Cenis Tunnel, is a very ill-regulated place ; but even the most irritable of tourists, meeting it on his way southward, will be disposed to consider it good-naturedly. There is far too much bustling and scrambling, and the facilities afforded you for the obligatory process of ripping open your luggage before the officers of the Italian custom-house are much scantier than should be ; but for myself there is something that deprecates irritation in the shabby green and grey uniforms of all the Italian officials who stand loafing about and watching the northern invaders scramble back into marching order. Wearing an administrative uniform doesn't necessarily spoil a man's temper, as in France one is sometimes led to believe ; for these excellent under-paid Italians carry theirs as lightly as possible, and their answers to your inquiries don't in the least bristle with rapiers, buttons and cockades. After leaving Modane you slide straight downhill into the Italy of your desire ; from which point the road edges, after the grand manner, along those great precipices that stand shoulder to shoulder, in a prodigious perpendicular file, till they finally admit you to a distant glimpse of the ancient capital of Piedmont.

Turin is no city of a name to conjure with, and I pay an extravagant tribute to subjective emotion in speaking of it as

ancient. But if the place is less bravely peninsular than
Florence and Rome, at least it is more in the scenic tradition
than New York and Paris ; and while I paced the great arcades
and looked at the fourth-rate shop windows I didn't scruple
to cultivate a shameless optimism. Relatively speaking, Turin
touches a chord ; but there is after all no reason in a large
collection of shabbily-stuccoed houses, disposed in a rigidly
rectangular manner, for passing a day of deep, still gaiety. The
only reason, I am afraid, is the old superstition of Italy—that
property in the very look of the written word, the evocation
of a myriad images, that makes any lover of the arts take
Italian satisfactions on easier terms than any others. The
written word stands for something that eternally tricks us ; we
juggle to our credulity even with such inferior apparatus as is
offered to our hand at Turin. I roamed all tne morning under
the tall porticoes, thinking it sufficient joy to take note of the
soft, warm air, of that local colour of things that is at once so
broken and so harmonious, and of the comings and goings, the
physiognomy and manners, of the excellent Turinese. I had
opened the old book again ; the old charm was in the style ;
I was in a more delightful world. I saw nothing surpassingly
beautiful or curious ; but your true taster of the most seasoned
of dishes finds well-nigh the whole mixture in any mouthful.
Above all on the threshold of Italy he knows again the solid
and perfectly definable pleasure of finding himself among the
traditions of the grand style in architecture. It must be said
that we have still to go there to recover the sense of the domiciliary mass. In northern cities there are beautiful houses,
picturesque and curious houses ; sculptured gables that hang
over the street, charming bay-windows, hooded doorways, elegant proportions, a profusion of delicate ornament ; but a good
specimen of an old Italian palazzo has a nobleness that is all
its own. We laugh at Italian " palaces," at their peeling paint,
their nudity, their dreariness ; but they have the great palatial

quality—elevation and extent.   They make of smaller things
the apparent abode of pigmies; they round their great arches
and interspace their huge windows with a proud indifference to
the cost of materials.   These grand proportions—the colossal
basements, the doorways that seem meant for cathedrals, the
far away cornices—impart by contrast a humble and *bourgeois*
expression to interiors founded on the sacrifice of the whole to
the part, and in which the air of grandeur depends largely on
the help of the upholsterer.   At Turin my first feeling was
really one of renewed shame for our meaner architectural manners.
If the Italians at bottom despise the rest of mankind and regard
them as barbarians, disinherited of the tradition of form, the
idea proceeds largely, no doubt, from our living in comparative
mole-hills.   They alone were really to build their civilisation.

An impression which on coming back to Italy I find even
stronger than when it was first received is that of the contrast
between the fecundity of the great artistic period and the
vulgarity there of the genius of to-day.   The first few hours
spent on Italian soil are sufficient to renew it, and the question I
allude to is, historically speaking, one of the oddest.   That the
people who but three hundred years ago had the best taste in the
world should now have the worst; that having produced the
noblest, loveliest, costliest works, they should now be given up
to the manufacture of objects at once ugly and paltry; that the
race of which Michael Angelo and Raphael, Leonardo and Titian
were characteristic should have no other title to distinction than
third-rate *genre* pictures and catchpenny statues—all this is a
frequent perplexity to the observer of actual Italian life.   The
flower of "great" art in these latter years ceased to bloom very
powerfully anywhere; but nowhere does it seem so drooping and
withered as in the shadow of the immortal embodiments of the
old Italian genius.   You go into a church or a gallery and feast
your fancy upon a splendid picture or an exquisite piece of sculpture, and on issuing from the door that has admitted you to the

beautiful past are confronted with something that has the effect of a very bad joke.   The aspect of your lodging—the carpets, the curtains, the upholstery in general, with their crude and violent colouring and their vulgar material—the trumpery things in the shops, the extreme bad taste of the dress of the women, the cheapness and baseness of every attempt at decoration in the cafés and railway-stations, the hopeless frivolity of everything that pretends to be a work of art—all this modern crudity runs riot over the relics of the great period.

We can do a thing for the first time but once; it is but once for all that we can have a pleasure in its freshness. This is a law not on the whole, I think, to be regretted, for we sometimes learn to know things better by not enjoying them too much.   It is certain, however, at the same time, that a visitor who has worked off the immediate ferment for this inexhaustibly interesting country has by no means entirely drained the cup.   After thinking of Italy as historical and artistic it will do him no great harm to think of her for a while as panting both for a future and for a balance at the bank; aspirations supposedly much at variance with the Byronic, the Ruskinian, the artistic, poetic, æsthetic manner of considering our eternally attaching peninsula.   He may grant—I don't say it is absolutely necessary—that its actual aspects and economics are ugly, prosaic, provokingly out of relation to the diary and the album; it is nevertheless true that, at the point things have come to, modern Italy in a manner imposes herself.   I hadn't been many hours in the country before that truth assailed me; and I may add that, the first irritation past, I found myself able to accept it.   For, if we think, nothing is more easy to understand than an honest ire on the part of the young Italy of to-day at being looked at by all the world as a kind of soluble pigment.   Young Italy, pre-occupied with its economical and political future, must be heartily tired of being admired for its eyelashes and its pose. In one of Thackeray's novels occurs a mention of a young artist who sent to the Royal Academy a picture representing "A Contadino dancing with a Trasteverina at the door of a Locanda, to the music of a Pifferaro." It is in this attitude and with these conventional accessories that the world has hitherto seen fit to represent young Italy, and one doesn't wonder that if the youth has any spirit he should at last begin to resent our insufferable æsthetic patronage. He has established a line of tram-cars in Rome, from the Porta del Popolo to the Ponte Molle, and it is on one of these democratic vehicles that I seem to see him taking his triumphant course down the vista of the future. I won't pretend to rejoice with him any more than I really do ; I won't pretend, as the sentimental tourists say about it all, as if it were the setting of an intaglio or the border of a Roman scarf, to "like" it. Like it or not, as we may, it is evidently destined to be ; I see a new Italy in the future which in many important respects will equal, if not surpass, the most enterprising sections of our native land. Perhaps by that time Chicago and San Francisco will have acquired a pose, and their sons and daughters will dance at the doors of *locande*.

However this may be, the accomplished schism between the old order and the new is the promptest moral of a fresh visit to this ever-suggestive part of the world. The old has become more and more a museum, preserved and perpetuated in the midst of the new, but without any further relation to it—it must be admitted indeed that such a relation is considerable— than that of the stock on his shelves to the shopkeeper, or of the Siren of the South to the showman who stands before his booth. More than once, as we move about nowadays in the Italian cities, there seems to pass before our eyes a vision of the coming years. It represents to our satisfaction an Italy united and prosperous, but altogether scientific and commercial. The Italy indeed that we sentimentalise and romance about was an ardently mercantile country ; though I suppose it loved not its ledgers less, but its frescoes and altar-pieces more. Scattered through this

paradise regained of trade—this country of a thousand ports—
we see a large number of beautiful buildings in which an endless
series of dusky pictures are darkening, dampening, fading, failing,
through the years.   By the doors of the beautiful buildings are
little turnstiles at which there sit a great many uniformed men
to whom the visitor pays a tenpenny fee.   Inside, in the vaulted
and frescoed chambers, the art of Italy lies buried as in a thousand
mausoleums.   It is well taken care of; it is constantly copied;
sometimes it is "restored"—as in the case of that beautiful boy-
figure of Andrea del Sarto at Florence, which may be seen at the
gallery of the Uffizi with its honourable duskiness quite peeled
off and heaven knows what raw, bleeding cuticle laid bare.   One
evening lately, near the same Florence, in the soft twilight, I
took a stroll among those encircling hills on which the massive
villas are mingled with the vaporous olives.   Presently I arrived
where three roads met at a wayside shrine, in which, before
some pious daub of an old-time Madonna, a little votive lamp
glimmered through the evening air.   The hour, the atmosphere,
the place, the twinkling taper, the sentiment of the observer, the
thought that some one had been rescued here from an assassin or
from some other peril and had set up a little grateful altar
in consequence, against the yellow-plastered wall of a tangled
podere; all this led me to approach the shrine with a reverent,
an emotional step.   I drew near it, but after a few steps I paused.
I became aware of an incongruous odour; it seemed to me
that the evening air was charged with a perfume which, although
to a certain extent familiar, had not hitherto associated itself with
rustic frescoes and wayside altars.   I wondered, I gently sniffed,
and the question so put left me no doubt.   The odour was that
of petroleum; the votive taper was nourished with the essence
of Pennsylvania.   I confess that I burst out laughing, and a
picturesque contadino, wending his homeward way in the dusk,
stared at me as if I were an iconoclast.   He noticed the petroleum only, I imagine, to snuff it fondly up; but to me the thing

H

served as a symbol of the Italy of the future.   There is a horse-car from the Porta del Popolo to the Ponte Molle, and the Tuscan shrines are fed with kerosene.

II

If it's very well meanwhile to come to Turin first it's better still to go to Genoa afterwards.   Genoa is the tightest topographic tangle in the world, which even a second visit helps you little to straighten out.   In the wonderful crooked, twisting, climbing, soaring, burrowing Genoese alleys the traveller is really up to his neck in the old Italian sketchability.   The pride of the place, I believe, is a port of great capacity, and the bequest of the late Duke of Galliera, who left four millions of dollars for the purpose of improving and enlarging it, will doubtless do much toward converting it into one of the great commercial stations of Europe.   But as, after leaving my hotel the afternoon I arrived, I wandered for a long time at hazard through the tortuous byways of the city, I said to myself, not without an accent of private triumph, that here at last was something it would be almost impossible to modernise.   I had found my hotel, in the first place, extremely entertaining—the Croce di Malta, as it is called, established in a gigantic palace on the edge of the swarming and not over-clean harbour.   It was the biggest house I had ever entered—the basement alone would have contained a dozen American caravansaries.   I met an American gentleman in the vestibule who (as he had indeed a perfect right to be) was annoyed by its troublesome dimensions—one was a quarter of an hour ascending out of the basement—and desired to know if it were a "fair sample" of the Genoese inns.   It appeared an excellent specimen of Genoese architecture generally; so far as I observed there were few houses perceptibly smaller than this Titanic tavern.   I lunched in a dusky ballroom whose ceiling was vaulted, frescoed and gilded with the fatal facility

of a couple of centuries ago, and which looked out upon another
ancient house-front, equally huge and equally battered, separated
from it only by a little wedge of dusky space—one of the principal streets, I believe, of Genoa—whence out of dim abysses
the population sent up to the windows (I had to crane out
very far to see it) a perpetual clattering, shuffling, chaffering
sound. Issuing forth presently into this crevice of a street I
found myself up to my neck in that element of the rich and
strange—as to visible and reproducible " effect," I mean—for
the love of which one revisits Italy. It offered itself indeed in
a variety of colours, some of which were not remarkable for
their freshness or purity. But their combined charm was not to
be resisted, and the picture glowed with the rankly human side
of southern low-life.

Genoa, as I have hinted, is the crookedest and most inco-
herent of cities; tossed about on the sides and crests of a dozen
hills, it is seamed with gullies and ravines that bristle with those
innumerable palaces for which we have heard from our earliest
years that the place is celebrated. These great structures, with
their mottled and faded complexions, lift their big ornamental
cornices to a tremendous height in the air, where, in a certain
indescribably forlorn and desolate fashion, overtopping each
other, they seem to reflect the twinkle and glitter of the warm
Mediterranean. Down about the basements, in the close crepuscular alleys, the people are for ever moving to and fro or
standing in their cavernous doorways and their dusky, crowded
shops, calling, chattering, laughing, lamenting, living their lives
in the conversational Italian fashion. I had for a long time
had no such vision of possible social pressure. I hadn't for
a long time seen people elbowing each other so closely or
swarming so thickly out of populous hives. A traveller is
often moved to ask himself whether it has been worth while to
leave his home—whatever his home may have been—only to
encounter new forms of human suffering, only to be reminded

that toil and privation, hunger and sorrow and sordid effort, are the portion of the mass of mankind. To travel is, as it were, to go to the play, to attend a spectacle; and there is something heartless in stepping forth into foreign streets to feast on " character " when character consists simply of the slightly different costume in which labour and want present themselves. These reflections were forced upon me as I strolled as through a twilight patched with colour and charged with stale smells; but after a time they ceased to bear me company. The reason of this, I think, is because—at least to foreign eyes—the sum of Italian misery is, on the whole, less than the sum of the Italian knowledge of life. That people should thank you, with a smile of striking sweetness, for the gift of twopence, is a proof, certainly, of extreme and constant destitution; but (keeping in mind the sweetness) it also attests an enviable ability not to be depressed by circumstances. I know that this may possibly be great nonsense; that half the time we are acclaiming the fine quality of the Italian smile the creature so constituted for physiognomic radiance may be in a sullen frenzy of impatience and pain. Our observation in any foreign land is extremely superficial, and our remarks are happily not addressed to the inhabitants themselves, who would be sure to exclaim upon the impudence of the fancy-picture.

The other day I visited a very picturesque old city upon a mountain-top, where, in the course of my wanderings, I arrived at an old disused gate in the ancient town-wall. The gate hadn't been absolutely forfeited; but the recent completion of a modern road down the mountain led most vehicles away to another egress. The grass-grown pavement, which wound into the plain by a hundred graceful twists and plunges, was now given up to ragged contadini and their donkeys, and to such wayfarers as were not alarmed at the disrepair into which it had fallen. I stood in the shadow of the tall old gateway admiring the scene, looking to right and left at the wonderful walls of the little town, perched on the edge of a shaggy precipice; at the circling mountains over against them; at the road dipping downward among the chestnuts and olives. There was no one within sight but a young man who slowly trudged upward with his coat slung over his shoulder and his hat upon his ear in the manner of a cavalier in an opera. Like an operatic performer too he sang as he came; the spectacle, generally, was operatic, and as his vocal flourishes reached my ear I said to myself that in Italy accident was always romantic and that such a figure had been exactly what was wanted to set off the landscape. It suggested in a high degree that knowledge of life for which I just now commended the Italians. I was turning back under the old gateway when the young man over-took me and, suspending his song, asked me if I could favour him with a match to light the hoarded remnant of a cigar. This request led, as I took my way again to the inn, to my falling into talk with him. He was a native of the ancient city, and answered freely all my inquiries as to its manners and customs and its note of public opinion. But the point of my anecdote is that he presently acknowledged himself a brooding young radical and communist, filled with hatred of the present Italian government, raging with discontent and crude political passion, professing a ridiculous hope that Italy would soon have, as France had had, her " '89," and declaring that he for his part would willingly lend a hand to chop off the heads of the king and the royal family. He was an unhappy, underfed, unemployed young man, who took a hard, grim view of every-thing and was operatic only quite in spite of himself. This made it very absurd of me to have looked at him simply as a graceful ornament to the prospect, an harmonious little figure in the middle distance. " Damn the prospect, damn the middle distance!" would have been all *his* philosophy. Yet but for the accident of my having gossipped with him I should have made him do service, in memory, as an example of sensuous optimism!

I am bound to say however that I believe a great deal of the sensuous optimism observable in the Genoese alleys and beneath the low, crowded arcades along the port was very real. Here every one was magnificently sunburnt, and there were plenty of those queer types, mahogany-coloured, bare-chested mariners with earrings and crimson girdles, that seem to people a southern seaport with the chorus of " Masaniello." But it is not fair to speak as if at Genoa there were nothing but low-life to be seen, for the place is the residence of some of the grandest people in the world. Nor are all the palaces ranged upon dusky alleys; the handsomest and most impressive form a splendid series on each side of a couple of very proper streets, in which there is plenty of room for a coach-and-four to approach the big doorways. Many of these doorways are open, revealing great marble staircases with couchant lions for balustrades and ceremonious courts surrounded by walls of sun-softened yellow. One of the great piles in the array is coloured a goodly red and contains in particular the grand people I just now spoke of. They live indeed on the third floor; but here they have suites of wonderful painted and gilded chambers, in which foreshortened frescoes also cover the vaulted ceilings and florid mouldings emboss the ample walls. These distinguished tenants bear the name of Vandyck, though they are members of the noble family of Brignole-Sale, one of whose children—the Duchess of Galliera—has lately given proof of nobleness in presenting the gallery of the red palace to the city of Genoa.

III

On leaving Genoa I repaired to Spezia, chiefly with a view of accomplishing a sentimental pilgrimage, which I in fact achieved in the most agreeable conditions. The Gulf of Spezia is now the headquarters of the Italian fleet, and there were several big iron-plated frigates riding at anchor in front of the town. The streets were filled with lads in blue flannel, who were receiving instruction at a schoolship in the harbour, and in the evening— there was a brilliant moon—the little breakwater which stretched out into the Mediterranean offered a scene of recreation to innumerable such persons. But this fact is from the point of view of the cherisher of quaintness of little account, for since it has become prosperous Spezia has grown ugly. The place is filled with long, dull stretches of dead wall and great raw expanses of artificial land. It wears that look of monstrous, of more than far-western newness which distinguishes all the creations of the young Italian State. Nor did I find any great compensation in an immense inn of recent birth, an establishment seated on the edge of the sea in anticipation of a *passeggiata* which is to come that way some five years hence, the region being in the meantime of the most primitive formation. The inn was filled with grave English people who looked respectable and bored, and there was of course a Church of England service in the gaudily-frescoed parlour. Neither was it the drive to Porto Venere that chiefly pleased me—a drive among vines and olives, over the hills and beside the Mediterranean, to a queer little crumbling village on a headland, as sweetly desolate and superannuated as the name it bears. There is a ruined church near the village, which occupies the site (according to tradition) of an ancient temple of Venus; and if Venus ever revisits her desecrated shrines she must sometimes pause a moment in that sunny stillness and listen to the murmur of the tideless sea at the base of the narrow promontory. If Venus sometimes comes there Apollo surely does as much; for close to the temple is a gateway surmounted by an inscription in Italian and English, which admits you to a curious, and it must be confessed rather cockneyfied, cave among the rocks. It was here, says the inscription, that the great Byron, swimmer and poet, "defied the waves of the Ligurian sea." The fact is interesting, though not supremely so; for Byron was always defying something, and if a slab had been put up wherever this performance came off these commemorative tablets would be in many parts of Europe as thick as milestones.

No; the great merit of Spezia, to my eye, is that I engaged a boat there of a lovely October afternoon and had myself rowed across the gulf—it took about an hour and a half—to the little bay of Lerici, which opens out of it. This bay of Lerici is charming; the bosky grey-green hills close it in, and on either side of the entrance, perched on a bold headland, a wonderful old crumbling castle keeps ineffectual guard. The place is classic to all English travellers, for in the middle of the curving shore is the now desolate little villa in which Shelley spent the last months of his short life. He was living at Lerici when he started on that short southern cruise from which he never returned. The house he occupied is strangely shabby and as sad as you may choose to find it. It stands directly upon the beach, with scarred and battered walls and a loggia of several arches opening to a little terrace with a rugged parapet, which, when the wind blows, must be drenched with the salt spray. The place is very lonely—all overwearied with sun and breeze and brine—very close to nature, as it was Shelley's passion to be. I can fancy a great lyric poet sitting on the terrace of a warm evening and feeling very far from England in the early years of the century. In that place, and with his genius, he would as a matter of course have heard in the voice of nature a sweetness which only the lyric movement could translate. It is a place where an English-speaking pilgrim himself may very honestly think thoughts and feel moved to lyric utterance. But I must content myself with saying in halting prose that I remember few episodes of Italian travel more sympathetic, as they have it here, than that perfect autumn afternoon; the half-hour's station on the little battered terrace of the villa; the climb to the singularly felicitous old castle that hangs above Lerici; the meditative lounge, in the fading light, on the vine-decked platform that looked out toward the sunset and the darkening mountains and, far below, upon the quiet sea, beyond which the pale-faced tragic villa stared up at the brightening moon.

IV

I had never known Florence more herself, or in other words more attaching, than I found her for a week in that brilliant October. She sat in the sunshine beside her yellow river like the little treasure-city she has always seemed, without commerce, without other industry than the manufacture of mosaic paper-weights and alabaster Cupids, without actuality or energy or earnestness or any of those rugged virtues which in most cases are deemed indispensable for civic cohesion; with nothing but the little unaugmented stock of her mediæval memories, her tender-coloured mountains, her churches and palaces, pictures and statues. There were very few strangers; one's detested fellow - pilgrim was infrequent; the native population itself seemed scanty; the sound of wheels in the streets was but occasional; by eight o'clock at night, apparently, every one had gone to bed, and the musing wanderer, still wandering and still musing, had the place to himself——had the thick shadow-masses of the great palaces, and the shafts of moonlight striking the polygonal paving-stones, and the empty bridges, and the silvered yellow of the Arno, and the stillness broken only by a home-ward step, a step accompanied by a snatch of song from a warm Italian voice. My room at the inn looked out on the river and was flooded all day with sunshine. There was an absurd orange-coloured paper on the walls; the Arno, of a hue not altogether different, flowed beneath; and on the other side of it rose a line of sallow houses, of extreme antiquity, crumbling and moulder-ing, bulging and protruding over the stream. (I seem to speak of their fronts; but what I saw was their shabby backs, which were exposed to the cheerful flicker of the river, while the fronts stood for ever in the deep damp shadow of a narrow mediæval street.) All this brightness and yellowness was a perpetual delight; it was a part of that indefinably charming colour which Florence always seems to wear as you look up and down at it from the river, and from the bridges and quays. This is a kind of grave radiance—a harmony of high tints—which I scarce know how to describe. There are yellow walls and green blinds and red roofs, there are intervals of brilliant brown and natural-looking blue; but the picture is not spotty nor gaudy, thanks to the distribution of the colours in large and comfortable masses, and to the washing-over of the scene by some happy softness of sunshine. The river-front of Florence is in short a delightful composition. Part of its charm comes of course from the generous aspect of those high-based Tuscan palaces which a renewal of acquaintance with them has again commended to me as the most dignified dwellings in the world. Nothing can be finer than that look of giving up the whole immense ground-floor to simple purposes of vestibule and staircase, of court and high-arched entrance; as if this were all but a massive pedestal for the real habitation and people weren't properly housed unless, to begin with, they should be lifted fifty feet above the pavement. The great blocks of the basement; the great intervals, horizontally and vertically, from window to window (telling of the height and breadth of the rooms within); the armorial shield hung forward at one of the angles; the wide-brimmed roof, overshadowing the narrow street; the rich old browns and yellows of the walls: these definite elements put themselves together with admirable art.

Take a Tuscan pile of this type out of its oblique situation in the town; call it no longer a palace, but a villa; set it down by a terrace on one of the hills that encircle Florence, place a row of high-waisted cypresses beside it, give it a grassy courtyard and a view of the Florentine towers and the valley of the Arno, and you will think it perhaps even more worthy of your

esteem. It was a Sunday noon, and brilliantly warm, when I
again arrived ; and after I had looked from my windows awhile
at that quietly-basking river-front I have spoken of I took my
way across one of the bridges and then out of one of the gates
—that immensely tall Roman Gate in which the space from the
top of the arch to the cornice (except that there is scarcely a
cornice, it is all a plain massive piece of wall) is as great, or
seems to be, as that from the ground to the former point.
Then I climbed a steep and winding way—much of it a little
dull if one likes, being bounded by mottled, mossy garden-walls
—to a villa on a hill-top, where I found various things that
touched me with almost too fine a point. Seeing them again,
often, for a week, both by sunlight and moonshine, I never quite
learned not to covet them ; not to feel that not being a part of
them was somehow to miss an exquisite chance. What a tranquil, contented life it seemed, with romantic beauty as a part of
its daily texture !—the sunny terrace, with its tangled *podere*
beneath it ; the bright grey olives against the bright blue sky ;
the long, serene, horizontal lines of other villas, flanked by their
upward cypresses, disposed upon the neighbouring hills ; the
richest little city in the world in a softly-scooped hollow at
one's feet, and beyond it the most appealing of views, the most
majestic, yet the most familiar. Within the villa was a great
love of art and a painting-room full of felicitous work, so that
if human life there confessed to quietness, the quietness was
mostly but that of the intent act. A beautiful occupation in
that beautiful position, what could possibly be better ? That
is what I spoke just now of envying—a way of life that doesn't
wince at such refinements of peace and ease. When labour self-
charmed presents itself in a dull or an ugly place we esteem it,
we admire it, but we scarce feel it to be the ideal of good
fortune. When, however, its votaries move as figures in an
ancient, noble landscape, and their walks and contemplations
are like a turning of the leaves of history, we seem to have

before us an admirable case of virtue made easy; meaning here by virtue contentment and concentration, a real appreciation of the rare, the exquisite though composite, medium of life. You needn't want a rush or a crush when the scene itself, the mere scene, shares with you such a wealth of consciousness.

It is true indeed that I might after a certain time grow weary of a regular afternoon stroll among the Florentine lanes; of sitting on low parapets, in intervals of flower-topped wall, and looking across at Fiesole or down the rich-hued valley of the Arno; of pausing at the open gates of villas and wondering at the height of cypresses and the depth of loggias; of walking home in the fading light and noting on a dozen westward-looking surfaces the glow of the opposite sunset. But for a week or so all this was delightful. The villas are innumerable, and if you're an aching alien half the talk is about villas. This one has a story; that one has another; they all look as if they had stories—none in truth predominantly gay. Most of them are offered to rent (many of them for sale) at prices unnaturally low; you may have a tower and a garden, a chapel and an expanse of thirty windows, for five hundred dollars a year. In imagination you hire three or four; you take possession and settle and stay. Your sense of the fineness of the finest is of something very grave and stately; your sense of the bravery of two or three of the best something quite tragic and sinister. From what does this latter impression come? You gather it as you stand there in the early dusk, with your eyes on the long, pale-brown façade, the enormous windows, the iron cages fastened to the lower ones. Part of the brooding expression of these great houses comes, even when they have not fallen into decay, from their look of having outlived their original use. Their extraordinary largeness and massiveness are a satire on their present fate. They weren't built with such a thickness of wall and depth of embrasure, such a solidity of staircase and superfluity of stone, simply to afford an economical winter residence to English and American families. I don't know whether it was the appearance of these stony old villas, which seemed so dumbly conscious of a change of manners, that threw a tinge of melancholy over the general prospect; certain it is that, having always found this note as of a myriad old sadnesses in solution in the view of Florence, it seemed to me now particularly strong. "Lovely, lovely, but it makes me 'blue,'" the sensitive stranger couldn't but murmur to himself as, in the late afternoon, he looked at the landscape from over one of the low parapets, and then, with his hands in his pockets, turned away indoors to candles and dinner.

V

Below, in the city, through all frequentation of streets and churches and museums, it was impossible not to have a good deal of the same feeling; but here the impression was more easy to analyse. It came from a sense of the perfect separateness of all the great productions of the Renaissance from the present and the future of the place, from the actual life and manners, the native ideal. I have already spoken of the way in which the vast aggregation of beautiful works of art in the Italian cities strikes the visitor nowadays—so far as present Italy is concerned—as the mere stock-in-trade of an impecunious but thrifty people. It is this spiritual solitude, this conscious disconnection of the great works of architecture and sculpture that deposits a certain weight upon the heart; when we see a great tradition broken we feel something of the pain with which we hear a stifled cry. But regret is one thing and resentment is another. Seeing one morning, in a shop-window, the series of *Mornings in Florence* published a few years since by Mr. Ruskin, I made haste to enter and purchase these amusing little books, some passages of which I remembered formerly to have read. I couldn't turn over many pages without observing that the "separateness" of the new and old which I just mentioned had produced in their author the liveliest irritation. With the more acute phases of this condition it was difficult to sympathise, for the simple reason, it seems to me, that it savours of arrogance to demand of any people, as a right of one's own, that they shall be artistic. "Be artistic yourselves!" is the very natural reply that young Italy has at hand for English critics and censors. When a people produces beautiful statues and pictures it gives us something more than is set down in the bond, and we must thank it for its generosity; and when it stops producing them or caring for them we may cease thanking, but we hardly have a right to begin and rail. The wreck of Florence, says Mr. Ruskin, "is now too ghastly and heart-breaking to any human soul that remembers the days of old;" and these desperate words are an allusion to the fact that the little square in front of the cathedral, at the foot of Giotto's Tower, with the grand Baptistery on the other side, is now the resort of a number of hackney-coaches and omnibuses. This fact is doubtless lamentable, and it would be a hundred times more agreeable to see among people who have been made the heirs of so priceless a work of art as the sublime campanile some such feeling about it as would keep it free even from the danger of defilement. A cab-stand is a very ugly and dirty thing, and Giotto's Tower should have nothing in common with such conveniences. But there is more than one way of taking such things, and the sensitive stranger who has been walking about for a week with his mind full of the sweetness and suggestiveness of a hundred Florentine places may feel at last in looking into Mr. Ruskin's little tracts that, discord for discord, there isn't much to choose between the importunity of the author's personal ill-humour and the incongruity of horse-pails and bundles of hay. And one may say this without being at all a partisan of the doctrine of the inevitableness of new desecrations. For my own part, I believe there are few things in this line that the new Italian spirit isn't capable of, and not many indeed that we aren't destined to see. Pictures and buildings won't be completely destroyed, because in that case the *forestieri*, scatterers of cash, would cease to arrive and the turn-stiles at the doors of the old palaces and convents, with the little patented slit for absorbing your half-franc, would grow quite rusty, would stiffen with disuse. But it's safe to say that the new Italy growing into an old Italy again will continue to take her elbow-room wherever she may find it.

I am almost ashamed to say what I did with Mr. Ruskin's little books. I put them into my pocket and betook myself to Santa Maria Novella. There I sat down and, after I had looked about for a while at the beautiful church, drew them forth one by one and read the greater part of them. Occupying one's self with light literature in a great religious edifice is perhaps as bad a piece of profanation as any of those rude dealings which Mr. Ruskin justly deplores; but a traveller has to make the most of odd moments, and I was waiting for a friend in whose company I was to go and look at Giotto's beautiful frescoes in the cloister of the church. My friend was a long time coming, so that I had an hour with Mr. Ruskin, whom I called just now a light *littérateur* because in these little Mornings in Florence he is for ever making his readers laugh. I remembered of course where I was, and in spite of my latent hilarity felt I had rarely got such a snubbing. I had really been enjoying the good old city of Florence, but I now learned from Mr. Ruskin that this was a scandalous waste of charity. I should have gone about with an imprecation on my lips, I should have worn a face three yards long. I had taken great pleasure in certain frescoes by Ghirlandaio in the choir of that very church; but it appeared from one of the little books that these frescoes were as naught. I had much admired Santa Croce and had thought the Duomo a very noble affair; but I had now the most positive assurance I knew nothing about them. After a while, if it was only ill-humour that was needed for doing honour to the city of the

Medici, I felt that I had risen to a proper level; only now it was Mr. Ruskin himself I had lost patience with, not the stupid Brunelleschi, not the vulgar Ghirlandaio. Indeed I lost patience altogether, and asked myself by what right this informal votary of form pretended to run riot through a poor charmed *flâneur's* quiet contemplations, his attachment to the noblest of pleasures, his enjoyment of the loveliest of cities. The little books seemed invidious and insane, and it was only when I remembered that I had been under no obligation to buy them that I checked myself in repenting of having done so.

Then at last my friend arrived and we passed together out of the church and, through the first cloister beside it, into a smaller enclosure where we stood a while to look at the tomb of the Marchesa Strozzi-Ridolfi, upon which the great Giotto has painted four superb little pictures. It was easy to see the pictures were superb; but I drew forth one of my little books again, for I had observed that Mr. Ruskin spoke of them. Hereupon I recovered my tolerance; for what could be better in this case, I asked myself, than Mr. Ruskin's remarks? They are in fact excellent and charming—full of appreciation of the deep and simple beauty of the great painter's work. I read them aloud to my companion; but my companion was rather, as the phrase is, "put off" by them. One of the frescoes—it is a picture of the birth of the Virgin—contains a figure coming through a door. "Of ornament," I quote, "there is only the entirely simple outline of the vase which the servant carries; of colour two or three masses of sober red and pure white, with brown and grey. That is all," Mr. Ruskin continues. "And if you are pleased with this you can see Florence. But if not, by all means amuse yourself there, if you find it amusing, as long as you like; you can never see it." *You can never see it.* This seemed to my friend insufferable, and I had to shuffle away the book again, so that we might look at the fresco with the unruffled geniality it deserves. We agreed afterwards, when in a more convenient place I read aloud a good many more passages from the precious tracts, that there are a great many ways of seeing Florence, as there are of seeing most beautiful and interesting things, and that it is very dry and pedantic to say that the happy vision depends upon our squaring our toes with a certain particular chalk-mark. We see Florence wherever and whenever we enjoy it, and for enjoying it we find a great many more pretexts than Mr. Ruskin seems inclined to allow. My friend and I convinced ourselves also, however, that the little books were an excellent purchase, on account of the great charm and felicity of much of their incidental criticism ; to say nothing, as I hinted just now, of their being extremely amusing. Nothing in fact is more comical than the familiar asperity of the author's style and the pedagogic fashion in which he pushes and pulls his unhappy pupils about, jerking their heads toward this, rapping their knuckles for that, sending them to stand in corners and giving them Scripture texts to copy. But it is neither the felicities nor the aberrations of detail, in Mr. Ruskin's writings, that are the main affair for most readers ; it is the general tone that, as I have said, puts them off or draws them on. For many persons he will never bear the test of being read in this rich old Italy, where art, so long as it really lived at all, was spontaneous, joyous, irresponsible. If the reader is in daily contact with those beautiful Florentine works which do still, in a way, force them-selves into notice through the vulgarity and cruelty of modern profanation, it will seem to him that this commentator's comment is pitched in the strangest falsetto key. " One may read a hundred pages of this sort of thing," said my friend, " without ever dream-ing that he is talking about *art*. You can say nothing worse about him than that." Which is perfectly true. Art is the one corner of human life in which we may take our ease. To justify our presence there the only thing demanded of us is that we shall have felt the representational impulse. In other con-nections our impulses are conditioned and embarrassed ; we are

I

allowed to have only so many as are consistent with those of our neighbours; with their convenience and well-being, with their convictions and prejudices, their rules and regulations. Art means an escape from all this. Wherever her shining standard floats the need for apology and compromise is over; there it is enough simply that we please or are pleased. There the tree is judged only by its fruits. If these are sweet the tree is justified —and not less so the consumer.

One may read a great many pages of Mr. Ruskin without getting a hint of this delightful truth; a hint of the not un-important fact that art after all is made for us and not we for art. This idea that the value of a work is in the amount of illusion it yields is conspicuous by its absence. And as for Mr. Ruskin's world's being a place—his world of art—where we may take life easily, woe to the luckless mortal who enters it with any such disposition. Instead of a garden of delight, he finds a sort of assize court in perpetual session. Instead of a place in which human responsibilities are lightened and suspended, he finds a region governed by a kind of Draconic legislation. His responsibilities indeed are tenfold increased; the gulf between truth and error is for ever yawning at his feet; the pains and penalties of this same error are advertised, in apocalyptic ter-minology, upon a thousand sign-posts; and the rash intruder soon begins to look back with infinite longing to the lost paradise of the artless. There can be no greater want of tact in dealing with those things with which men attempt to ornament life than to be perpetually talking about "error." A truce to all rigidities is the law of the place; the only thing absolute there is that some force and some charm have worked. The grim old bearer of the scales excuses herself; she feels this not to be her province. Differences here are not iniquity and righteousness; they are simply variations of temperament, kinds of curiosity. We are not under theological government.

VI

It was very charming, in the bright, warm days, to wander from one corner of Florence to another, paying one's respects again to remembered masterpieces. It was pleasant also to find that memory had played no tricks and that the rarest things of an earlier year were as rare as ever. To enumerate these felicities would take a great deal of space; for I never had been more struck with the mere quantity of brilliant Florentine work. Even giving up the Duomo and Santa Croce to Mr. Ruskin as very ill-arranged edifices, the list of the Florentine treasures is almost inexhaustible. Those long outer galleries of the Uffizi had never beguiled me more; sometimes there were not more than two or three figures standing there, Baedeker in hand, to break the charming perspective. One side of this upstairs portico, it will be remembered, is entirely composed of glass; a continuity of old-fashioned windows, draped with white curtains of rather primitive fashion, which hang there till they acquire a perceptible tone. The light, passing through them, is softly filtered and diffused; it rests mildly upon the old marbles—chiefly antique Roman busts—which stand in the narrow intervals of the casements. It is projected upon the numerous pictures that cover the opposite wall and that are not by any means, as a general thing, the gems of the great collection; it imparts a faded brightness to the old ornamental arabesques upon the painted wooden ceiling, and it makes a great soft shining upon the marble floor, in which, as you look up and down, you see the strolling tourists and the motionless copyists almost reflected. I don't know why I should find all this very pleasant, but in fact, I have seldom gone into the Uffizi without walking the length of this third-story cloister, between the (for the most part) third-rate canvases and panels and the faded cotton curtains. Why is it that in Italy we see a charm in things in regard to which in other countries we always take vulgarity for granted? If in the city of New York a great museum of the arts were to be provided, by way of decoration, with a species of verandah inclosed on one side by a series of small-paned windows draped in dirty linen, and furnished on the other with an array of pictorial feebleness, the place being surmounted by a thinly-painted wooden roof, strongly suggestive of summer heat, of winter cold, of frequent leakage, those amateurs who had had the advantage of foreign travel would be at small pains to conceal their contempt.

Contemptible or respectable, to the judicial mind, this quaint old loggia of the Uffizi admitted me into twenty chambers where I found as great a number of ancient favourites. I don't know that I had a warmer greeting for any old friend than for Andrea del Sarto, that most touching of painters who is not one of the first. But it was on the other side of the Arno that I found him in force, in those dusky drawing-rooms of the Pitti Palace to which you take your way along the tortuous tunnel that wanders through the houses of Florence and is supported by the little goldsmiths' booths on the Ponte Vecchio. In the rich insufficient light of these beautiful rooms, where, to look at the pictures, you sit in damask chairs and rest your elbows on tables of malachite, the elegant Andrea becomes deeply effective. Before long he has drawn you close. But the great pleasure, after all, was to revisit the earlier masters, in those specimens of them chiefly that bloom so unfadingly on the big plain walls of the Academy. Fra Angelico and Filippo Lippi, Botticelli and Lorenzo di Credi are the clearest, the sweetest and best of all painters; as I sat for an hour in their company, in the cold great hall of the institution I have mentioned—there are shabby rafters above and an immense expanse of brick tiles below, and many bad pictures as well as good—it seemed to me more than ever that if one really had to choose one couldn't do better than choose here. You may rest at your ease at the

Academy, in this big first room—at the upper end especially, on the left—because more than many other places it savours of old Florence. More for instance, in reality, than the Bargello, though the Bargello makes great pretensions. Beautiful and masterful though the Bargello is, it smells too strongly of restoration, and, much of old Italy as still lurks in its furbished and renovated chambers, it speaks even more distinctly of the ill-mannered young kingdom that has—as "unavoidably" as you please—lifted down a hundred delicate works of sculpture from the convent-walls where their pious authors placed them. If the early Tuscan painters are exquisite I can think of no praise pure enough for the sculptors of the same period, Donatello and Luca della Robbia, Matteo Civitale and Mina da Fiesole, who, as I refreshed my memory of them, seemed to me to leave absolutely nothing to be desired in the way of straightness of inspiration and grace of invention. The Bargello is full of early Tuscan sculpture, most of the pieces of which have come from suppressed religious houses; and even if the visitor be an ardent liberal he is uncomfortably conscious of the rather brutal process by which it has been collected. One can hardly envy young Italy the number of odious things she has had to do.

The railway journey from Florence to Rome has been altered both for the better and for the worse; for the better in that it has been shortened by a couple of hours; for the worse inasmuch as when about half the distance has been traversed the train deflects to the west and leaves the beautiful old cities of Assisi, Perugia, Terni, Narni, unvisited. Of old it was possible to call at these places, in a manner, from the window of the train; even if you didn't stop, as you probably couldn't, every time you passed, the immensely interesting way in which, like a loosened belt on an aged and shrunken person, their ample walls held them easily together was something well worth noting. Now, however, for compensation, the express train to Rome stops at Orvieto, and in consequence. . . . In consequence what?

What is the result of the stop of an express train at Orvieto? As I glibly wrote that sentence I suddenly paused, aware of the queer stuff I was uttering. That an express train would graze the base of the horrid purple mountain from the apex of which this dark old Catholic city uplifts the glittering front of its cathedral—that might have been foretold by a keen observer of contemporary manners. But that it would really have the grossness to hang about is a fact over which, as he records it, an inveterate, a perverse cherisher of the sense of the past order, the order still largely prevailing at the time of his first visit to Italy, may well make what is vulgarly called an ado. The train does stop at Orvieto, not very long, it is true, but long enough to let you out. The same phenomenon takes place on the following day, when, having visited the city, you get in again. I availed myself without scruple of both of these occasions, having formerly neglected to drive to the place in a post-chaise. But frankly, the railway-station being in the plain and the town on the summit of an extraordinary hill, you have time to forget the puffing indiscretion while you wind upwards to the city-gate. The position of Orvieto is superb—worthy of the "middle distance" of an eighteenth-century landscape. But, as every one knows, the splendid Cathedral is the proper attraction of the spot, which, indeed, save for this fine monument and for its craggy and crumbling ramparts, is a meanly arranged and, as Italian cities go, not particularly impressive little town. I spent a beautiful Sunday there and took in the charming church. I gave it my best attention, though on the whole I fear I found it inferior to its fame. A high concert of colour, however, is the densely carved front, richly covered with radiant mosaics. The old white marble of the sculptured portions is as softly yellow as ancient ivory; the large exceedingly bright pictures above them flashed and twinkled in the glorious weather. Very striking and interesting the theological frescoes of Luca Signorelli, though I have seen compositions of this general order that appealed to me more. Characteristically fresh, finally, the clear-faced saints and seraphs, in robes of pink and azure, whom Fra Angelico has painted upon the ceiling of the great chapel, along with a noble sitting figure—more expressive of movement than most of the creations of this pictorial peace-maker—of Christ in judgment. Yet the interest of the cathedral of Orvieto is mainly not the visible result, but the historical process that lies behind it; those three hundred years of the applied devotion of a people of which an American scholar has written an admirable account.[1]

1877.

[1] Charles Eliot Norton, *Study and Travel in Italy*.

A ROMAN HOLIDAY

IT is certainly sweet to be merry at the right moment; but the right moment hardly seems to me the ten days of the Roman Carnival. It was my rather cynical suspicion perhaps that they wouldn't keep to my imagination the brilliant promise of legend; but I have been justified by the event and have been decidedly less conscious of the festal influences of the season than of the inalienable gravity of the place. There was a time when the Carnival was a serious matter—that is a heartily joyous one; but, thanks to the seven-league boots the kingdom of Italy has lately donned for the march of progress in quite other directions, the fashion of public revelry has fallen woefully out of step. The state of mind and manners under which the Carnival was kept in generous good faith I doubt if an American can exactly conceive: he can only say to himself that for a month in the year there must have been things—things considerably of humiliation—it was comfortable to forget. But now that Italy is made the Carnival is unmade; and we are not especially tempted to envy the attitude of a population who have lost their relish for play and not yet acquired to any striking extent an enthusiasm for work. The spectacle on the Corso has seemed to me, on the whole, an illustration of that great breach with the past of which Catholic Christendom felt the somewhat muffled shock in September 1870. A traveller acquainted with the fully papal Rome, coming back any time during the past winter, must have immediately noticed that something momentous had happened —something hostile to the elements of picture and colour and "style." My first warning was that ten minutes after my arrival I found myself face to face with a newspaper stand. The impossibility in the other days of having anything in the journalistic line but the *Osservatore Romano* and the *Voce della Verità* used to seem to me much connected with the extraordinary leisure of thought and stillness of mind to which the place admitted you. But now the slender piping of the Voice of Truth is stifled by the raucous note of eventide vendors of the *Capitale*, the *Libertà* and the *Fanfulla*; and Rome reading unexpurgated news is another Rome indeed. For every subscriber to the *Libertà* there may well be an antique masker and reveller less. As striking a sign of the new régime is the extraordinary increase of population. The Corso was always a well-filled street, but now it's a perpetual crush. I never cease to wonder where the new-comers are lodged, and how such spotless flowers of fashion as the gentlemen who stare at the carriages can bloom in the atmosphere of those *camere mobiliate* of which I have had glimpses. This, however, is their own question, and bravely enough they meet it. They proclaimed somehow, to the first freshness of my wonder, as I say, that by force of numbers Rome had been secularised. An Italian dandy is a figure visually to reckon with, but these goodly throngs of them scarce offered compensation for the absent monsignori, treading the streets in their purple stockings and followed by the solemn servants who returned on their behalf the bows of the meaner sort; for the mourning gear of the cardinals' coaches that formerly glittered with scarlet and swung with the weight of the footmen clinging behind; for the certainty that you'll not, by the best of traveller's luck, meet the Pope sitting deep in the shadow of his great chariot with uplifted fingers like some inaccessible idol in his shrine. You may meet the King indeed, who is as ugly, as imposingly ugly, as some idols, though not so inaccessible. The other day as I passed the Quirinal he drove up in a low carriage with a single attendant; and a group of men and women who had been waiting near the gate rushed at him with a number of folded papers. The carriage slackened pace and he pocketed their offerings with a business-like air—that of a good-natured man accepting hand-bills at a street-corner. Here was a monarch at his palace gate receiving petitions from his subjects—being adjured to right their wrongs. The scene ought to have thrilled me, but some-how it had no more intensity than a woodcut in an illustrated newspaper. Homely I should call it at most; admirably so, certainly, for there were lately few sovereigns standing, I believe, with whom their people enjoyed these filial hand-to-hand relations. The King this year, however, has had as little to do with the Carnival as the Pope, and the innkeepers and Americans have marked it for their own.

It was advertised to begin at half-past two o'clock of a certain Saturday, and punctually at the stroke of the hour, from my room across a wide court, I heard a sudden multiplication of sounds and confusion of tongues in the Corso. I was writing to a friend for whom I cared more than for any mere romp; but as the minutes elapsed and the hubbub deepened curiosity got the better of affection, and I remembered that I was really within eye-shot of an affair the fame of which had ministered to the day-dreams of my infancy. I used to have a scrap-book with a coloured print of the starting of the bedizened wild horses, and the use of a library rich in keepsakes and annuals with a frontispiece commonly of a masked lady in a balcony, the heroine of a delightful tale further on. Agitated by these tender memories I descended into the street; but I confess I looked in vain for a masked lady who might serve as a frontis-piece, in vain for any object whatever that might adorn a tale. Masked and muffled ladies there were in abundance; but their masks were of ugly wire, perfectly resembling the little covers placed upon strong cheese in German hotels, and their drapery was a shabby water-proof with the hood pulled over their chignons. They were armed with great tin scoops or funnels, with which they solemnly shovelled lime and flour out of bushel-baskets and down on the heads of the people in the street. They were packed into balconies all the way along the straight vista of the Corso, in which their calcareous shower maintained a dense, gritty, unpalatable fog. The crowd was compact in the street, and the Americans in it were tossing back confetti out of great satchels hung round their necks. It was quite the "you're another" sort of repartee, and less seasoned than I had hoped with the airy mockery tradition hangs about this festival. The scene was striking, in a word ; but somehow not as I had dreamed of its being. I stood regardful, I suppose, but with a peculiarly tempting blankness of visage, for in a moment I received half a bushel of flour on my too-philosophic head. Decidedly it was an ignoble form of humour. I shook my ears like an emergent diver, and had a sudden vision of how still and sunny and solemn, how peculiarly and undisturbedly themselves, how secure from any intrusion less sympathetic than one's own, certain outlying parts of Rome must just then be. The Carnival had received its death-blow in my imagination ; and it has been ever since but a thin and dusky ghost of pleasure that has flitted at intervals in and out of my consciousness.

I turned my back accordingly on the Corso and wandered away to the grass-grown quarters delightfully free even from the possibility of a fellow-countryman. And so having set myself an example I have been keeping Carnival by strolling perversely along the silent circumference of Rome. I have doubtless lost a great deal. The Princess Margaret has occupied a balcony opposite the open space which leads into Via Condotti and, I believe, like the discreet princess she is, has dealt in no missiles but bonbons, bouquets and white doves. I would have waited half an hour any day to see the Princess Margaret hold a dove on her forefinger ; but I never chanced to notice any preparation for that effect. And yet do what you

will you can't really elude the Carnival.   As the days elapse
it filters down into the manners of the common people, and
before the week is over the very beggars at the church-doors
seem to have gone to the expense of a domino.   When you
meet these specimens of dingy drollery capering about in dusky
back-streets at all hours of the day and night, meet them flitting
out of black doorways between the greasy groups that cluster
about Roman thresholds, you feel that a love of "pranks," the
more vivid the better, must from far back have been implanted
in the Roman temperament with a strong hand.   An unsophisticated American is wonderstruck at the number of persons, of
every age and various conditions, whom it costs nothing in the
nature of an ingenuous blush to walk up and down the streets
in the costume of a theatrical supernumerary.   Fathers of
families do it at the head of an admiring progeniture; aunts
and uncles and grandmothers do it; all the family does it,
with varying splendour but with the same good conscience.
"A pack of babies!" the doubtless too self-conscious alien
pronounces it for its pains, and tries to imagine himself strutting
along Broadway in a battered tin helmet and a pair of yellow
tights.   Our vices are certainly different; it takes those of the
innocent sort to be so ridiculous.   A self-consciousness lapsing
so easily, in fine, strikes me as so near a relation to amenity,
urbanity and general gracefulness that, for myself, I should
be sorry to lay a tax on it, lest these other commodities should
also cease to come to market.

I was rewarded, when I had turned away with my ears full
of flour, by a glimpse of an intenser life than the dingy foolery
of the Corso.   I walked down by the back streets to the steps
mounting to the Capitol—that long inclined plane, rather,
broken at every two paces, which is the unfailing disappointment, I believe, of tourists primed for retrospective raptures.
Certainly the Capitol seen from this side isn't commanding.
The hill is so low, the ascent so narrow, Michael Angelo's

architecture in the quadrangle at the top so meagre, the whole place somehow so much more of a mole-hill than a mountain, that for the first ten minutes of your standing there Roman history seems suddenly to have sunk through a trap-door. It emerges however on the other side, in the Forum; and here meanwhile, if you get no sense of the sublime, you get gradually a sense of exquisite composition. Nowhere in Rome is more colour, more charm, more sport for the eye. The mild incline, during the winter months, is always covered with lounging sun-seekers, and especially with those more constantly obvious members of the Roman population—beggars, soldiers, monks and tourists. The beggars and peasants lie kicking their heels along that grandest of loafing-places the great steps of the Ara Cœli. The dwarfish look of the Capitol is intensified, I think, by the neighbourhood of this huge blank staircase, mouldering away in disuse, the weeds thick in its crevices, and climbing to the rudely solemn façade of the church. The sunshine glares on this great unfinished wall only to light up its featureless despair, its expression of conscious, irremediable incompleteness. Sometimes, massing its rusty screen against the deep blue sky, with the little cross and the sculptured porch casting a clear-cut shadow on the bricks, it seems to have even more than a Roman desolation, it confusedly suggests Spain and Africa—lands with no latent *risorgimenti*, with absolutely nothing but a fatal past. The legendary wolf of Rome has lately been accommodated with a little artificial grotto, among the cacti and the palms, in the fantastic triangular garden squeezed between the steps of the church and the ascent to the Capitol, where she holds a perpetual levee and "draws" apparently as powerfully as the Pope himself. Above, in the piazzetta before the stuccoed palace which rises so jauntily on a basement of thrice its magnitude, are more loungers and knitters in the sun, seated round the massively inscribed base of the statue of Marcus Aurelius. Hawthorne has perfectly expressed the attitude of this admirable figure in saying that it extends its arm with "a command which is in itself a benediction." I doubt if any statue of king or captain in the public places of the world has more to commend it to the general heart. Irrecoverable simplicity—residing so in irrecoverable Style—has no sturdier representative. Here is an impression that the sculptors of the last three hundred years have been laboriously trying to reproduce; but contrasted with this mild old monarch their prancing horsemen suggest a succession of riding-masters taking out young ladies' schools. The admirably human character of the figure survives the rusty decomposition of the bronze and the slight "debasement" of the art; and one may call it singular that in the capital of Christendom the portrait most suggestive of a Christian conscience is that of a pagan emperor.

You recover in some degree your stifled hopes of sublimity as you pass beyond the palace and take your choice of either curving slope to descend into the Forum. Then you see that the little stuccoed edifice is but a modern excrescence on the mighty cliff of a primitive construction, whose great squares of porous tufa, as they underlie each other, seem to resolve themselves back into the colossal cohesion of unhewn rock. There are prodigious strangenesses in the union of this airy and comparatively fresh-faced superstructure and these deep-plunging, hoary foundations; and few things in Rome are more entertaining to the eye than to measure the long plumb-line which drops from the inhabited windows of the palace, with their little over-peeping balconies, their muslin curtains and their bird-cages, down to the rugged constructional work of the Republic. In the Forum proper the sublime is eclipsed again, though the late extension of the excavations gives a chance for it.

Nothing in Rome helps your fancy to a more vigorous backward flight than to lounge on a sunny day over the railing which guards the great central researches. It "says" more things to you than you can repeat to see the past, the ancient world, as you stand there, bodily turned up with the spade and transformed from an immaterial, inaccessible fact of time into a matter of soils and surfaces. The pleasure is the same—in kind—as what you enjoy at Pompeii, and the pain the same. It wasn't here, however, that I found my compensation for forfeiting the spectacle on the Corso, but in a little church at the end of the narrow byway which diverges up the Palatine from just beside the Arch of Titus. This byway leads you between high walls, then takes a bend and introduces you to a long row of rusty, dusty little pictures of the stations of the cross. Beyond these stands a small church with a front so modest that you hardly recognise it till you see the leather curtain. I never see a leather curtain without lifting it ; it is sure to cover a constituted *scene* of some sort—good, bad or indifferent. The scene this time was meagre —whitewash and tarnished candlesticks and mouldy muslin flowers being its principal features. I shouldn't have remained if I hadn't been struck with the attitude of the single worshipper —a young priest kneeling before one of the side-altars, who, as I entered, lifted his head and gave me a sidelong look so charged with the languor of devotion that he immediately became an object of interest. He was visiting each of the altars in turn and kissing the balustrade beneath them. He was alone in the church, and indeed in the whole region. There were no beggars even at the door ; they were plying their trade on the skirts of the Carnival. In the entirely deserted place he alone knelt for religion, and as I sat respectfully by it seemed to me I could hear in the perfect silence the far-away uproar of the maskers. It was my late impression of these frivolous people, I suppose, joined with the extraordinary gravity of the young priest's face —his pious fatigue, his droning prayer and his isolation—that gave me just then and there a supreme vision of the religious passion, its privations and resignations and exhaustions and its terribly small share of amusement. He was young and strong and evidently of not too refined a fibre to enjoy the Carnival ;

but, planted there with his face pale with fasting and his knees stiff with praying, he seemed so stern a satire on it and on the crazy thousands who were preferring it to *his* way, that I half expected to see some heavenly portent out of a monastic legend come down and confirm his choice. Yet I confess that though I wasn't enamoured of the Carnival myself his seemed a grim preference and this forswearing of the world a terrible game— a gaining one only if your zeal never falters ; a hard fight when it does. In such an hour, to a stout young fellow like the hero of my anecdote, the smell of incense must seem horribly stale and the muslin flowers and gilt candlesticks to figure no great bribe. And it wouldn't have helped him much to think that not so very far away, just beyond the Forum, in the Corso, there was sport for the million, and for nothing. I doubt on the other hand whether my young priest had thought of this.' He had made himself a temple out of the very elements of his innocence, and his prayers followed each other too fast for the tempter to slip in a whisper. And so, as I say, I found a solider fact of human nature than the love of *coriandoli.*

One of course never passes the Colosseum without paying it one's respects—without going in under one of the hundred portals and crossing the long oval and sitting down awhile, generally at the foot of the cross in the centre. I always feel, as I do so, as if I were seated in the depths of some Alpine valley. The upper portions of the side toward the Esquiline look as remote and lonely as an Alpine ridge, and you raise your eyes to their rugged sky-line, drinking in the sun and silvered by the blue air, with much the same feeling with which you would take in a grey cliff on which an eagle might lodge. This roughly mountainous quality of the great ruin is its chief interest ; beauty of detail has pretty well vanished, especially since the high-grow-ing wild-flowers have been plucked away by the new government, whose functionaries, surely, at certain points of their task, must have felt as if they shared the dreadful trade of those who gather samphire. Even if you are on your way to the Lateran you won't grudge the twenty minutes it will take you, on leaving the Colosseum, to turn away under the Arch of Constantine, whose noble battered bas-reliefs, with the chain of tragic statues —fettered, drooping barbarians—round its summit, I assume you to have profoundly admired, toward the piazzetta of the church of San Giovanni e Paolo, on the slope of Cælian. No spot in Rome can show a cluster of more charming accidents. The ancient brick apse of the church peeps down into the trees of the little wooded walk before the neighbouring church of San Gregorio, intensely venerable beneath its excessive modernisation ; and a series of heavy brick buttresses, flying across to an opposite wall, overarches the short, steep, paved passage which leads into the small square. This is flanked on one side by the long mediæval portico of the church of the two saints, sustained by eight time-blackened columns of granite and marble. On another rise the great scarce-windowed walls of a Passionist convent, and on the third the portals of a grand villa, whose tall porter, with his cockade and silver-topped staff, standing sublime behind his grating, seems a kind of mundane St. Peter, I suppose, to the beggars who sit at the church door or lie in the sun along the farther slope which leads to the gate of the convent. The place always seems to me the perfection of an out-of-the-way corner—a place you would think twice before telling people about, lest you should find them there the next time you were to go. It is such a group of objects, singly and in their happy combination, as one must come to Rome to find at one's house door ; but what makes it peculiarly a picture is the beautiful dark red campanile of the church, which stands embedded in the mass of the convent. It begins, as so many things in Rome begin, with a stout foundation of antique travertine, and rises high, in delicately quaint mediæval brickwork—little tiers and apertures sustained on miniature columns and adorned with small cracked slabs of green and yellow marble, inserted almost at random.

K

When there are three or four brown-breasted contadini sleeping in the sun before the convent doors, and a departing monk leading his shadow down over them, I think you will not find anything in Rome more *sketchable*.

If you stop, however, to observe everything worthy of your water-colours you will never reach St. John Lateran. My business was much less with the interior of that vast and empty, that cold clean temple, which I have never found peculiarly interesting, than with certain charming features of its surrounding precinct— the crooked old court beside it, which admits you to the Baptistery and to a delightful rear-view of the queer architectural odds and ends that may in Rome compose a florid ecclesiastical façade. There are more of these, a stranger jumble of chance detail, of lurking recesses and wanton projections and inexplicable windows, than I have memory or phrase for; but the gem of the collection is the oddly perched peaked turret, with its yellow travertine welded upon the rusty brickwork, which was not meant to be suspected, and the brickwork retreating beneath and leaving it in the odd position of a tower *under* which you may see the sky. As to the great front of the church overlooking the Porta San Giovanni, you are not admitted behind the scenes; the term is quite in keeping, for the architecture has a vastly theatrical air. It is extremely imposing—that of St. Peter's alone is more so; and when from far off on the Campagna you see the colossal images of the mitred saints along the top standing distinct against the sky, you forget their coarse construction and their inflated draperies. The view from the great space which stretches from the church steps to the city wall is the very prince of views. Just beside you, beyond the great alcove of mosaic, is the Scala Santa, the marble staircase which (says the legend) Christ descended under the weight of Pilate's judgment, and which all Christians must forever ascend on their knees; before you is the city gate which opens upon the Via Appia Nuova, the long gaunt file of arches of the Claudian aqueduct, their jagged ridge stretching away like the vertebral column of some monstrous mouldering skeleton, and upon the blooming brown and purple flats and dells of the Campagna and the glowing blue of the Alban Mountains, spotted with their white, high-nestling towns; while to your left is the great grassy space, lined with dwarfish mulberry-trees, which stretches across to the damp little sister-basilica of Santa Croce in Gerusalemme. During a former visit to Rome I lost my heart to this idle tract,[1] and wasted much time in sitting on the steps of the church and watching certain white-cowled friars who were sure to be passing there for the delight of my eyes. There are fewer friars now, and there are a great many of the king's recruits, who inhabit the ex-conventual barracks adjoining Santa Croce and are led forward to practise their goose-step on the sunny turf. Here too the poor old cardinals who are no longer to be seen on the Pincio descend from their mourning-coaches and relax their venerable knees. These members alone still testify to the traditional splendour of the princes of the Church; for as they advance the lifted black petticoat reveals a flash of scarlet stockings and makes you groan at the victory of civilisation over colour.

If St. John Lateran disappoints you internally, you have an easy compensation in pacing the long lane which connects it with Santa Maria Maggiore and entering the singularly perfect nave of that most delightful of churches. The first day of my stay in Rome under the old dispensation I spent in wandering at random through the city, with accident for my *valet-de-place*. It served me to perfection and introduced me to the best things; among others to an immediate happy relation with Santa Maria Maggiore. First impressions, memorable impressions, are generally irrecoverable; they often leave one the wiser, but they rarely return in the same form. I remember, of my coming uninformed and unprepared into the place of worship and of

[1] Utterly overbuilt and gone—1909.

curiosity that I have named, only that I sat for half an hour on the edge of the base of one of the marble columns of the beautiful nave and enjoyed a perfect revel of—what shall I call it?—taste, intelligence, fancy, perceptive emotion? The place proved so endlessly suggestive that perception became a throbbing confusion of images, and I departed with a sense of knowing a good deal that is not set down in Murray. I have seated myself more than once again at the base of the same column; but you live your life only once, the parts as well as the whole. The obvious charm of the church is the elegant grandeur of the nave—its perfect shapeliness and its rich simplicity, its long double row of white marble columns and its high flat roof, embossed with intricate gildings and mouldings. It opens into a choir of an extraordinary splendour of effect, which I recommend you to look out for of a fine afternoon. At such a time the glowing western light, entering the high windows of the tribune, kindles the scattered masses of colour into sombre brightness, scintillates on the great solemn mosaic of the vault, touches the porphyry columns of the superb baldachino with ruby lights, and buries its shining shafts in the deep-toned shadows that hang about frescoes and sculptures and mouldings. The deeper charm even than in such things, however, is the social or historic note or tone or atmosphere of the church—I fumble, you see, for my right expression; the sense it gives you, in common with most of the Roman churches, and more than any of them, of having been prayed in for several centuries by an endlessly curious and complex society. It takes no great attention to let it come to you that the authority of Italian Catholicism has lapsed not a little in these days; not less also perhaps than to feel that, as they stand, these deserted temples were the fruit of a society leavened through and through by ecclesiastical manners, and that they formed for ages the constant background of the human drama. They are, as one may say, the *churchiest* churches in Europe—the fullest of gathered memories, of the experience of

their office. There's not a figure one has read of in old-world
annals that isn't to be imagined on proper occasion kneeling
before the lamp-decked Confession beneath the altar of Santa
Maria Maggiore. One sees after all, however, even among the
most palpable realities, very much what the play of one's imagination projects there ; and I present my remarks simply as a
reminder that one's constant excursions into these places are not
the least interesting episodes of one's walks in Rome.

I had meant to give a simple illustration of the church-
habit, so to speak, but I have given it at such a length as leaves
scant space to touch on the innumerable topics brushed by the
pen that begins to take Roman notes. It is by the aimless
flânerie which leaves you free to follow capriciously every hint of
entertainment that you get to know Rome. The greater part of
the life about you goes on in the streets ; and for an observer
fresh from a country in which town scenery is at the least
monotonous incident and character and picture seem to abound.
I become conscious with compunction, let me hasten to add,
that I have launched myself thus on the subject of Roman
churches and Roman walks without so much as a preliminary
allusion to St. Peter's. One is apt to proceed thither on rainy
days with intentions of exercise—to put the case only at that—
and to carry these out body and mind. Taken as a walk not
less than as a church, St. Peter's of course reigns alone. Even
for the profane "constitutional" it serves where the Boulevards,
where Piccadilly and Broadway, fall short, and if it didn't offer
to our use the grandest area in the world it would still offer
the most diverting. Few great works of art last longer to the
curiosity, to the perpetually transcended attention. You think
you have taken the whole thing in, but it expands, it rises
sublime again, and leaves your measure itself poor. You never
let the ponderous leather curtain bang down behind you—your
weak lift of a scant edge of whose padded vastness resembles
the liberty taken in folding back the parchment corner of some

mighty folio page—without feeling all former visits to have
been but missed attempts at apprehension and the actual to
achieve your first real possession. The conventional question
is ever as to whether one hasn't been "disappointed in the size,"
but a few honest folk here and there, I hope, will never cease
to say no. The place struck me from the first as the hugest
thing conceivable—a real exaltation of one's idea of space; so
that one's entrance, even from the great empty square which
either glares beneath the deep blue sky or makes of the cool
far-cast shadow of the immense front something that resembles
a big slate-coloured country on a map, seems not so much a
going in somewhere as a going out. The mere man of pleasure
in quest of new sensations might well not know where to better
his encounter there of the sublime shock that brings him, within
the threshold, to an immediate gasping pause. There are days
when the vast nave looks mysteriously vaster than on others
and the gorgeous baldachino a longer journey beyond the far-
spreading tessellated plain of the pavement, and when the light
has yet a quality which lets things loom their largest, while the
scattered figures—I mean the human, for there are plenty of
others—mark happily the scale of items and parts. Then you
have only to stroll and stroll and gaze and gaze; to watch the
glorious altar-canopy lift its bronze architecture, its colossal
embroidered contortions, like a temple within a temple, and
feel yourself, at the bottom of the abysmal shaft of the dome,
dwindle to a crawling dot.

Much of the constituted beauty resides in the fact that it
is all general beauty, that you are appealed to by no specific
details, or that these at least, practically never importunate, are
as taken for granted as the lieutenants and captains are taken
for granted in a great standing army—among whom indeed
individual aspects may figure here the rather shifting range of
decorative dignity in which details, when observed, often prove
poor (though never not massive and substantially precious) and

sometimes prove ridiculou' The sculptures, with the sole exception of Michael Angelo's ineffable " Pièta," which lurks obscurely
in a side-chapel—this indeed to my sense the rarest artistic *combination* of the greatest things the hand of man has produced—
are either bad or indifferent; and the universal incrustation of
marble, though sumptuous enough, has a less brilliant effect
than much later work of the same sort, that for instance of
St. Paul's without the Walls. The supreme beauty is the
splendidly sustained simplicity of the whole. The thing represents a prodigious imagination extraordinarily strained, yet
strained, at its happiest pitch, without breaking. Its happiest
pitch I say, because this is the only creation of its strenuous
author in presence of which you are in presence of serenity.
You may invoke the idea of ease at St. Peter's without a sense
of sacrilege—which you can hardly do, if you are at all spiritually nervous, in Westminster Abbey or Notre Dame. The vast
enclosed clearness has much to do with the idea. There are
no shadows to speak of, no marked effects of shade; only effects
of light innumerable—points at which this element seems to
mass itself in airy density and scatter itself in enchanting gradations and cadences. It performs the office of gloom or of
mystery in Gothic churches; hangs like a rolling mist along the
gilded vault of the nave, melts into bright interfusion the
mosaic scintillations of the dome, clings and clusters and lingers,
animates the whole huge and otherwise empty shell. A good
Catholic, I suppose, is the same Catholic anywhere, before the
grandest as well as the humblest altars; but to a visitor not
formally enrolled St. Peter's speaks less of aspiration than of
full and convenient assurance. The soul infinitely expands
there, if one will, but all on its quite human level. It marvels
at the reach of our dream and the immensity of our resources.
To be so impressed and put in our place, we say, is to be
sufficiently "saved"; we can't be more than that in heaven
itself; and what specifically celestial beauty such a show or such

a substitute may lack it makes up for in certainty and tangibility. And yet if one's hours on the scene are not actually spent in praying, the spirit seeks it again as for the finer comfort, for the blessing, exactly, of its example, its protection and its exclusion. When you are weary of the swarming democracy of your fellow-tourists, of the unremunerative aspects of human nature on Corso and Pincio, of the oppressively frequent combination of coronets on carriage panels and stupid faces in carriages, of addled brains and lacquered boots, of ruin and dirt and decay, of priests and beggars and takers of advantage, of the myriad tokens of a halting civilisation, the image of the great temple depresses the balance of your doubts, seems to rise above even the highest tide of vulgarity and make you still believe in the heroic will and the heroic act. It's a relief, in other words, to feel that there's nothing but a cab-fare between your pessimism and one of the greatest of human achievements.

This might serve as a Lenten peroration to these remarks of mine which have strayed so woefully from their jovial text, save that I ought fairly to confess that my last impression of the Carnival was altogether Carnivalesque. The merry-making of Shrove Tuesday had life and felicity; the dead letter of tradition broke out into nature and grace. I pocketed my scepticism and spent a long afternoon on the Corso. Almost every one was a masker, but you had no need to conform; the pelting rain of confetti effectually disguised you. I can't say I found it all very exhilarating; but here and there I noticed a brighter episode—a capering clown inflamed with contagious jollity, some finer humourist forming a circle every thirty yards to crow at his indefatigable sallies. One clever performer so especially pleased me that I should have been glad to catch a glimpse of the natural man. You imagined for him that he was taking a prodigious intellectual holiday and that his gaiety was in inverse ratio to his daily mood. Dressed as a needy scholar, in an ancient evening-coat and with a rusty black hat and gloves

fantastically patched, he carried a little volume carefully under
his arm. His humours were in excellent taste, his whole manner
the perfection of genteel comedy. The crowd seemed to relish
him vastly, and he at once commanded a gleefully attentive
audience. Many of his sallies I lost; those I caught were
excellent. His trick was often to begin by taking some one
urbanely and caressingly by the chin and complimenting him on
the *intelligenza della sua fisionomia*. I kept near him as long as
I could; for he struck me as a real ironic artist, cherishing a
disinterested, and yet at the same time a motived and a moral,
passion for the grotesque. I should have liked, however—if
indeed I shouldn't have feared—to see him the next morning, or
when he unmasked that night over his hard-earned supper in a
smoky *trattoria*. As the evening went on the cloud thickened
and became a motley press of shouting, pushing, scrambling,
everything but squabbling, revellers. The rain of missiles ceased
at dusk, but the universal deposit of chalk and flour was trampled
into a cloud made lurid by flaring pyramids of the gas-lamps
that replaced for the occasion the stingy Roman luminaries.
Early in the evening came off the classic exhibition of the
moccoletti, which I but half saw, like a languid reporter resigned
beforehand to be cashiered for want of enterprise. From the
mouth of a side-street, over a thousand heads, I caught a huge
slow-moving illuminated car, from which blue-lights and rockets
and Roman candles were in course of discharge, meeting all
in a dim fuliginous glare far above the house-tops. It was
like a glimpse of some public orgy in ancient Babylon. In the
small hours of the morning, walking homeward from a private
entertainment, I found Ash-Wednesday still kept at bay. The
Corso, flaring with light, smelt like a circus. Every one was
taking friendly liberties with every one else and using up the
dregs of his festive energy in convulsive hootings and gym-
nastics. Here and there certain indefatigable spirits, clad all
in red after the manner of devils and leaping furiously about

with torches, were supposed to affright you. But they shared the universal geniality and bequeathed me no midnight fears as a pretext for keeping Lent, the *carnevale dei preti*, as I read in that profanely radical sheet the *Capitale*. Of this too I have been having glimpses. Going lately into Santa Francesca Romana, the picturesque church near the Temple of Peace, I found a feast for the eyes—a dim crimson-toned light through curtained windows, a great festoon of tapers round the altar, a bulging girdle of lamps before the sunken shrine beneath, and a dozen white-robed Dominicans scattered in the happiest composition on the pavement. It was better than the *moccoletti*.

1873.

ROMAN RIDES

I SHALL always remember the first I took: out of the Porta del Popolo, to where the Ponte Molle, whose single arch sustains a weight of historic tradition, compels the sallow Tiber to flow between its four great-mannered ecclesiastical statues, over the crest of the hill and along the old posting-road to Florence. It was mild midwinter, the season peculiarly of colour on the Roman Campagna; and the light was full of that mellow purple glow, that tempered intensity, which haunts the after-visions of those who have known Rome like the memory of some supremely irresponsible pleasure. An hour away I pulled up and at the edge of a meadow gazed away for some time into remoter distances. Then and there, it seemed to me, I measured the deep delight of knowing the Campagna. But I saw more things in it than I can easily tell. The country rolled away around me into slopes and dells of long-drawn grace, chequered with purple and blue and blooming brown. The lights and shadows were at play on the Sabine Mountains—an alternation of tones so exquisite as to be conveyed only by some fantastic comparison to sapphire and amber. In the foreground a contadino in his cloak and peaked hat jogged solitary on his ass; and here and there in the distance, among blue undulations, some white village, some gray tower, helped deliciously to make the picture the typical "Italian landscape" of old-fashioned art. It was so bright and yet so sad, so still and yet so charged, to the supersensuous ear, with the murmur of an extinguished life, that you could only say it was intensely and adorably strange, could only impute to the whole overarched scene an unsurpassed secret for bringing tears of appreciation to no matter how ignorant—archeologically ignorant —eyes. To ride once, in these conditions, is of course to ride again and to allot to the Campagna a generous share of the time one spends in Rome.

It is a pleasure that doubles one's horizon, and one can scarcely say whether it enlarges or limits one's impression of the city proper. It certainly makes St. Peter's seem a trifle smaller and blunts the edge of one's curiosity in the Forum. It must be the effect of the experience, at all extended, that when you think of Rome afterwards you will think still respectfully and regretfully enough of the Vatican and the Pincio, the streets and the picture-making street life; but will even more wonder, with an irrepressible contraction of the heart, when again you shall feel yourself bounding over the flower-smothered turf, or pass from one framed picture to another beside the open arches of the crumbling aqueducts. You look back at the City so often from some grassy hill-top—hugely compact within its walls, with St. Peter's overtopping all things and yet seeming small, and the vast girdle of marsh and meadow receding on all sides to the mountains and the sea—that you come to remember it at last as hardly more than a respectable parenthesis in a great sweep of generalisation. Within the walls, on the other hand, you think of your intended ride as the most romantic of all your possibilities; of the Campagna generally as an illimitable experience. One's rides certainly give Rome an inordinate scope for the reflective—by which I suppose I mean after all the æsthetic and the "esoteric"—life. To dwell in a city which, much as you grumble at it, is after all very fairly a modern city; with crowds and shops and theatres and cafés and balls and receptions and dinner-parties and all the modern confusion of social pleasures and pains; to have at your door the good and evil of it all; and yet to be able in half an hour to gallop away and leave it a hundred miles, a hundred years, behind, and to look at the tufted broom glowing on a lonely tower-top in the still blue air, and the pale pink asphodels trembling none the less for the stillness, and the shaggy-legged shepherds leaning on their sticks in motionless brotherhood with the heaps of ruin, and the scrambling goats and staggering little kids treading out wild desert smells from the top of hollow-sounding mounds ; and then to come back through one of the great gates and a couple of hours later find yourself in the "world," dressed, introduced, entertained, inquiring, talking about "Middlemarch" to a young English lady or listening to Neapolitan songs from a gentleman in a very low-cut shirt—all this is to lead in a manner a double life and to gather from the hurrying hours more impressions than a mind of modest capacity quite knows how to dispose of.

I touched lately upon this theme with a friend who, I fancied, would understand me, and who immediately assured me that he had just spent a day that this mingled diversity of sensation made to the days one spends elsewhere what an uncommonly good novel may be to the daily paper. "There was an air of idleness about it, if you will," he said, "and it was certainly pleasant enough to have been wrong. Perhaps, being after all unused to long stretches of dissipation, this was why I had a half-feeling that I was reading an odd chapter in the history of a person very much more of a *héros de roman* than myself." Then he proceeded to relate how he had taken a long ride with a lady whom he extremely admired. "We turned off from the Tor di Quinto Road to that castellated farm-house you know of—once a Ghibelline fortress—whither Claude Lorraine used to come to paint pictures of which the surrounding landscape is still so artistically, so compositionally, suggestive. We went into the inner court, a cloister almost, with the carven capitals of its loggia columns, and looked at a handsome child swinging shyly against the half-opened door of a room whose impenetrable shadow, behind her, made her, as it were, a sketch in bituminous water-colours. We talked with the farmer, a handsome, pale, fever-tainted fellow with a well-to-do air that didn't in the least deter his affability from a turn compatible with the acceptance of small coin; and then we galloped away and away over the meadows which stretch with hardly a break to Veii. The day was strangely delicious, with a cool grey sky and just a touch of moisture in the air stirred by our rapid motion. The Campagna, in the colourless even light, was more solemn and romantic than ever; and a ragged shepherd, driving a meagre straggling flock, whom we stopped to ask our way of, was a perfect type of pastoral, weather-beaten misery. He was precisely the shepherd for the foreground of a scratchy etching. There were faint odours of spring in the air, and the grass here and there was streaked with great patches of daisies; but it was spring with a foreknowledge of autumn, a day to be enjoyed with a substrain of sadness, the foreboding of regret, a day somehow to make one feel as if one had seen and felt a great deal—quite, as I say, like a *héros de roman*. Touching such characters, it was the illustrious Pelham, I think, who, on being asked if he rode, replied that he left those violent exercises to the ladies. But under such a sky, in such an air, over acres of daisied turf, a long, long gallop is certainly a supersubtle joy. The elastic bound of your horse is the poetry of motion; and if you are so happy as to add to it not the prose of companionship riding comes almost to affect you as a spiritual exercise. My gallop, at any rate," said my friend, "threw me into a mood which gave an extraordinary zest to the rest of the day." He was to go to a dinner-party at a villa on the edge of Rome, and Madame X——, who was also going, called for him in her carriage. "It was a long drive," he went on, "through the Forum, past the Colosseum. She told me a long story about a most interesting person. Toward the end my eyes caught through the carriage window a slab of rugged sculptures. We were passing under the Arch of Constantine. In the hall pavement of the villa is a rare antique mosaic—one of the largest and most perfect; the ladies on their way to the drawing-room trail over it the flounces of Worth. We drove home late, and there's my day."

On your exit from most of the gates of Rome you have generally half-an-hour's progress through winding lanes, many of which are hardly less charming than the open meadows. On foot the walls and high hedges would vex you and spoil your walk; but in the saddle you generally overtop them, to an endless peopling of the minor vision. Yet a Roman wall in the springtime is for that matter almost as interesting as anything it conceals. Crumbling grain by grain, coloured and mottled to a hundred tones by sun and storm, with its rugged structure of brick extruding through its coarse complexion of peeling stucco, its creeping lacework of wandering ivy starred with miniature violets, and its wild fringe of stouter flowers against the sky—it is as little as possible a blank partition; it is practically a luxury of landscape. At the moment at which I write, in mid-April, all the ledges and cornices are wreathed with flaming poppies, nodding there as if they knew so well what faded greys and yellows are an offset to their scarlet. But the best point in a dilapidated enclosing surface of vineyard or villa is of course the gateway, lifting its great arch of cheap rococo scroll-work, its balls and shields and mossy dish-covers—as they always perversely figure to me—and flanked with its dusky cypresses. I never pass one without taking out my mental sketch-book and jotting it down as a vignette in the insubstantial record of my ride. They are as sad and dreary as if they led to the moated grange where Mariana waited in desperation for something to happen; and it's easy to take the usual inscription over the porch as a recommendation to those who enter to renounce all hope of anything but a glass of more or less agreeably acrid *vino romano*. For what you chiefly see over the walls and at the end of the straight short avenue of rusty cypresses are the appurtenances of a *vigna*—a couple of acres of little upright sticks blackening in the sun, and a vast sallow-faced, scantily windowed mansion, whose expression denotes little of the life of the mind beyond what goes to the driving of a hard bargain over the tasted hogsheads. If Mariana is there she certainly has no pile of old magazines to beguile her leisure. The life of the mind, if the term be in any application here not ridiculous, appears to any asker of curious questions, as he wanders about Rome, the very thinnest deposit of the past. Within the rococo gateway, which itself has a vaguely æsthetic self-consciousness, at the end of the cypress walk, you will probably see a mythological group in rusty marble—a Cupid and Psyche, a Venus and Paris, an Apollo and Daphne—the relic of an age when a Roman proprietor thought it fine to patronise the arts. But I imagine you are safe in supposing it to constitute the only allusion savouring of culture that has been made on the premises for three or four generations.

There is a franker cheerfulness—though certainly a proper amount of that forlornness which lurks about every object to which the Campagna forms a background—in the primitive little taverns where, on the homeward stretch, in the waning light, you are often glad to rein up and demand a bottle of their best. Their best and their worst are indeed the same, though with a shifting price, and plain *vino bianco* or *vino rosso* (rarely both) is the sole article of refreshment in which they deal. There is a ragged bush over the door, and within, under a dusky vault, on crooked cobble-stones, sit half-a-dozen contadini in their indigo jackets and goatskin breeches and with their elbows on the table. There is generally a rabble of infantile beggars at the door, pretty enough in their dusty rags, with their fine eyes and intense Italian smile, to make you forget your private vow of doing your individual best to make these people, whom you like so much, unlearn their old vices. Was Porta Pia bombarded three years ago that Peppino should still grow up to whine for a copper? But the

Italian shells had no direct message for Peppino's stomach—and you are going to a dinner-party at a villa. So Peppino " points " an instant for the copper in the dust and grows up a Roman beggar. The whole little place represents the most primitive form of hostelry ; but along any of the roads leading out of the city you may find establishments of a higher type, with Garibaldi, superbly mounted and foreshortened, painted on the wall, or a lady in a low-necked dress opening a fictive lattice with irresistible hospitality, and a yard with the classic vine-wreathed arbour casting thin shadows upon benches and tables draped and cushioned with the white dust from which the highways from the gates borrow most of their local colour. None the less, I say, you avoid the highroads, and, if you are a person of taste, don't grumble at the occasional need of following the walls of the city. City walls, to a properly constituted American, can never be an object of indifference ; and it is emphatically " no end of a sensation" to pace in the shadow of this massive cincture of Rome. I have found myself, as I skirted its base, talking of trivial things, but never without a sudden reflection on the deplorable impermanence of first impressions. A twelve-month ago the raw plank fences of a Boston suburb, inscribed with the virtues of healing drugs, bristled along my horizon : now I glance with idle eyes at a compacted antiquity in which a more learned sense may read portentous dates and signs—Servius, Aurelius, Honorius. But even to idle eyes the prodigious, the continuous thing bristles with eloquent passages. In some places, where the huge brickwork is black with time and certain strange square towers look down at you with still blue eyes, the Roman sky peering through lidless loopholes, and there is nothing but white dust in the road and solitude in the air, I might take myself for a wandering Tartar touching on the confines of the Celestial Empire. The wall of China must have very much such a gaunt robustness. The colour of the Roman ramparts is everywhere fine, and their rugged

L

patchwork has been subdued by time and weather into a mellow harmony that the brush only asks to catch up. On the northern side of the city, behind the Vatican, St. Peter's and the Trastevere, I have seen them glowing in the late afternoon with the tones of ancient bronze and rusty gold. Here at various points they are embossed with the Papal insignia, the tiara with its flying bands and crossed keys; to the high style of which the grace that attaches to almost any lost cause—even if not quite the "tender" grace of a day that is dead—considerably adds a style. With the dome of St. Peter's resting on their cornice and the hugely clustered architecture of the Vatican rising from them as from a terrace, they seem indeed the valid bulwark of an ecclesiastical city. Vain bulwark, alas! sighs the sentimental tourist, fresh from the meagre entertainment of this latter Holy Week. But he may find monumental consolation in this neighbourhood at a source where, as I pass, I never fail to apply for it. At half-an-hour's walk beyond Porta San Pancrazio, beneath the wall of the Villa Doria, is a delightfully pompous ecclesiastical gateway of the seventeenth century, erected by Paul V. to commemorate his restoration of the aqueducts through which the stream bearing his name flows towards the fine florid portico protecting its clear-sheeted outgush on the crest of the Janiculan. It arches across the road in the most ornamental manner of the period, and one can hardly pause before it without seeming to assist at a ten minutes' revival of old Italy—without feeling as if one were in a cocked hat and sword and were coming up to Rome, in another mood than Luther's, with a letter of recommendation to the mistress of a cardinal.

The Campagna differs greatly on the two sides of the Tiber; and it is hard to say which, for the rider, has the greater charm. The half-dozen rides you may take from Porta San Giovanni possess the perfection of traditional Roman interest and lead you through a far-strewn wilderness of ruins—a scattered maze of tombs and towers and nameless fragments of antique masonry.

The landscape here has two great features; close before you on one side is the long, gentle swell of the Alban Hills, deeply, fantastically blue in most weathers, and marbled with the vague white masses of their scattered towns and villas. It would be difficult to draw the hard figure to a softer curve than that with which the heights sweep from Albano to the plain; this a perfect example of the classic beauty of line in the Italian landscape —that beauty which, when it fills the background of a picture, makes us look in the foreground for a broken column couched upon flowers and a shepherd piping to dancing nymphs. At your side, constantly, you have the broken line of the Claudian Aqueduct, carrying its broad arches far away into the plain. The meadows along which it lies are not the smoothest in the world for a gallop, but there is no pleasure greater than to wander near it. It stands knee-deep in the flower-strewn grass, and its rugged piers are hung with ivy as the columns of a church are draped for a festa. Every archway is a picture, massively framed, of the distance beyond—of the snow-tipped Sabines and lonely Soracte. As the spring advances the whole Campagna smiles and waves with flowers; but I think they are nowhere more rank and lovely than in the shifting shadow of the aqueducts, where they muffle the feet of the columns and smother the half-dozen brooks which wander in and out like silver meshes between the legs of a file of giants. They make a niche for themselves too in every crevice and tremble on the vault of the empty conduits. The ivy hereabouts in the springtime is peculiarly brilliant and delicate; and though it cloaks and muffles these Roman fragments far less closely than the castles and abbeys of England it hangs with the light elegance of all Italian vegetation. It is partly doubtless because their mighty outlines are still unsoftened that the aqueducts are so impressive. They seem the very source of the solitude in which they stand; they look like architectural spectres and loom through the light mists of their grassy desert, as you recede along the line, with the same

insubstantial vastness as if they rose out of Egyptian sands.   It
is a great neighbourhood of ruins, many of which, it must be
confessed, you have applauded in many an album.   But station
a peasant with sheepskin coat and bandaged legs in the shadow
of a tomb or tower best known to drawing-room art, and scatter
a dozen goats on the mound above him, and the picture has a
charm which has not yet been sketched away.

The other quarter of the Campagna has wider fields and
smoother turf and perhaps a greater number of delightful rides ;
the earth is sounder, and there are fewer pitfalls and ditches.
The land for the most part lies higher and catches more wind,
and the grass is here and there for great stretches as smooth and
level as a carpet.   You have no Alban Mountains before you,
but you have in the distance the waving ridge of the nearer
Apennines, and west of them, along the course of the Tiber, the
long seaward level of deep-coloured fields, deepening as they
recede to the blue and purple of the sea itself.   Beyond them,
of a very clear day, you may see the glitter of the Mediterranean.
These are the occasions perhaps to remember most fondly, for
they lead you to enchanting nooks, and the landscape has details
of the highest refinement.   Indeed when my sense reverts to
the lingering impressions of so blest a time, it seems a fool's
errand to have attempted to express them, and a waste of words
to do more than recommend the reader to go citywards at twilight of the end of March, making for Porta Cavalleggieri, and
note what he sees.   At this hour the Campagna is to the last
point its melancholy self, and I remember roadside " effects " of
a strange and intense suggestiveness.   Certain mean, mouldering
villas behind grass-grown courts have an indefinably sinister
look ; there was one in especial of which it was impossible not to
argue that a despairing creature must have once committed suicide
there, behind bolted door and barred window, and that no one
has since had the pluck to go in and see why he never came out.
Every wayside mark of manners, of history, every stamp of the

past in the country about Rome, touches my sense to a thrill, and I may thus exaggerate the appeal of very common things. This is the more likely because the appeal seems ever to rise out of heaven knows what depths of ancient trouble. To delight in the aspects of *sentient* ruin might appear a heartless pastime, and the pleasure, I confess, shows the note of perversity. The sombre and the hard are as common an influence from southern things as the soft and the bright, I think ; sadness rarely fails to assault a northern observer when he misses what he takes for comfort. Beauty is no compensation for the loss, only making it more poignant. Enough beauty of climate hangs over these Roman cottages and farm-houses—beauty of light, of atmosphere and of vegetation ; but their charm for the maker-out of the stories in things is the way the golden air shows off their desolation. Man lives more with Nature in Italy than in New or than in Old England ; she does more work for him and gives him more holidays than in our short-summered climes, and his home is therefore much more bare of devices for helping him to do without her, forget her and forgive her. These reflections are perhaps the source of the character you find in a moss-coated stone stairway climbing outside of a wall ; in a queer inner court, befouled with rubbish and drearily bare of convenience ; in an ancient quaintly carven well, worked with infinite labour from an overhanging window ; in an arbour of time-twisted vines under which you may sit with your feet in the dirt and remember as a dim fable that there are races for which the type of domestic allurement is the parlour hearth-rug. For reasons apparent or otherwise these things amuse me beyond expression, and I am never weary of staring into gateways, of lingering by dreary, shabby, half-barbaric farm-yards, of feasting a foolish gaze on sun-cracked plaster and unctuous indoor shadows.

I mustn't forget, however, that it's not for wayside effects that one rides away behind St. Peter's, but for the strong sense of wandering over boundless space, of seeing great classic lines of landscape, of watching them dispose themselves into pictures so full of "style" that you can think of no painter who deserves to have you admit that they suggest him—hardly knowing whether it is better pleasure to gallop far and drink deep of air and grassy distance and the whole delicious opportunity, or to walk and pause and linger, and try and grasp some ineffaceable memory of sky and colour and outline. Your pace can hardly help falling into a contemplative measure at the time, everywhere so wonderful, but in Rome so persuasively divine, when the winter begins palpably to soften and quicken. Far out on the Campagna, early in February, you feel the first vague earthly emanations, which in a few weeks come wandering into the heart of the city and throbbing through the close, dark streets. Springtime in Rome is an immensely poetic affair ; but you must stand often far out in the ancient waste, between grass and sky, to measure its deep, full, steadily accelerated rhythm. The winter has an incontestable beauty, and is pre-eminently the time of colour—the time when it is no affectation, but homely verity, to talk about the "purple" tone of the atmosphere. As February comes and goes your purple is streaked with green and the rich, dark bloom of the distance begins to lose its intensity. But your loss is made up by other gains ; none more precious than that inestimable gain to the ear—the disembodied voice of the lark. It comes with the early flowers, the white narcissus and the cyclamen, the half-buried violets and the pale anemones, and makes the whole atmosphere ring like a vault of tinkling glass. You never see the source of the sound, and are utterly unable to localise his note, which seems to come from everywhere at once, to be some hundred-throated voice of the air. Sometimes you fancy you just catch him, a mere vague spot against the blue, an intenser throb in the universal pulsation of light. As the weeks go on the flowers multiply and the deep blues and purples of the hills, turning to azure and violet, creep higher toward the narrowing snow-line of the Sabines. The temperature rises, the first hour of your ride you feel the heat, but you beguile it with brushing the hawthorn-blossoms as you pass along the hedges, and catching at the wild rose and honeysuckle ; and when you get into the meadows there is stir enough in the air to lighten the dead weight of the sun. The Roman air, however, is not a tonic medicine, and it seldom suffers exercise to be all exhilarating. It has always seemed to me indeed part of the charm of the latter that your keenest consciousness is haunted with a vague languor. Occasionally when the sirocco blows that sensation becomes strange and exquisite. Then, under the grey sky, before the dim distances which the south-wind mostly brings with it, you seem to ride forth into a world from which all hope has departed and in which, in spite of the flowers that make your horse's footfalls soundless, nothing is left save some queer probability that your imagination is unable to measure, but from which it hardly shrinks. This quality in the Roman element may now and then "relax" you almost to ecstasy ; but a season of sirocco would be an overdose of morbid pleasure. You may at any rate best feel the peculiar beauty of the Campagna on those mild days of winter when the mere quality and temper of the sunshine suffice to move the landscape to joy, and you pause on the brown grass in the sunny stillness and, by listening long enough, almost fancy you hear the shrill of the midsummer cricket. It is detail and ornament that vary from month to month, from week to week even, and make your returns to the same places a constant feast of unexpectedness ; but the great essential features of the prospect preserve throughout the year the same impressive serenity. Soracte, be it January or May, rises from its blue horizon like an island from the sea and with an elegance of contour which no mood of the year can deepen or diminish. You know it well ; you have seen it often in the mellow backgrounds of Claude ; and it has such an irresistibly classic, academic air that while you look at it you begin to take your saddle for a faded old arm-chair in a palace gallery. A month's rides in different directions will show you a dozen prime Claudes. After I had seen them all I went piously to the Doria gallery to refresh my memory of its two famous specimens and to enjoy to the utmost their delightful air of reference to something that had become a part of my personal experience. Delightful it certainly is to feel the common element in one's own sensibility and those of a genius whom that element has helped to do great things. Claude must have haunted the very places of one's personal preference and adjusted their divine undulations to his splendid scheme of romance, his view of the poetry of life. He was familiar with aspects in which there wasn't a single uncompromising line. I saw a few days ago a small finished sketch from his hand, in the possession of an American artist, which was almost startling in its clear reflection of forms unaltered by the two centuries that have dimmed and cracked the paint and canvas.

This unbroken continuity of the impressions I have tried to indicate is an excellent example of the intellectual background of all enjoyment in Rome. It effectually prevents pleasure from becoming vulgar, for your sensation rarely begins and ends with itself; it reverberates—it recalls, commemorates, resuscitates something else. At least half the merit of everything you enjoy must be that it suits you absolutely; but the larger half here is generally that it has suited some one else and that you can never flatter yourself you have discovered it. It has been addressed to some use a million miles out of your range, and has had great adventures before ever condescending to please you. It was in admission of this truth that my discriminating friend who showed me the Claudes found it impossible to designate a certain delightful region which you enter at the end of an hour's riding from Porta Cavalleggieri as anything but Arcadia. The exquisite correspondence of the term in this case altogether revived its faded bloom; here veritably the oaten pipe must have stirred the windless air and the satyrs have laughed among

the brookside reeds. Three or four long grassy dells stretch
away in a chain between low hills over which delicate trees are so
discreetly scattered that each one is a resting place for a shepherd. The elements of the scene are simple enough, but the
composition has extraordinary refinement. By one of those
happy chances which keep observation in Italy always in her best
humour a shepherd had thrown himself down under one of the
trees in the very attitude of Melibœus. He had been washing
his feet, I suppose, in the neighbouring brook, and had found it
pleasant afterwards to roll his short breeches well up on his
thighs. Lying thus in the shade, on his elbow, with his naked
legs stretched out on the turf and his soft peaked hat over his
long hair crushed back like the veritable bonnet of Arcady, he
was exactly the figure of the background of this happy valley.
The poor fellow, lying there in rustic weariness and ignorance,
little fancied that he was a symbol of old-world meanings to
new-world eyes.

Such eyes may find as great a store of picturesque meanings
in the cork-woods of Monte Mario, tenderly loved of all eques-
trians. These are less severely pastoral than our Arcadia, and
you might more properly lodge there a damosel of Ariosto than
a nymph of Theocritus. Among them is strewn a lovely
wilderness of flowers and shrubs, and the whole place has such a
charming woodland air, that, casting about me the other day for
a compliment, I declared that it reminded me of New Hamp-
shire. My compliment had a double edge, and I had no sooner
uttered it than I smiled—or sighed—to perceive in all the
undiscriminated botany about me the wealth of detail, the idle
elegance and grace of Italy alone, the natural stamp of the land
which has the singular privilege of making one love her unsancti-
fied beauty all but as well as those features of one's own country
toward which nature's small allowance doubles that of one's own
affection. For this effect of casting a spell no rides have more
value than those you take in Villa Doria or Villa Borghese ; or

don't take, possibly, if you prefer to reserve these particular regions—the latter in especial—for your walking hours. People do ride, however, in both villas, which deserve honourable mention in this regard. Villa Doria, with its noble site, its splendid views, its great groups of stone-pines, so clustered and yet so individual, its lawns and flowers and fountains, its altogether princely disposition, is a place where one may pace, well mounted, of a brilliant day, with an agreeable sense of its being rather a more elegant pastime to balance in one's stirrups than to trudge on even the smoothest gravel. But at Villa Borghese the walkers have the best of it; for they are free of those adorable outlying corners and bosky byways which the rumble of barouches never reaches. In March the place becomes a perfect epitome of the spring. You cease to care much for the melancholy greenness of the disfeatured statues which has been your chief winter's intimation of verdure; and before you are quite conscious of the tender streaks and patches in the great quaint grassy arena round which the Propaganda students, in their long skirts, wander slowly, like dusky seraphs revolving the gossip of Paradise, you spy the brave little violets uncapping their azure brows beneath the high-stemmed pines. One's walks here would take us too far, and one's pauses detain us too long, when in the quiet parts under the wall one comes across a group of charming small school-boys in full-dress suits and white cravats, shouting over their play in clear Italian, while a grave young priest, beneath a tree, watches them over the top of his book. It sounds like nothing, but the force behind it and the frame round it, the setting, the air, the chord struck, make it a hundred wonderful things.

1873.

ROMAN NEIGHBOURHOODS

I MADE a note after my first stroll at Albano to the effect that I had been talking of the " picturesque " all my life, but that now for a change I beheld it. I had been looking all winter across the Campagna at the free-flowing outline of the Alban Mount, with its half-dozen towns shining on its purple side even as vague sun-spots in the shadow of a cloud, and thinking it simply an agreeable incident in the varied background of Rome. But now that during the last few days I have been treating it as a foreground, have been suffering St. Peter's to play the part of a small mountain on the horizon, with the Campagna swimming mistily through the ambiguous lights and shadows of the interval, I find the interest as great as in the best of the by-play of Rome. The walk I speak of was just out of the village, to the south, toward the neighbouring town of L'Ariccia, neighbouring these twenty years, since the Pope (the late Pope, I was on the point of calling him) threw his superb viaduct across the deep ravine which divides it from Albano. At the risk of seeming to fantasticate I confess that the Pope's having built the viaduct—in this very recent antiquity —made me linger there in a pensive posture and marvel at the march of history and at Pius the Ninth's beginning already to profit by the sentimental allowances we make to vanished powers. An ardent *nero* then would have had his own way with me and obtained a frank admission that the Pope was indeed a father to his people. Far down into the charming valley which slopes out the ancestral woods of the Chigis into the level Campagna winds the steep stone-paved road at the bottom of which, in the good old days, tourists in no great hurry saw the mules and oxen tackled to their carriage for the opposite ascent. And indeed even an impatient tourist might have been content to lounge back in his jolting chaise and look out at the mouldy foundations of the little city plunging into the verdurous flank of the gorge. Questioned, as a cherisher of quaintness, as to the best "bit" hereabouts, I should certainly name the way in which the crumbling black houses of these ponderous villages plant their weary feet on the flowery edges of all the steepest chasms. Before you enter one of them you invariably find yourself lingering outside its pretentious old gateway to see it clutched and stitched to the stony hillside by this rank embroidery of the wildest and bravest things that grow. Just at this moment nothing is prettier than the contrast between their dusky ruggedness and the tender, the yellow and pink and violet fringe of that mantle. All this you may observe from the viaduct at the Ariccia; but you must wander below to feel the full force of the eloquence of our imaginary *papalino*. The pillars and arches of pale grey peperino arise in huge tiers with a magnificent spring and solidity. The older Romans built no better; and the work has a deceptive air of being one of their sturdy bequests which help one to drop another sigh over the antecedents the Italians of to-day are so eager to repudiate. Will those *they* give their descendants be as good?

At the Ariccia, in any case, I found a little square with a couple of mossy fountains, occupied on one side by a vast dusky-faced Palazzo Chigi and on the other by a goodly church with an imposing dome. The dome, within, covers the whole edifice and is adorned with some extremely elegant stucco-work of the seventeenth century. It gave a great value to this fine old decoration that preparations were going forward for a local festival and that the village carpenter was hanging certain mouldy strips of crimson damask against the piers of the vaults. The damask might have been of the seventeenth

century too, and a group of peasant-women were seeing it
unfurled with evident awe. I regarded it myself with interest
—it seemed so the tattered remnant of a fashion that had gone
out for ever. I thought again of the poor disinherited Pope,
wondering whether, when such venerable frippery will no
longer bear the carpenter's nails, any more will be provided. It
was hard to fancy anything but shreds and patches in that musty
tabernacle. Wherever you go in Italy you receive some such
intimation as this of the shrunken proportions of Catholicism,
and every church I have glanced into on my walks hereabouts
has given me an almost pitying sense of it. One finds one's self
at last—without fatuity, I hope—feeling sorry for the solitude
of the remaining faithful. It's as if the churches had been made
so for the world, in its social sense, and the world had so irrevo-
cably moved away. They are in size out of all modern proportion to the local needs, and the only thing at all alive in
the melancholy waste they collectively form is the smell of stale
incense. There are pictures on all the altars by respectable
third-rate painters ; pictures which I suppose once were ordered
and paid for and criticised by worshippers who united taste with
piety. At Genzano, beyond the Ariccia, rises on the grey village
street a pompous Renaissance temple whose imposing nave and
aisles would contain the population of a capital. But where is
the *taste* of the Ariccia and Genzano ? Where are the choice
spirits for whom Antonio Raggi modelled the garlands of his
dome and a hundred clever craftsmen imitated Guido and
Caravaggio ? Here and there, from the pavement, as you pass,
a dusky crone interlards her devotions with more profane importunities, or a grizzled peasant on rusty-jointed knees, tilted
forward with his elbows on a bench, reveals the dimensions of
the patch in his blue breeches. But where is the connecting
link between Guido and Caravaggio and those poor souls for
whom an undoubted original is only a something behind a row
of candlesticks, of no very clear meaning save that you must

bow to it? You find a vague memory of it at best in the useless grandeurs about you, and you seem to be looking at a structure of which the stubborn earth-scented foundations alone remain, with the carved and painted shell that bends above them, while the central substance has utterly crumbled away.

I shall seem to have adopted a more meditative pace than befits a brisk constitutional if I say that I also fell a-thinking before the shabby façade of the old Chigi Palace. But it seemed somehow in its grey forlornness to respond to the sadly super-annuated expression of the opposite church; and indeed in any condition what self-respecting cherisher of quaintness can forbear to do a little romancing in the shadow of a provincial palazzo? On the face of the matter, I know, there is often no very salient peg to hang a romance on. A sort of dusky blankness invests the establishment, which has often a rather imbecile old age. But a hundred brooding secrets lurk in this inexpressive mask, and the Chigi Palace did duty for me in the suggestive twilight as the most haunted of houses. Its basement walls sloped outward like the beginning of a pyramid, and its lower windows were covered with massive iron cages. Within the doorway, across the court, I saw the pale glimmer of flowers on a terrace, and I made much, for the effect of the roof, of a great covered loggia or belvedere with a dozen window-panes missing or mended with paper. Nothing gives one a stronger impression of old manners than an ancestral palace towering in this haughty fashion over a shabby little town; you hardly stretch a point when you call it an impression of feudalism. The scene may pass for feudal to American eyes, for which a hundred windows on a façade mean nothing more exclusive than a hotel kept (at the most invidious) on the European plan. The mouldy grey houses on the steep crooked street, with their black cavernous archways pervaded by bad smells, by the braying of asses and by human intonations hardly more musical, the haggard and tattered peasantry staring at you with hungry-heavy eyes, the brutish-looking monks (there are still enough to point a moral), the soldiers, the mounted constables, the dirt, the dreariness, the misery, and the dark overgrown palace frowning over it all from barred window and guarded gateway—what more than all this do we dimly descry in a mental image of the dark ages? For all his desire to keep the peace with the vivid image of things if it be only vivid enough, the votary of this ideal may well occasionally turn over such values with the wonder of what one takes them as paying for. They pay sometimes for such sorry "facts of life." At Genzano, out of the very midst of the village squalor, rises the Palazzo Cesarini, separated from its gardens by a dirty lane. Between peasant and prince the contact is unbroken, and one would suppose Italian good-nature sorely taxed by their mutual allowances; that the prince in especial must cultivate a firm impervious shell. There are no comfortable townsfolk about him to remind him of the blessings of a happy mediocrity of fortune. When he looks out of his window he sees a battered old peasant against a sunny wall sawing off his dinner from a hunch of black bread.

I must confess, however, that "feudal" as it amused me to find the little piazza of the Ariccia, it appeared to threaten in no manner an exasperated rising. On the contrary, the afternoon being cool, many of the villagers were contentedly muffled in those ancient cloaks, lined with green baize, which, when tossed over the shoulder and surmounted with a peaked hat, form one of the few lingering remnants of "costume" in Italy; others were tossing wooden balls light-heartedly enough on the grass outside the town. The egress on this side is under a great stone archway thrown out from the palace and surmounted with the family arms. Nothing could better confirm your theory that the townsfolk are groaning serfs. The road leads away through the woods, like many of the roads hereabouts, among trees less remarkable for their size than for their picturesque contortions and posturings. The woods, at the moment at which I write, are full of the raw green light of early spring, a *jour* vastly becoming to the various complexions of the wild flowers that cover the waysides. I have never seen these untended parterres in such lovely exuberance; the sturdiest pedestrian becomes a lingering idler if he allows them to catch his eye. The pale purple cyclamen, with its hood thrown back, stands up in masses as dense as tulip-beds; and here and there in the duskier places great sheets of forget-me-not seem to exhale a faint blue mist. These are the commonest plants; there are dozens more I know no name for—a rich profusion in especial of a beautiful five-petalled flower whose white texture is pencilled with hair-strokes certain fair copyists I know of would have to hold their breath to imitate. An Italian oak has neither the girth nor the height of its English brothers, but it contrives in proportion to be perhaps even more effective. It crooks its back and twists its arms and clinches its hundred fists with the queerest extravagance, and wrinkles its bark into strange rugosities from which its first scattered sprouts of yellow green seem to break out like a morbid fungus. But the tree which has the greatest charm to northern eyes is the cold grey-green ilex, whose clear crepuscular shade drops against a Roman sun a veil impenetrable, yet not oppressive. The ilex has even less colour than the cypress, but it is much less funereal, and a landscape in which it is frequent may still be said to smile faintly, though by no means to laugh. It abounds in old Italian gardens, where the boughs are trimmed and interlocked into vaulted corridors in which, from point to point, as in the niches of some dimly frescoed hall, you see mildewed busts stare at you with a solemnity which the even grey light makes strangely intense. A humbler relative of the ilex, though it does better things than help broken-nosed emperors to look dignified, is the olive, which covers many of the neighbouring hillsides with its little smoky puffs of foliage. A stroke of composition I never weary of is that long blue stretch of the Campagna which makes a high horizon and rests on this vaporous base of olive-tops. A reporter intent upon a simile might liken it to the ocean seen above the smoke of watch-fires kindled on the strand.

To do perfect justice to the wood-walk away from the Ariccia I ought to touch upon the birds that were singing vespers as I passed. But the reader would find my rhapsody as poor entertainment as the programme of a concert he had been unable to attend. I have no more learning about bird-music than would help me to guess that a dull dissyllabic refrain in the heart of the wood came from the cuckoo; and when at moments I heard a twitter of fuller tone, with a more suggestive modulation, I could only *hope* it was the nightingale. I have listened for the nightingale more than once in places so charming that his song would have seemed but the articulate expression of their beauty, and have never heard much beyond a provoking snatch or two—a prelude that came to nothing. In spite of a natural grudge, however, I generously believe him a great artist or at least a great genius—a creature who despises any prompting short of absolute inspiration. For the rich, the multitudinous melody around me seemed but the offering to my ear of the prodigal spirit of tradition. The wood was ringing with sound because it was twilight, spring and Italy. It was also because of these good things and various others besides that I relished so keenly my visit to the Capuchin convent upon which I emerged after half-an-hour in the wood. It stands above the town, on the slope of the Alban Mount, and its wild garden climbs away behind it and extends its melancholy influence. Before it is a small stiff avenue of trimmed live-oaks which conducts you to a grotesque little shrine beneath the staircase ascending to the church. Just here, if you are apt to grow timorous at twilight, you may take a very pretty fright; for as you draw near you catch behind the grating of the shrine the startling semblance of a gaunt and livid monk. A sickly lamplight plays

down upon his face, and he stares at you from cavernous eyes
with a dreadful air of death in life. Horror of horrors, you
murmur, is this a Capuchin penance? You discover of course
in a moment that it is only a Capuchin joke, that the monk is
a pious dummy and his spectral visage a matter of the paint-
brush. You resent his intrusion on the surrounding loveliness;
and as you proceed to demand entertainment at their convent
you pronounce the Capuchins very foolish fellows. This declaration, as I made it, was supported by the conduct of the simple
brother who opened the door of the cloister in obedience to my
knock and, on learning my errand, demurred about admitting
me at so late an hour. If I would return on the morrow morning he'd be most happy. He broke into a blank grin when I
assured him that this was the very hour of my desire and that
the garish morning light would do no justice to the view. These
were mysteries beyond his ken, and it was only his good-nature
(of which he had plenty) and not his imagination that was
moved. So that when, passing through the narrow cloister and
out upon the grassy terrace, I saw another cowled brother
standing with folded hands profiled against the sky, in admirable harmony with the scene, I questioned his knowing the uses
for which he is still most precious. This, however, was surely
too much to ask of him, and it was cause enough for gratitude
that, though he was there before me, he was not a fellow-
tourist with an opera-glass slung over his shoulder. There was
support to my idea of the convent in the expiring light, for the
scene was in its way unsurpassable. Directly below the terrace
lay the deep-set circle of the Alban Lake, shining softly through
the light mists of evening. This beautiful pool—it is hardly
more—occupies the crater of a prehistoric volcano, a perfect cup,
shaped and smelted by furnace-fires. The rim of the cup, rising
high and densely wooded round the placid stone-blue water, has
a sort of natural artificiality. The sweep and contour of the long
circle are admirable; never was a lake so charmingly lodged. It

is said to be of extraordinary depth ; and though stone-blue
water seems at first a very innocent substitute for boiling lava
it has a sinister look which betrays its dangerous antecedents.
The winds never reach it and its surface is never ruffled ; but
its deep-bosomed placidity seems to cover guilty secrets, and you
fancy it in communication with the capricious and treacherous
forces of nature. Its very colour is of a joyless beauty, a blue as
cold and opaque as a solidified sheet of lava. Streaked and
wrinkled by a mysterious motion of its own, it affects the very
type of a legendary pool, and I could easily have believed that I
had only to sit long enough into the evening to see the ghosts of
classic nymphs and naiads cleave its sullen flood and beckon me
with irresistible arms. Is it because its shores are haunted with
these vague Pagan influences that two convents have risen there
to purge the atmosphere? From the Capuchin terrace you look
across at the grey Franciscan monastery of Palazzuola, which is
not less romantic certainly than the most obstinate myth it may
have exorcised. The Capuchin garden is a wild tangle of great
trees and shrubs and clinging, trembling vines which in these hard
days are left to take care of themselves ; a weedy garden, if there
ever was one, but none the less charming for that, in the deepening dusk, with its steep grassy vistas struggling away into impenetrable shadow. I braved the shadow for the sake of
climbing upon certain little flat-roofed crumbling pavilions that
rise from the corners of the further wall and give you a wider
and lovelier view of lake and hills and sky.

I have perhaps justified to the reader the mild proposition
with which I started—convinced him, that is, that Albano is
worth a walk. It may be a different walk each day, moreover,
and not resemble its predecessors save by its keeping in the
shade. "Galleries" the roads are prettily called, and with the
justice that they are vaulted and draped overhead and hung
with an immense succession of pictures. As you follow the
few miles from Genzano to Frascati you have perpetual views

of the Campagna framed by clusters of trees; the vast iridescent expanse of which completes the charm and comfort of your verdurous dusk. I compared it just now to the sea, and with a good deal of truth, for it has the same incalculable lights and shades, the same confusion of glitter and gloom. But I have seen it at moments—chiefly in the misty twilight—when it resembled less the waste of waters than something more portentous, the land itself in fatal dissolution. I could believe the fields to be dimly surging and tossing and melting away into quicksands, and that one's very last chance of an impression was taking place. A view, however, which has the merit of being really as interesting as it seems, is that of the Lake of Nemi; which the enterprising traveller hastens to compare with its sister sheet of Albano. Comparison in this case is particularly odious, for in order to prefer one lake to the other you have to discover faults where there are none. Nemi is a smaller circle, but lies in a deeper cup, and if with no grey Franciscan pile to guard its woody shores, at least, in the same position, the little high-perched black town to which it gives its name and which looks across at Genzano on the opposite shore as Palazzuola regards Castel Gandolfo. The walk from the Ariccia to Genzano is charming, most of all when it reaches a certain grassy piazza from which three public avenues stretch away under a double row of stunted and twisted elms. The Duke Cesarini has a villa at Genzano—I mentioned it just now— whose gardens overhang the lake; but he has also a porter in a faded rakish-looking livery who shakes his head at your proffered franc unless you can reinforce it with a permit countersigned at Rome. For this annoying complication of dignities he is justly to be denounced; but I forgive him for the sake of that ancestor who in the seventeenth century planted this shady walk. Never was a prettier approach to a town than by these low-roofed light-chequered corridors. Their only defect is that they prepare you for a town of rather more rustic coquetry than Genzano exhibits. It has quite the usual allowance, the common cynicism, of accepted decay, and looks dismally as if its best families had all fallen into penury together and lost the means of keeping anything better than donkeys in their great dark, vaulted basements and mending their broken window-panes with anything better than paper. It was on the occasion of this drear Genzano that I had a difference of opinion with a friend who maintained that there was nothing in the same line so pretty in Europe as a pretty New England village. The proposition seemed to a cherisher of quaintness on the face of it inacceptable; but calmly considered it has a measure of truth. I am not fond of chalk-white painted planks, certainly; I vastly prefer the dusky tones of ancient stucco and peperino; but I succumb on occasion to the charms of a vine-shaded porch, of tulips and dahlias glowing in the shade of high-arching elms, of heavy-scented lilacs bending over a white paling to brush your cheek.

"I prefer Siena to Lowell," said my friend; "but I prefer Farmington to such a thing as this." In fact an Italian village is simply a miniature Italian city, and its various parts imply a town of fifty times the size. At Genzano are neither dahlias nor lilacs, and no odours but foul ones. Flowers and other graces are all confined to the high-walled precincts of Duke Cesarini, to which you must obtain admission twenty miles away. The houses on the other hand would generally lodge a New England cottage, porch and garden and high-arching elms included, in one of their cavernous basements. These vast grey dwellings are all of a fashion denoting more generous social needs than any they serve nowadays. They speak of better days and of a fabulous time when Italy was either not shabby or could at least " carry off " her shabbiness. For what follies are they doing penance? Through what melancholy stages have their fortunes ebbed? You ask these questions as you choose the shady side of the long blank street and watch the hot sun glare upon the dust-coloured walls and pause before the fetid gloom of open doors.

I should like to spare a word for mouldy little Nemi, perched upon a cliff high above the lake, at the opposite side ; but after all, when I had climbed up into it from the water-side, passing beneath a great arch which I suppose once topped a gateway, and counted its twenty or thirty apparent inhabitants peeping at me from black doorways, and looked at the old round tower at whose base the village clusters, and declared that it was all queer, queer, desperately queer, I had said all that is worth saying about it. Nemi has a much better appreciation of its lovely position than Genzano, where your only view of the lake is from a dunghill behind one of the houses. At the foot of the round tower is an overhanging terrace, from which you may feast your eyes on the only fresh-ness they find in these dusky human hives—the blooming seam, as one may call it, of strong wild-flowers which binds the crumbling walls to the face of the cliff. Of Rocca di Papa I must say as little. It consorted generally with the bravery of its name ; but the only object I made a note of as I passed through it on my way to Monte Cavo, which rises directly above it, was a little black house with a tablet in its face setting forth that Massimo d'Azeglio had dwelt there. The story of his sojourn is not the least attaching episode in his delightful *Ricordi*. From the summit of Monte Cavo is a prodigious view, which you may enjoy with whatever good-nature is left you by the reflection that the modern Passionist convent occupy-ing this admirable site was erected by the Cardinal of York (grandson of James II.) on the demolished ruins of an imme-morial temple of Jupiter : the last foolish act of a foolish race. For me I confess this folly spoiled the convent, and the convent all but spoiled the view ; for I kept thinking how fine it would have been to emerge upon the old pillars and sculptures from the lava pavement of the Via Triumphalis, which wanders grass-grown and untrodden through the woods. A convent, however, which nothing spoils is that of Palazzuola, to which I paid my respects on this same occasion. It rises on a lower spur of Monte Cavo, on the edge, as we have seen, of the Alban Lake, and though it occupies a classic site, that of early Alba Longa, it displaced nothing more precious than memories and legends so dim that the antiquarians are still quarrelling about them. It has a meagre little church and the usual sham Perugino with a couple of tinsel crowns for the Madonna and the Infant inserted into the canvas; and it has also a musty old room hung about with faded portraits and charts and queer ecclesiastical knick-knacks, which borrowed a mysterious interest from the sudden assurance of the simple Franciscan brother who accompanied me that it was the room of the Son of the King of Portugal. But my peculiar pleasure was the little thick-shaded garden which adjoins the convent and commands from its massive artificial foundations an enchanting view of the lake. Part of it is laid out in cabbages and lettuce, over which a rubicund brother, with his frock tucked up, was bending with a solicitude which he interrupted to remove his skull-cap and greet me with the unsophisticated sweet-humoured smile that every now and then in Italy does so much to make you forget the ambiguities of monachism. The rest is occupied by cypresses and other funereal umbrage, making a dank circle round an old cracked fountain black with water-moss. The parapet of the terrace is furnished with good stone seats where you may lean on your elbows to gaze away a sunny half-hour and, feeling the general charm of the scene, declare that the best mission of such a country in the world has been simply to produce, in the way of prospect and picture, these masterpieces of mildness. Mild here as a dream the whole attained effect, mild as resignation, mild as one's thoughts of another life. Such a session wasn't surely an experience of the irritable flesh; it was the deep degustation, on a summer's day, of something immortally expressed by a man of genius.

From Albano you may take your way through several ancient little cities to Frascati, a rival centre of *villeggiatura*, the road following the hillside for a long morning's walk and passing through alternations of denser and clearer shade—the dark vaulted alleys of ilex and the brilliant corridors of fresh-sprouting oak. The Campagna is beneath you continually, with the sea beyond Ostia receiving the silver arrows of the sun upon its chased and burnished shield, and mighty Rome, to the north, lying at no great length in the idle immensity around it. The highway passes below Castel Gandolfo, which stands perched on an eminence behind a couple of gateways surmounted with the Papal tiara and twisted cordon; and I have more than once chosen the roundabout road for the sake of passing beneath these pompous insignia. Castel Gandolfo is indeed an ecclesiastical village and under the peculiar protection of the Popes, whose huge summer-palace rises in the midst of it like a rural Vatican. In speaking of the road to Frascati I necessarily revert to my first impressions, gathered on the occasion of the feast of the Annunziata, which falls on the 25th of March and is celebrated by a peasants' fair. As Murray strongly recommends you to visit this spectacle, at which you are promised a brilliant exhibition of all the costumes of modern Latium, I took an early train to Frascati and measured, in company with a prodigious stream of humble pedestrians, the half-hour's interval to Grotta Ferrata, where the fair is held. The road winds along the hillside, among the silver-sprinkled olives and through a charming wood where the ivy seemed tacked upon the oaks by women's fingers and the birds were singing to the late anemones. It was covered with a very jolly crowd of vulgar pleasure-takers, and the only creatures not in a state of manifest hilarity were the pitiful little overladen, overbeaten donkeys (who surely deserve a chapter to themselves in any description of these neighbour-

hoods) and the horrible beggars who were thrusting their sores
and stumps at you from under every tree. Every one was
shouting, singing, scrambling, making light of dust and distance and filling the air with that childlike jollity which the
blessed Italian temperament never goes roundabout to conceal.
There is no crowd surely at once so jovial and so gentle as an
Italian crowd, and I doubt if in any other country the tightly
packed third-class car in which I went out from Rome would
have introduced me to so much smiling and so little swearing.
Grotta Ferrata is a very dirty little village, with a number of
raw new houses baking on the hot hillside and nothing to charm
the fond gazer but its situation and its old fortified abbey. After
pushing about among the shabby little booths and declining a
number of fabulous bargains in tinware, shoes and pork, I was
glad to retire to a comparatively uninvaded corner of the
abbey and divert myself with the view. This grey ecclesiastical
stronghold is a thoroughly scenic affair, hanging over the hillside on plunging foundations which bury themselves among the
dense olives. It has massive round towers at the corners and a
grass-grown moat, enclosing a church and a monastery. The fore-
court, within the abbatial gateway, now serves as the public
square of the village and in fair-time of course witnesses the
best of the fun. The best of the fun was to be found in certain
great vaults and cellars of the abbey, where wine was in free
flow from gigantic hogsheads. At the exit of these trickling
grottos shady trellises of bamboo and gathered twigs had been
improvised, and under them a grand guzzling proceeded.
All of which was so in the fine old style that I was roughly
reminded of the wedding-feast of Gamacho. The banquet was
far less substantial of course, but it had a note as of immemorial
manners that couldn't fail to suggest romantic analogies to a
pilgrim from the land of no cooks. There was a feast of reason
close at hand, however, and I was careful to visit the famous
frescoes of Domenichino in the adjoining church. It sounds

rather brutal perhaps to say that, when I came back into the clamorous little piazza, the sight of the peasants swilling down their sour wine appealed to me more than the masterpieces—Murray calls them so—of the famous Bolognese. It amounts after all to saying that I prefer Teniers to Domenichino; which I am willing to let pass for the truth. The scene under the rickety trellises was the more suggestive of Teniers that there were no costumes to make it too Italian. Murray's attractive statement on this point was, like many of his statements, much truer twenty years ago than to-day. Costume is gone or fast going; I saw among the women not a single crimson bodice and not a couple of classic head-cloths. The poorer sort, dressed in vulgar rags of no fashion and colour, and the smarter ones in calico gowns and printed shawls of the vilest modern fabric, had honoured their dusky tresses but with rich applications of grease. The men are still in jackets and breeches, and, with their slouched and pointed hats and open-breasted shirts and rattling leather leggings, may remind one sufficiently of the Italian peasant as he figured in the woodcuts familiar to our infancy. After coming out of the church I found a delightful nook—a queer little terrace before a more retired and tranquil drinking-shop—where I called for a bottle of wine to help me to guess why I " drew the line " at Domenichino.

This little terrace was a capricious excrescence at the end of the piazza, itself simply a greater terrace; and one reached it, picturesquely, by ascending a short inclined plane of grass-grown cobble-stones and passing across a little dusky kitchen through whose narrow windows the light of the mighty landscape beyond touched up old earthen pots. The terrace was oblong and so narrow that it held but a single small table, placed lengthwise; yet nothing could be pleasanter than to place one's bottle on the polished parapet. Here you seemed by the time you had emptied it to be swinging forward into immensity—hanging poised above the Campagna. A beautiful gorge with a twinkling stream wandered down the hill far below you, beyond which Marino and Castel Gandolfo peeped above the trees. In front you could count the towers of Rome and the tombs of the Appian Way. I don't know that I came to any very distinct conclusion about Domenichino; but it was perhaps because the view was perfection that he struck me as more than ever mediocrity. And yet I don't think it was one's bottle of wine, either, that made one after all maudlin about him; it was the sense of the foolishly usurped in his tenure of fame, of the derisive in his ever having been put forward. To say so indeed savours of flogging a dead horse, but it is surely an unkind stroke of fate for him that Murray assures ten thousand Britons every winter in the most emphatic manner that his Communion of St. Jerome is the "second finest picture in the world." If this were so one would certainly here in Rome, where such institutions are convenient, retire into the very nearest convent; with such a world one would have a standing quarrel. And yet this sport of destiny is an interesting case, in default of being an interesting painter, and I would take a moderate walk, in most moods, to see one of his pictures. He is so supremely good an example of effort detached from inspiration and school-merit divorced from spontaneity, that one of his fine frigid performances ought to hang in a conspicuous place in every academy of design. Few things of the sort contain more urgent lessons or point a more precious moral; and I would have the head-master in the drawing-school take each ingenuous pupil by the hand and lead him up to the Triumph of David or the Chase of Diana or the red-nosed Persian Sibyl and make him some such little speech as the following: "This great picture, my son, was hung here to show you how you must *never* paint; to give you a perfect specimen of what in its boundless generosity the providence of nature created for our fuller knowledge—an artist whose development was a negation. The great thing in art is charm, and the great thing in charm is spontaneity.

Domenichino, having talent, is here and there an excellent model—he was devoted, conscientious, observant, industrious; but now that we've seen pretty well what can simply be learned do its best, these things help him little with us, because his imagination was cold. It loved nothing, it lost itself in nothing, its efforts never gave it the heartache. It went about trying this and that, concocting cold pictures after cold receipts, dealing in the second-hand, in the ready-made, and putting into its performances a little of everything but itself. When you see so many things in a composition you might suppose that among them all some charm might be born; yet they're really but the hundred mouths through which you may hear the unhappy thing murmur 'I'm dead!' It's by the simplest thing it has that a picture lives—by its temper. Look at all the great talents, Domenichino as well as at Titian; but think less of dogma than of plain nature, and I can almost promise you that yours will remain true." This is very little to what the æsthetic sage I have imagined *might* say; and we are after all unwilling to let our last verdict be an unkind one on any great bequest of human effort. The faded frescoes in the chapel at Grotta Ferrata leave us a memory the more of man's effort to dream beautifully; and they thus mingle harmoniously enough with our multifold impressions of Italy, where dreams and realities have both kept such pace and so strangely diverged. It was absurd—that was the truth—to be critical at all among the appealing old Italianisms round me and to treat the poor exploded Bolognese more harshly than, when I walked back to Frascati, I treated the charming old water-works of the Villa Aldobrandini. I confound these various products of antiquated art in a genial absolution, and should like especially to tell how fine it was to watch this prodigious fountain come tumbling down its channel of mouldy rock-work, through its magnificent vista of ilex, to the fantastic old hemicycle where a dozen tritons and naiads sit posturing to receive it. The sky above the ilexes was incredibly blue and the ilexes themselves incredibly black; and to see the young white moon peeping above the trees you could easily have fancied it was midnight. I should like furthermore to expatiate on Villa Mondragone, the most grandly impressive hereabouts, of all such domestic monuments. The great Casino in the midst is as big as the Vatican, which it strikingly resembles, and it stands perched on a terrace as vast as the parvise of St. Peter's, looking straight away over black cypress-tops into the shining vastness of the Campagna. Everything somehow seemed immense and solemn; there was nothing small but certain little nestling blue shadows on the Sabine Mountains, to which the terrace seems to carry you wonderfully near. The place has been for some time lost to private uses, since it figures fantastically in a novel of George Sand—*La Daniella*—and now, in quite another way, as a Jesuit college for boys. The afternoon was perfect, and as it waned it filled the dark alleys with a wonderful golden haze. Into this came leaping and shouting a herd of little collegians with a couple of long-skirted Jesuits striding at their heels. We all know—I make the point for my antithesis—the monstrous practices of these people; yet as I watched the group I verily believe I declared that if I had a little son he should go to Mondragone and receive their crooked teachings for the sake of the other memories, the avenues of cypress and ilex, the view of the Campagna, the atmosphere of antiquity. But doubtless when a sense of "mere character," shameless incomparable character, has brought one to this it is time one should pause.

THE AFTER-SEASON IN ROME

ONE may at the blest end of May say without injustice to anybody that the state of mind of many a *forestiero* in Rome is one of intense impatience for the moment when all other *forestieri* shall have taken themselves off. One may confess to this state of mind and be no misanthrope. The place has passed so completely for the winter months into the hands of the barbarians that that estimable character the passionate pilgrim finds it constantly harder to keep his passion clear. He has a rueful sense of impressions perverted and adulterated ; the all-venerable visage disconcerts us by a vain eagerness to see itself mirrored in English, American, German eyes. It isn't simply that you are never first or never alone at the classic or historic spots where you have dreamt of persuading the shy *genius loci* into confidential utterance ; it isn't simply that St. Peter's, the Vatican, the Palatine, are forever ringing with the false note of the languages without style : it is the general oppressive feeling that the city of the soul has become for the time a monstrous mixture of watering-place and curiosity-shop and that its most ardent life is that of the tourists who haggle over false intaglios and yawn through palaces and temples. But you are told of a happy time when these abuses begin to pass away, when Rome becomes Rome again and you may have her all to yourself. "You may like her more or less now," I was assured at the height of the season ; "but you must wait till the month of May, when she'll give you *all* she has, to love her. Then the foreigners, or the excess of them, are gone ; the galleries and ruins are empty, and the place," said my informant, who was a happy Frenchman of the Académie de France, "*renaît à elle-même*." Indeed I was haunted all winter by an irresistible pre-vision of what Rome *must* be in declared spring. Certain charming places seemed to murmur : "Ah, this is nothing ! Come back at the right weeks and see the sky above us almost black with its excess of blue, and the new grass already deep, but still vivid, and the white roses tumble in odorous spray and the warm radiant air distil gold for the smelting-pot that the *genius loci* then dips his brush into before making play with it, in his inimitable way, for the general effect of complexion."

A month ago I spent a week in the country, and on my return, the first time I approached the Corso, became conscious of a change. Something delightful had happened, to which at first I couldn't give a name, but which presently shone out as the fact that there were but half of many people present and that these were chiefly the natural or the naturalised. We had been docked of half our irrelevance, our motley excess, and now physically, morally, æsthetically there was elbow-room. In the afternoon I went to the Pincio, and the Pincio was almost dull. The band was playing to a dozen ladies who lay in landaus poising their lace-fringed parasols ; but they had scarce more than a light-gloved dandy apiece hanging over their carriage doors. By the parapet to the great terrace that sweeps the city stood but three or four interlopers looking at the sunset and with their Baedekers only just showing in their pockets—the sunsets not being down among the tariffed articles in these precious volumes. I went so far as to hope for them that, like myself, they were, under every precaution, taking some amorous intellectual liberty with the scene.

Practically I violate thus the instinct of monopoly, since it's a shame not to publish that Rome in May is indeed exquisitely worth your patience. I have just been so gratified at finding myself in undisturbed possession for a couple of hours of the

Museum of the Lateran that I can afford to be magnanimous. It's almost as if the old all-papal paradise had come back. The weather for a month has been perfect, the sky an extravagance of blue, the air lively enough, the nights cool, nippingly cool, and the whole ancient greyness lighted with an irresistible smile. Rome, which in some moods, especially to new-comers, seems a place of almost sinister gloom, has an occasional art, as one knows her better, of brushing away care by the grand gesture with which some splendid impatient mourning matron—just the Niobe of Nations, surviving, emerging and looking about her again—might pull off and cast aside an oppression of muffling crape. This admirable power still temperamentally to react and take notice lurks in all her darkness and dirt and decay—a something more careless and hopeless that our thrifty northern cheer, and yet more genial and urbane than the Parisian spirit of *blague*. The collective Roman nature is a healthy and hearty one, and you feel it abroad in the streets even when the sirocco blows and the medium of life seems to proceed more or less from the mouth of a furnace. But who shall analyse even the simplest Roman impression ? It is compounded of so many things, it says so much, it involves so much, it so quickens the intelligence and so flatters the heart, that before we fairly grasp the case the imagination has marked it for her own and exposed us to a perilous likelihood of talking nonsense about it.

The smile of Rome, as I have called it, and its insidious message to those who incline to ramble irresponsibly and take things as they come, is ushered in with the first breath of spring, and then grows and grows with the advancing season till it wraps the whole place in its tenfold charm. As the process develops you can do few better things than go often to Villa Borghese and sit on the grass—on a stout bit of drapery—and watch its exquisite stages. It has a frankness and a sweetness beyond any relenting of *our* clumsy climates even when ours leave off their damnable faces and begin. Nature departs from every reserve with a confidence that leaves one at a loss where, as it were, to look—leaves one, as I say, nothing to do but to lay one's head among the anemones at the base of a high-stemmed pine and gaze up crestward and skyward along its slanting silvery column. You may watch the whole business from a dozen of these choice standpoints and have a different villa for it every day in the week. The Doria, the Ludovisi, the Medici, the Albani, the Wolkonski, the Chigi, the Mellini, the Massimo —there are more of them, with all their sights and sounds and odours and memories, than you have senses for. But I prefer none of them to the Borghese, which is free to all the world at all times and yet never crowded; for when the whirl of carriages is great in the middle regions you may find a hundred untrodden spots and silent corners, tenanted at the worst by a group of those long-skirted young Propagandists who stalk about with solemn angularity, each with a book under his arm, like silhouettes from a mediæval missal, and "compose" so extremely well with the still more processional cypresses and with stretches of golden-russet wall overtopped by ultramarine. And yet if the Borghese is good the Medici is strangely charming, and you may stand in the little belvedere which rises with such surpassing oddity out of the dusky heart of the Boschetto at the latter establishment—a miniature presentation of the wood of the Sleeping Beauty—and look across at the Ludovisi pines lifting their crooked parasols into a sky of what a painter would call the most morbid blue, and declare that the place where *they* grow is the most delightful in the world. Villa Ludovisi has been all winter the residence of the lady familiarly known in Roman society as "Rosina," Victor Emmanuel's morganatic wife, the only familiarity, it would seem, that she allows, for the grounds were rigidly closed, to the inconsolable regret of old Roman sojourners. Just as the nightingales began to sing, however, the quasi-august *padrona* departed, and the public, with certain restrictions, have been

N

admitted to hear them. The place takes, where it lies, a princely ease, and there could be no better example of the expansive tendencies of ancient privilege than the fact that its whole vast extent is contained by the city walls. It has in this respect very much the same enviable air of having got up early that marks the great intramural demesne of Magdalen College at Oxford. The stern old ramparts of Rome form the outer enclosure of the villa, and hence a series of "striking scenic effects" which it would be unscrupulous flattery to say you can imagine. The grounds are laid out in the formal last-century manner; but nowhere do the straight black cypresses lead off the gaze into vistas of a melancholy more charged with associations—poetic, romantic, historic; nowhere are there grander smoother walls of laurel and myrtle.

I recently spent an afternoon hour at the little Protestant cemetery close to St. Paul's Gate, where the ancient and the modern world are insidiously contrasted. They make between them one of the solemn places of Rome—although indeed when funereal things are so interfused it seems ungrateful to call them sad. Here is a mixture of tears and smiles, of stones and flowers, of mourning cypresses and radiant sky, which gives us the impression of our looking back at death from the brighter side of the grave. The cemetery nestles in an angle of the city wall, and the older graves are sheltered by a mass of ancient brickwork, through whose narrow loopholes you peep at the wide purple of the Campagna. Shelley's grave is here, buried in roses—a happy grave every way for the very type and figure of the Poet. Nothing could be more impenetrably tranquil than this little corner in the bend of the protecting rampart, where a cluster of modern ashes is held tenderly in the rugged hand of the Past. The past is tremendously embodied in the hoary pyramid of Caius Cestius, which rises hard by, half within the wall and half without, cutting solidly into the solid blue of the sky and casting its pagan shadow upon the grass of English

graves—that of Keats, among them—with an effect of poetic
justice. It is a wonderful confusion of mortality and a grim
enough admonition of our helpless promiscuity in the crucible
of time. But the most touching element of all is the appeal of
the pious English inscriptions among all these Roman memories;
touching because of their universal expression of that trouble
within trouble, misfortune in a foreign land. Something special
stirs the heart through the fine Scriptural language in which
everything is recorded. The echoes of massive Latinity with
which the atmosphere is charged suggest nothing more majestic
and monumental. I may seem unduly to refine, but the in-
junction to the reader in the monument to Miss Bathurst,
drowned in the Tiber in 1824, "If thou art young and lovely,
build not thereon, for she who lies beneath thy feet in death
was the loveliest flower ever cropt in its bloom," affects us
irresistibly as a case for tears on the spot. The whole elaborate
inscription indeed says something over and beyond all it does
say. The English have the reputation of being the most reticent
people in the world, and as there is no smoke without fire I
suppose they have done something to deserve it; yet who can
say that one doesn't constantly meet the most startling examples
of the insular faculty to "gush?" In this instance the mother
of the deceased takes the public into her confidence with surprising frankness and omits no detail, seizing the opportunity
to mention by the way that she had already lost her husband
by a most mysterious visitation. The appeal to one's attention
and the confidence in it are withal most moving. The whole
record has an old-fashioned gentility that makes its frankness
tragic. You seem to hear the garrulity of passionate grief.

To be choosing these positive commonplaces of the Roman
tone for a theme when there are matters of modern moment
going on may seem none the less to require an apology. But I
make no claim to your special correspondent's faculty for getting
an "inside" view of things, and I have hardly more than a

pictorial impression of the Pope's illness and of the discussion of
the Law of the Convents.   Indeed I am afraid to speak of the
Pope's illness at all, lest I should say something egregiously
heartless about it, recalling too forcibly that unnatural husband
who was heard to wish that his wife would "either" get well———!
He had his reasons, and Roman tourists have theirs in the shape
of a vague longing for something spectacular at St. Peter's.   If
it takes the sacrifice of somebody to produce it let somebody
then be sacrificed.   Meanwhile we have been having a glimpse
of the spectacular side of the Religious Corporations Bill.
Hearing one morning a great hubbub in the Corso I stepped
forth upon my balcony.   A couple of hundred men were strolling
slowly down the street with their hands in their pockets, shouting in unison "Abbasso il ministero!" and huzzaing in chorus.
Just beneath my window they stopped and began to murmur
"Al Quirinale, al Quirinale!"   The crowd surged a moment
gently and then drifted to the Quirinal, where it scuffled harmlessly with half-a-dozen of the king's soldiers.   It ought to have
been impressive, for what was it, strictly, unless the seeds of
revolution?   But its carriage was too gentle and its cries too
musical to send the most timorous tourist to packing his trunk.
As I began with saying : in Rome, in May, everything has an
amiable side, even popular uprisings.

FROM A ROMAN NOTE-BOOK

DECEMBER 28, 1872.—In Rome again for the last three days—that second visit which, when the first isn't followed by a fatal illness in Florence, the story goes that one is doomed to pay. I didn't drink of the Fountain of Trevi on the eve of departure the other time; but I feel as if I had drunk of the Tiber itself. Nevertheless as I drove from the station in the evening I wondered what I should think of it at this first glimpse hadn't I already known it. All manner of evil perhaps. Paris, as I passed along the Boulevards three evenings before to take the train, was swarming and glittering as befits a great capital. Here, in the black, narrow, crooked, empty streets, I saw nothing I would fain regard as eternal. But there were new gas-lamps round the spouting Triton in Piazza Barberini and a newspaper stall on the corner of the Condotti and the Corso—salient signs of the emancipated state. An hour later I walked up to Via Gregoriana by Piazza di Spagna. It was all silent and deserted, and the great flight of steps looked surprisingly small. Everything seemed meagre, dusky, provincial. Could Rome after all really *be* a world-city? That queer old rococo garden gateway at the top of the Gregoriana stirred a dormant memory; it awoke into a consciousness of the delicious mildness of the air, and very soon, in a little crimson drawing-room, I was reconciled and re-initiated. . . . Everything is dear (in the way of lodgings) but it hardly matters, as everything is taken and some one else paying for it. I must make up my mind to a bare perch. But it seems poorly perverse here to aspire to an "interior" or to be conscious of the economic side of life. The æsthetic is so intense that you feel you should live on the taste of it, should extract the nutritive essence of the atmosphere. For positively it's *such* an atmosphere! The weather is perfect, the sky as blue as the most exploded tradition fames it, the whole air glowing and throbbing with lovely colour. . . . The glitter of Paris is now all gaslight. And oh the monotonous miles of rain-washed asphalte!

December 30*th*.—I have had nothing to do with the "ceremonies." In fact I believe there have hardly been any—no midnight mass at the Sistine chapel, no silver trumpets at St. Peter's. Everything is remorselessly clipped and curtailed—the Vatican in deepest mourning. But I saw it in its superbest scarlet in '69 . . . I went yesterday with L. to the Colonna gardens—an adventure that would have reconverted me to Rome if the thing weren't already done. It's a rare old place—rising in mouldy bosky terraces and mossy stairways and winding walks from the back of the palace to the top of the Quirinal. It's the grand style of gardening, and resembles the present natural manner as a chapter of Johnsonian rhetoric resembles a piece of clever contemporary journalism. But it's a better style in horticulture than in literature; I prefer one of the long-drawn blue-green Colonna vistas, with a maimed and mossy-coated garden goddess at the end, to the finest possible quotation from a last-century classic. Perhaps the best thing there is the old orangery with its trees in fantastic terra-cotta tubs. The late afternoon light was gilding the monstrous jars and suspending golden chequers among the golden-fruited leaves. Or perhaps the best thing is the broad terrace with its mossy balustrade and its benches; also its view of the great naked Torre di Nerone (I think) which might look stupid if the rosy brickwork didn't take such a colour in the blue air. Delightful, at any rate, to stroll and talk there in the afternoon sunshine.

January 2*nd*, 1873.—Two or three drives with A.—one to St. Paul's without the Walls and back by a couple of old churches on the Aventine. I was freshly struck with the rare distinction of the little Protestant cemetery at the Gate, lying in the shadow of the black sepulchral Pyramid and the thick-growing black cypresses. Bathed in the clear Roman light the place is heartbreaking for what it asks you—in such a world as *this*—to renounce. If it should "make one in love with death to lie there," that's only if death should be conscious. As the case stands the weight of a tremendous past presses upon the flowery sod, and the sleeper's mortality feels the contact of all the mortality with which the brilliant air is tainted. . . . The restored Basilica is incredibly splendid. It seems a last pompous effort of formal Catholicism, and there are few more striking emblems of later Rome—the Rome foredoomed to see Victor Emmanuel in the Quirinal, the Rome of abortive councils and unheeded anathemas. It rises there, gorgeous and useless, on its miasmatic site, with an air of conscious bravado— a florid advertisement of the superabundance of faith. Within it's magnificent, and its magnificence has no shabby spots—a rare thing in Rome. Marble and mosaic, alabaster and malachite, lapis and porphyry, incrust it from pavement to cornice and flash back their polished lights at each other with such a splendour of effect that you seem to stand at the heart of some immense prismatic crystal. One has to come to Italy to know marbles and love them. I remember the fascination of the first great show of them I met in Venice—at the Scalzi and Gesuiti. Colour has in no other form so cool and unfading a purity and lustre. Softness of tone and hardness of substance—isn't that the sum of the artist's desire? G., with his beautiful caressing, open-lipped Roman utterance, so easy to understand and, to my ear, so finely suggestive of genuine Latin, not our horrible Anglo-Saxon and Protestant kind, urged upon us the charms of a return by the Aventine and the sight of a couple of old churches. The best is Santa Sabina, a very fine old structure of the fifth century, mouldering in its dusky solitude and consuming its own antiquity. What a massive heritage Christianity and Catholicism are leaving here! What a substantial fact, in all its decay, this memorial Christian temple outliving its uses among the sunny gardens and vineyards! It has a noble nave, filled with a stale smell which (like that of the onion) brought tears to my eyes, and bordered with twenty-four fluted marble columns of Pagan origin. The crudely primitive little mosaics along the entablature are extremely curious. A Dominican monk, still young, who showed us the church, seemed a creature generated from its musty shadows and odours. His physiognomy was wonderfully *de l'emploi*, and his voice, most agreeable, had the strangest jaded humility. His lugubrious salute and sanctimonious impersonal appropriation of my departing franc would have been a master-touch on the stage. While we were still in the church a bell rang that he had to go and answer, and as he came back and approached us along the nave he made with his white gown and hood and his cadaverous face, against the dark church background, one of those pictures which, thank the Muses, have not yet been reformed out of Italy. It was the exact illustration, for insertion in a text, of heaven knows how many old romantic and conventional literary Italianisms—plays, poems, mysteries of Udolpho. We got back into the carriage and talked of profane things and went home to dinner—drifting recklessly, it seemed to me, from æsthetic luxury to social.

On the 31st we went to the musical vesper-service at the Gesù—hitherto done so splendidly before the Pope and the cardinals. The manner of it was eloquent of change—no Pope, no cardinals, and indifferent music; but a great *mise-en-scène* nevertheless. The church is gorgeous; late Renaissance, of great proportions, and full, like so many others, but in a preeminent degree, of seventeenth and eighteenth century Romanism. It doesn't impress the imagination, but richly feeds the curiosity, by which I mean one's sense of the curious; suggests no legends, but innumerable anecdotes à la Stendhal. There is a vast dome, filled with a florid concave fresco of tumbling fore-shortened angels, and all over the ceilings and cornices a wonderful outlay of dusky gildings and mouldings. There are various Bernini saints and seraphs in stucco-sculpture, astride of the tablets and door-tops, backing against their rusty machinery of coppery *nimbi* and egg-shaped cloudlets. Marble, damask and tapers in gorgeous profusion. The high altar a great screen of twinkling chandeliers. The choir perched in a little loft high up in the right transept, like a balcony in a side-scene at the opera, and indulging in surprising roulades and flourishes. . . . Near me sat a handsome, opulent-looking nun—possibly an abbess or prioress of noble lineage. Can a holy woman of such a complexion listen to a fine operatic barytone in a sumptuous temple and receive none but ascetic impressions? What a cross-fire of influences does Catholicism provide!

January 4th.—A drive with A. out of Porta San Giovanni and along Via Appia Nuova. More and more beautiful as you get well away from the walls and the great view opens out before you—the rolling green-brown dells and flats of the Campagna, the long, disjointed arcade of the aqueducts, the deep-shadowed blue of the Alban hills, touched into pale lights by their scattered towns. We stopped at the ruined basilica of San Stefano, an affair of the fifth century, rather meaningless without a learned companion. But the perfect little sepulchral chambers of the Pancratii, disinterred beneath the church, tell their own tale—in their hardly dimmed frescoes, their beautiful sculptured coffin and great sepulchral slab. Better still the tomb of the Valerii adjoining it—a single chamber with an arched roof, covered with stucco mouldings perfectly intact, exquisite figures and arabesques as sharp and delicate as if the plasterer's scaffold had just been taken from under them. Strange enough to think of these things—so many of them as there are—surviving their immemorial eclipse in this perfect shape and coming up like long-lost divers from the sea of time.

January 16*th*.—A delightful walk last Sunday with F. to Monte Mario. We drove to Porta Angelica, the little gate hidden behind the right wing of Bernini's colonnade, and strolled thence up the winding road to the Villa Mellini, where one of the greasy peasants huddled under the wall in the sun admits you for half a franc into the finest old ilex-walk in Italy. It is all vaulted grey-green shade with blue Campagna stretches in the interstices. The day was perfect; the still sunshine, as we sat at the twisted base of the old trees, seemed to have the drowsy hum of midsummer—with that charm of Italian vegetation that comes to us as its confession of having scenically served, to weariness at last, for some pastoral these many centuries a classic. In a certain cheapness and thinness of substance—as compared with the English stoutness, never left athirst—it reminds me of our own, and it is relatively dry enough and pale enough to explain the contempt of many unimaginative Britons. But it has an idle abundance and wantonness, a romantic shabbiness and dishevelment. At the Villa Mellini is the famous lonely pine which "tells" so in the landscape from other points, bought off from the axe by (I believe) Sir George Beaumont, commemorated in a like connection in Wordsworth's great sonnet. He at least was not an unimaginative Briton. As you stand under it, its far-away shallow dome, supported on a single column almost white enough to be marble, seems to dwell in the dizziest depths of the blue. Its pale grey-blue boughs and its silvery stem make a wonderful harmony with the ambient air. The Villa Mellini is full of the elder Italy of one's imagination—the Italy of Boccaccio and Ariosto. There are twenty places where the Florentine story-tellers might have sat round on the grass. Outside the villa walls, beneath the over-crowding orange-boughs, straggled old Italy as well—but not in Boccaccio's velvet: a row of ragged and livid contadini, some simply stupid in their squalor, but some downright brigands of romance, or of reality, with matted locks and terribly sullen eyes.

A couple of days later I walked for old acquaintance sake over to San Onofrio on the Janiculan. The approach is one of the dirtiest adventures in Rome, and though the view is fine from the little terrace, the church and convent are of a meagre and musty pattern. Yet here—almost like pearls in a dung-hill—are hidden mementos of two of the most exquisite of Italian minds. Torquato Tasso spent the last months of his life here, and you may visit his room and various warped and faded relics. The most interesting is a cast of his face taken after death—looking, like all such casts, almost more than mortally gallant and distinguished. But who should look all ideally so if not he? In a little shabby, chilly corridor adjoining is a fresco of Leonardo, a Virgin and Child with the *donatorio*. It is very small, simple and faded, but it has all the artist's magic, that mocking, illusive refinement and hint of a vague *arrière-pensée* which mark every stroke of Leonardo's brush. Is it the perfection of irony or the perfection of tenderness? What does he mean, what does he affirm, what does he deny? Magic wouldn't be magic, nor the author of such things stand so absolutely alone, if we were ready with an explanation. As I glanced from the picture to the poor stupid little red-faced brother at my side I wondered if the thing mightn't pass for an elegant epigram on monasticism. Certainly, at any rate, there is more intellect in it than under all the monkish tonsures it has seen coming and going these three hundred years.

January 21*st.*—The last three or four days I have regularly spent a couple of hours from noon baking myself in the sun of the Pincio to get rid of a cold. The weather perfect and the crowd (especially to-day) amazing. Such a staring, lounging, dandified, amiable crowd! Who does the vulgar stay-at-home work of Rome? All the grandees and half the foreigners are there in their carriages, the *bourgeoisie* on foot staring at them and the beggars lining all the approaches. The great difference between public places in America and Europe is in the number of unoccupied people of every age and condition sitting about early and late on benches and gazing at you, from your hat to your boots, as you pass. Europe is certainly the continent of the practised stare. The ladies on the Pincio have to run the gauntlet; but they seem to do so complacently enough. The European woman is brought up to the sense of having a definite part in the way of manners or manner to play in public. To lie back in a barouche alone, balancing a parasol and seeming to ignore the extremely immediate gaze of two serried ranks of male creatures on each side of her path, save here and there to recognise one of them with an imperceptible nod, is one of her daily duties. The number of young men here who, like the cœnobites of old, lead the purely contemplative life is enormous. They muster in especial force on the Pincio, but the Corso all day is thronged with them. They are well-dressed, good-humoured, good-looking, polite; but they seem never to do a harder stroke of work than to stroll from the Piazza Colonna to the Hôtel de Rome or *vice versâ*. Some of them don't even stroll, but stand leaning by the hour against the doorways, sucking the knobs of their canes, feeling their back hair and settling their shirt-cuffs. At my cafe in the morning several stroll in already (at nine o'clock) in light, in "evening" gloves. But they order nothing, turn on their heels, glance at the mirrors and stroll out again. When it rains they herd under the *portes-cochères* and in the smaller cafes. . . . Yesterday Prince Humbert's little *primogenito* was on the Pincio in an open landau with his governess. He's a sturdy blond little man and the image of the King. They had stopped to listen to the music, and the crowd was planted about the carriage-wheels, staring and criticising under the child's snub little nose. It appeared bold cynical curiosity, without the slightest manifestation of "loyalty," and it gave me a singular sense of the vulgarisation of Rome under the new régime. When the Pope drove abroad it was a solemn spectacle; even if you neither kneeled nor uncovered you were irresistibly impressed. But the Pope never stopped to listen to opera tunes, and he had no little popelings, under the charge of superior nurse-maids, whom you might take liberties with. The family at the Quirinal make something of a merit, I believe, of their modest and inexpensive way of life. The merit is great; yet, representationally, what a change for the worse from an order which proclaimed stateliness a part of its essence! The divinity that doth hedge a king must be pretty well on the wane. But how many more fine old traditions will the extremely sentimental traveller miss in the Italians over whom that little jostled prince in the landau will have come into his kinghood? . . . The Pincio continues to beguile; it's a great resource. I am forever being reminded of the " æsthetic luxury," as I called it above, of living in Rome. To be able to choose of an afternoon for a lounge (respectfully speaking) between St. Peter's and the high precinct you approach by the gate just beyond Villa Medici— counting nothing else—is a proof that if in Rome you may suffer from ennui, at least your ennui has a throbbing soul in it. It is something to say for the Pincio that you don't always choose St. Peter's. Sometimes I lose patience with its parade of eternal idleness, but at others this very idleness is balm to one's conscience. Life on just these terms seems so easy, so monotonously sweet, that you feel it would be unwise, would be really unsafe, to change. The Roman air is charged with an elixir, the Roman cup seasoned with some insidious drop, of which the action is fatally, yet none the less agreeably, " lowering."

January 26th.—With S. to the Villa Medici—perhaps on the whole the most enchanting place in Rome. The part of the garden called the Boschetto has an incredible, impossible charm; an upper terrace, behind locked gates, covered with a little dusky forest of evergreen oaks. Such a dim light as of a fabled, haunted place, such a soft suffusion of tender grey-green tones, such a company of gnarled and twisted little miniature trunks— dwarfs playing with each other at being giants—and such a

shower of golden sparkles drifting in from the vivid west! At
the end of the wood is a steep, circular mound, up which the
short trees scramble amain, with a long mossy staircase climbing
up to a belvedere. This staircase, rising suddenly out of the
leafy dusk to you don't see where, is delightfully fantastic.
You expect to see an old woman in a crimson petticoat and with
a distaff come hobbling down and turn into a fairy and offer you
three wishes. I should name for my own first wish that one
didn't have to be a Frenchman to come and live and dream and
work at the Académie de France. Can there be for a while a
happier destiny than that of a young artist conscious of talent
and of no errand but to educate, polish and perfect it, trans-
planted to these sacred shades? One has fancied Plato's
Academy—his gleaming colonnades, his blooming gardens and
Athenian sky; but was it as good as this one, where Monsieur
Hébert does the Platonic? The blessing in Rome is not that
this or that or the other isolated object is so very unsurpassable;
but that the general air so contributes to interest, to impressions
that are not as any other impressions anywhere in the world.
And from this general air the Villa Medici has distilled an
essence of its own—walled it in and made it delightfully private.
The great façade on the gardens is like an enormous rococo
clock-face all incrusted with images and arabesques and tablets.
What mornings and afternoons one might spend there, brush in
hand, unpreoccupied, untormented, pensioned, satisfied—either
persuading one's self that one would be "doing something" in
consequence or not caring if one shouldn't be.

At a later date—middle of March.—A ride with S. W. out of
the Porta Pia to the meadows beyond the Ponte Nomentana—
close to the site of Phaon's villa where Nero in hiding had himself
stabbed. It all spoke as things here only speak, touching more
chords than one can *now* really know or say. For these are
predestined memories and the stuff that regrets are made of;
the mild divine efflorescence of spring, the wonderful landscape,

the talk suspended for another gallop. . . . Returning, we dismounted at the gate of the Villa Medici and walked through the twilight of the vaguely perfumed, bird-haunted alleys to H.'s studio, hidden in the wood like a cottage in a fairy tale. I spent there a charming half-hour in the fading light, looking at the pictures while my companion discoursed of her errand. The studio is small and more like a little salon ; the painting refined, imaginative, somewhat morbid, full of consummate French ability. A portrait, idealised and etherealised, but a likeness of Mme. de —— (from last year's Salon) in white satin, quantities of lace, a coronet, diamonds and pearls ; a striking combination of brilliant silvery tones. A "Femme Sauvage," a naked dusky girl in a wood, with a wonderfully clever pair of shy, passionate eyes. The author is different enough from any of the numerous American artists. They may be producers, but he's a product as well—a product of influences of a sort of which we have as yet no general command. One of them is his charmed lapse of life in that unprofessional-looking little studio, with his enchanted wood on one side and the plunging wall of Rome on the other.

January 30th.—A drive the other day with a friend to Villa Madama, on the side of Monte Mario ; a place like a page out of one of Browning's richest evocations of this clime and civilisation. Wondrous in its haunting melancholy, it might have inspired half "The Ring and the Book" at a stroke. What a grim commentary on history such a scene—what an irony of the past ! The road up to it through the outer enclosure is almost impassable with mud and stones. At the end, on a terrace, rises the once elegant Casino, with hardly a whole pane of glass in its façade, reduced to its sallow stucco and degraded ornaments. The front away from Rome has in the basement a great loggia, now walled in from the weather, preceded by a grassy belittered platform with an immense sweeping view of the Campagna ; the sad-looking, more than sad-looking, evil-looking, Tiber beneath (the colour of gold, the sentimentalists say, the colour of mustard, the realists) ; a great vague stretch beyond, of various complexions and uses ; and on the horizon the ever-iridescent mountains. The place has become the shabbiest farm-house, with muddy water in the old *pièces d'eau* and dung-hills on the old parterres. The "feature" is the contents of the loggia : a vaulted roof and walls decorated by Giulio Romano ; exquisite stucco-work and still brilliant frescoes ; arabesques and figurini, nymphs and fauns, animals and flowers —gracefully lavish designs of every sort. Much of the colour —especially the blues—still almost vivid, and all the work wonderfully ingenious, elegant and charming. Apartments so decorated can have been meant only for the recreation of people greater than any we know, people for whom life was impudent ease and success. Margaret Farnese was the lady of the house, but where she trailed her cloth of gold the chickens now scamper between your legs over rotten straw. It is all inexpressibly dreary. A stupid peasant scratching his head, a couple of critical Americans picking their steps, the walls tattered and befouled breast-high, dampness and decay striking in on your heart, and the scene overbowed by these heavenly frescoes, mouldering there in their airy artistry ! It's poignant ; it provokes tears ; it tells so of the waste of effort. Something human seems to pant beneath the grey pall of time and to implore you to rescue it, to pity it, to stand by it somehow. But you leave it to its lingering death without compunction, almost with pleasure ; for the place seems vaguely crime-haunted—paying at least the penalty of some hard immorality. The end of a Renaissance pleasure-house. Endless for the didactic observer the moral, abysmal for the story-seeker the tale.

February 12*th*.—Yesterday to the Villa Albani. Over-formal and (as my companion says) too much like a tea-garden ; but with beautiful stairs and splendid geometrical lines of immense box-hedge, intersected with high pedestals supporting little antique busts. The light to-day magnificent; the Alban hills of an intenser broken purple than I had yet seen them—their white towns blooming upon it like vague projected lights. It was like a piece of very modern painting, and a good example of how Nature has at times a sort of mannerism which ought to make us careful how we condemn out of hand the more refined and affected artists. The collection of marbles in the Casino (Winckelmann's)' admirable and to be seen again. The famous Antinous crowned with lotus a strangely beautiful and impressive thing. The "Greek manner," on the showing of something now and again encountered here, moves one to feel that even for purely romantic and imaginative effects it surpasses any since invented. If there be not imagination, even in our comparatively modern sense of the word, in the baleful beauty of that perfect young profile there is none in "Hamlet" or in "Lycidas." There is five hundred times as much as in "The Transfiguration." With this at any rate to point to it's not for sculpture not professedly to produce any emotion producible by painting. There are numbers of small and delicate fragments of bas-reliefs of exquisite grace, and a huge piece (two combatants—one, on horseback, beating down another—murder made eternal and beautiful) attributed to the Parthenon and certainly as grandly impressive as anything in the Elgin marbles. S. W. suggested again the Roman villas as a "subject." Excellent if one could find a feast of facts à la Stendhal. A lot of vague ecstatic descriptions and anecdotes wouldn't at all pay. There have been too many already. Enough facts are recorded, I suppose; one should discover them and soak in them for a twelvemonth. And yet a Roman villa, in spite of statues, ideas and atmosphere, affects me as of a scanter human and social *portée*, a shorter, thinner reverberation, than an old English country-house, round which experience seems piled so thick. But this perhaps is either hair-splitting or "racial" prejudice.

March 9th.—The Vatican is still deadly cold; a couple

o

of hours there yesterday with R. W. E. Yet he, illustrious and enviable man, fresh from the East, had no overcoat and wanted none. Perfect bliss, I think, would be to live in Rome without thinking of overcoats. The Vatican seems very familiar, but strangely smaller than of old. I never lost the sense before of confusing vastness. *Sancta simplicitas !* All my old friends however stand there in undimmed radiance, keeping most of them their old pledges. I am perhaps more struck now with the enormous amount of padding—the number of third-rate, fourth-rate things that weary the eye desirous to approach freshly the twenty and thirty best. In spite of the padding there are dozens of treasures that one passes regretfully; but the impression of the whole place is the great thing—the feeling that through these solemn vistas flows the source of an incalculable part of our present conception of Beauty.

April 10th.—Last night, in the rain, to the Teatro Valle to see a comedy of Goldoni in Venetian dialect—"I Quattro Rustighi." I could but half follow it; enough, however, to be sure that, for all its humanity of irony, it wasn't so good as Molière. The acting was capital—broad, free and natural; the play of talk easier even than life itself; but, like all the Italian acting I have seen, it was wanting in *finesse*, that shade of the shade by which, and by which alone, one really knows art. I contrasted the affair with the evening in December last that I walked over (also in the rain) to the Odéon and saw the "Plaideurs" and the "Malade Imaginaire." There, too, was hardly more than a handful of spectators; but what rich, ripe, fully representational and above all intellectual comedy, and what polished, educated playing ! These Venetians in particular, however, have a marvellous *entrain* of their own; they seem even less than the French to recite. In some of the women—ugly, with red hands and shabby dresses—an extraordinary gift of natural utterance, of seeming to invent joyously as they go.

Later.—Last evening in H.'s box at the Apollo to hear
Ernesto Rossi in "Othello." He shares supremacy with
Salvini in Italian tragedy. Beautiful great theatre with boxes
you can walk about in; brilliant audience. The Princess
Margaret was there—I have never been to the theatre that
she was not—and a number of other princesses in neighbouring boxes. G. G. came in and instructed us that they were
the M., the L., the P., &c. Rossi is both very bad and very
fine; bad where anything like taste and discretion is required,
but "all there," and more than there, in violent passion. The
last act reduced too much, however, to mere exhibitional sensibility. The interesting thing to me was to observe the Italian
conception of the part—to see how crude it was, how little
it expressed the hero's moral side, his depth, his dignity—anything more than his being a creature terrible in mere tantrums.
The great point was his seizing Iago's head and whacking it
half-a-dozen times on the floor, and then flinging him twenty
yards away. It was wonderfully done, but in the doing of it
and in the evident relish for it in the house there was I scarce
knew what force of easy and thereby rather cheap expression.

April 27*th.*—A morning with L. B. at Villa Ludovisi, which
we agreed that we shouldn't soon forget. The villa now
belongs to the King, who has lodged his morganatic wife
there. There is nothing so blissfully *right* in Rome, nothing
more consummately consecrated to style. The grounds and
gardens are immense, and the great rusty-red city wall stretches
away behind them and makes the burden of the seven hills seem
vast without making *them* seem small. There is everything—
dusky avenues trimmed by the clippings of centuries, groves and
dells and glades and glowing pastures and reedy fountains and
great flowering meadows studded with enormous slanting pines.
The day was delicious, the trees all one melody, the whole place
a revelation of what Italy and hereditary pomp can do together.
Nothing could be more in the grand manner than this garden

view of the city ramparts, lifting their fantastic battlements above the trees and flowers. They are all tapestried with vines and made to serve as sunny fruit-walls—grim old defence as they once were; now giving nothing but a splendid buttressed privacy. The sculptures in the little Casino are few, but there are two great ones—the beautiful sitting Mars and the head of the great Juno, the latter thrust into a corner behind a shutter. These things it's almost impossible to praise; we can only mark them well and keep them clear, as we insist on silence to hear great music. . . . If I don't praise Guercino's Aurora in the greater Casino, it's for another reason; this is certainly a very muddy masterpiece. It figures on the ceiling of a small low hall; the painting is coarse and the ceiling too near. Besides, it's unfair to pass straight from the Greek mythology to the Bolognese. We were left to roam at will through the house; the custode shut us in and went to walk in the park. The apartments were all open, and I had an opportunity to re-construct, from its *milieu* at least, the character of a morganatic queen. I saw nothing to indicate that it was not amiable; but I should have thought more highly of the lady's discrimination if she had had the Juno removed from behind her shutter. In such a house, girdled about with such a park, methinks I could be amiable—and perhaps discriminating too. The Ludovisi Casino is small, but the perfection of the life of ease might surely be led there. There are English houses enough in wondrous parks, but they expose you to too many small needs and observances—to say nothing of a red-faced butler dropping his *h*'s. You are oppressed with the detail of accommodation. Here the billiard-table is old-fashioned, perhaps a trifle crooked; but you have Guercino above your head, and Guercino, after all, is almost as good as Guido. The rooms, I noticed, all pleased by their shape, by a lovely proportion, by a mass of delicate ornamentation on the high concave ceilings. One might live over again in them some deliciously benighted life of a forgotten type—with graceful old *sale*, and immensely thick walls, and a winding stone staircase, and a view from the loggia at the top; a view of twisted parasol-pines balanced, high above a wooden horizon, against a sky of faded sapphire.

May 17th.—It was wonderful yesterday at St. John Lateran. The spring now has turned to perfect summer; there are cascades of verdure over all the walls; the early flowers are a fading memory, and the new grass knee-deep in the Villa Borghese. The winter aspect of the region about the Lateran is one of the best things in Rome; the sunshine is nowhere so golden and the lean shadows nowhere so purple as on the long grassy walk to Santa Croce. But yesterday I seemed to see nothing but green and blue. The expanse before Santa Croce was vivid green; the Campagna rolled away in great green billows, which seemed to break high about the gaunt aqueducts; and the Alban Hills, which in January and February keep shifting and melting along the whole scale of azure, were almost monotonously fresh, and had lost some of their finer modelling. But the sky was ultramarine and everything radiant with light and warmth—warmth which a soft steady breeze kept from excess. I strolled some time about the church, which has a grand air enough, though I don't seize the point of view of Miss ——, who told me the other day how vastly finer she thought it than St. Peter's. But on Miss ——'s lips this seemed a very pretty paradox. The choir and transepts have a sombre splendour, and I like the old vaulted passage with its slabs and monuments behind the choir. The charm of charms at St. John Lateran is the admirable twelfth-century cloister, which was never more charming than yesterday. The shrubs and flowers about the ancient well were blooming away in the intense light, and the twisted pillars and chiselled capitals of the perfect little colonnade seemed to enclose them like the sculptured rim of a precious vase. Standing out among the flowers you may look up and see a section of the summit of the great façade of the church. The robed and mitred apostles, bleached and rain-washed by the ages, rose into the blue air like huge snow figures. I spent at the incorporated museum a subsequent hour of fond vague attention, having it quite to myself. It is rather scantily stocked, but the great cool halls open out impressively one after the other, and the wide spaces between the statues seem to suggest at first that each is a masterpiece. I was in the loving mood of one's last days in Rome, and when I had nothing else to admire I admired the magnificent thickness of the embrasures of the doors and windows. If there were no objects of interest at all in the Lateran the palace would be worth walking through every now and then, to keep up one's idea of solid architecture. I went over to the Scala Santa, where was no one but a very shabby priest sitting like a ticket-taker at the door. But he let me pass, and I ascended one of the profane lateral stairways and treated myself to a glimpse of the Sanctum Sanctorum. Its threshold is crossed but once or twice a year, I believe, by three or four of the most exalted divines, but you may look into it freely enough through a couple of gilded lattices. It is very sombre and splendid, and conveys the impression of a very holy place. And yet somehow it suggested irreverent thoughts ; it had to my fancy—perhaps on account of the lattice—an Oriental, a Mahometan note. I expected every moment to see a sultana appear in a silver veil and silken trousers and sit down on the crimson carpet.

Farewell, packing, the sharp pang of going. One would like to be able after five months in Rome to sum up, for tribute and homage, one's experience, one's gains, the whole adventure of one's sensibility. But one has really vibrated too much— the addition of so many items isn't easy. What is simply clear is the sense of an acquired passion for the place and of an incalculable number of gathered impressions. Many of these have been intense and momentous, but one has trodden on the other—there are always the big fish that swallow up the little—and one can hardly say what has become of them. They store themselves noiselessly away, I suppose, in the dim but safe places of memory and "taste," and we live in a quiet faith that they will emerge into vivid relief if life or art should demand them. As for the passion we needn't perhaps trouble ourselves about that. Fifty swallowed palmfuls of the Fountain of Trevi couldn't make us more ardently sure that we shall at any cost come back.

1873.

A FEW OTHER ROMAN
NEIGHBOURHOODS

IF I find my old notes, in all these Roman connections, inevitably bristle with the spirit of the postscript, so I give way to this prompting to the extent of my scant space and with the sense of other occasions awaiting me on which I shall have to do no less. The impression of Rome was repeatedly to renew itself for the author of these now rather antique and artless accents; was to overlay itself again and again with almost heavy thicknesses of experience, the last of which is, as I write, quite fresh to memory; and he has thus felt almost ashamed to drop his subject (though it be one that tends so easily to turn to the infinite) as if the law of change had in all the years had nothing to say to his case. It's of course but of his case alone that he speaks—wondering little what he may make of it for the profit of others by an attempt, however brief, to point the moral of the matter, or in other words compare the musing *mature* visitor's " feeling about Rome " with that of the extremely agitated, even if though extremely inexpert, consciousness reflected in the previous pages. The actual, the current Rome affects him as a world governed by new conditions altogether and ruefully pleading that sorry fact in the ear of the antique wanderer wherever he may yet mournfully turn for some re-capture of what he misses. The city of his first unpremeditated rapture shines to memory, on the other hand, in the manner of a lost paradise the rustle of whose gardens is still just audible enough in the air to make him wonder if some sudden turn, some recovered vista, mayn't lead him back to the thing itself. My genial, my helpful tag, at this point, would doubtless properly resolve itself, for the reader, into a clue toward some such successful ingenuity of quest ; a remark I make, I may add, even while reflecting that the Paradise isn't apparently at all "lost" to visitors not of my generation. It is the seekers of *that* remote and romantic tradition who have seen it, from one period of ten, or even of five, years to another, systematically and remorselessly built out from their view. Their helpless plaint, their sense of the generally irrecoverable and unspeakable, is not, however, what I desire here most to express ; I should like, on the contrary, with ampler opportunity, positively to enumerate the cases, the cases of contact, impression, experience, in which the cold ashes of a long-chilled passion may fairly feel themselves made to glow again. No one who has ever loved Rome as Rome could be loved in youth and before her poised basketful of the finer appeals to fond fancy was actually upset, wants to stop loving her ; so that our bleeding and wounded, though perhaps not wholly moribund, loyalty attends us as a hovering admonitory, anticipatory ghost, one of those magnanimous life-companions who before complete extinction designate to the other member of the union their approved successor. So it is at any rate that I conceive the pilgrim old enough to have become aware in all these later years of what he misses to be counselled and pacified in the interest of recognitions that shall a little make up for it.

It was this wisdom I was putting into practice, no doubt, for instance, when I lately resigned myself to motoring of a splendid June day "out to" Subiaco ; as a substitute for a resignation that had anciently taken, alas, but the form of my never getting there at all. Everything that day, moreover, seemed right, surely ; everything on certain other days that were like it through their large indebtedness, at this, that and the other point, to the last new thing, seemed so right that they come back to me now, after a moderate interval, in the full light of that unchallenged felicity. I couldn't at all gloriously recall, for instance, as I floated to Subiaco on vast brave wings, how on the occasion of my first visit to Rome, thirty-eight years before, I had devoted certain evenings, evenings of artless " preparation " in my room at the inn, to the perusal of Alphonse Dantier's admirable *Monastères Benedictins d'Italie*, taking piously for granted that I should get myself somehow conveyed to Monte Cassino and to Subiaco at least : such an affront to the passion of curiosity, the generally infatuated state then kindled, would any suspicion of my foredoomed, my all but interminable, privation during visits to come have seemed to me. Fortune, in the event, had never favoured my going, but I was to give myself up at last to the sense of her quite taking me by the hand, and that is how I now think of our splendid June day at Subiaco. The note of the wondrous place itself is conventional " wild " Italy raised to the highest intensity, the ideally, the sublimely conventional and wild, complete and supreme in itself, without a disparity or a flaw ; which character of perfect picturesque orthodoxy seemed more particularly to begin for me, I remember, as we passed, on our way, through that indescribable and indestructible Tivoli, where the jumble of the elements of the familiarly and exploitedly, the all too notoriously fair and queer, was more violent and vociferous than ever—so the whole spectacle there seemed at once to rejoice in cockneyfication and to resist it. There at least I had old memories to renew—including that, in especial, from a few years back, of one of the longest, hottest, dustiest return-drives to Rome that the Campagna on a sirocco day was ever to have treated me to.

That was to be more than made up on this later occasion by an hour of early evening, snatched on the run back to Rome, that remains with me as one of those felicities we are wise to leave for ever just as they are, just, that is, where they fell,

never attempting to renew or improve them. So happy a chance
was it that ensured me at the afternoon's end a solitary stroll
through the Villa d'Este, where the day's invasion, whatever it
might have been, had left no traces and where I met nobody in
the great rococo passages and chambers, and in the prodigious
alleys and on the repeated flights of tortuous steps, but the
haunting Genius of Style, into whose noble battered old face, as
if it had come out clearer in the golden twilight and on recognition of response so deeply moved, I seemed to exhale my
sympathy. This was truly, amid a conception and order of
things all mossed over from disuse, but still without a form
abandoned or a principle disowned, one of the hours that one
doesn't forget. The ruined fountains seemed strangely to *wait*,
in the stillness and under cover of the approaching dusk, not
to begin ever again to play, also, but just only to be tenderly
imagined to do so; quite as everything held its breath, at the
mystic moment, for the drop of the cruel and garish exposure,
for the Spirit of the place to steal forth and go his round. The
vistas of the innumerable mighty cypresses ranged themselves,
in their files and companies, like beaten heroes for their
captain's review; the great artificial "works" of every description, cascades, hemicycles, all graded and grassed and stone-
seated as for floral games, mazes and bowers and alcoves and
grottos, brave indissoluble unions of the planted and the
builded symmetry, with the terraces and staircases that overhang and the arcades and cloisters that underspread, made
common cause together as for one's taking up a little, in kindly
lingering wonder, the "feeling" out of which they have sprung.
One didn't see it, under the actual influence, one wouldn't for
the world have seen it, as that they longed to be justified, during
a few minutes in the twenty-four hours, of their absurdity of
pomp and circumstance—but only that they asked for company,
once in a way, as they were so splendidly formed to give it,
and that the best company, in a changed world, at the end of

time, what could they hope it to be but just the lone, the dawdling person of taste, the visitor with a flicker of fancy, not to speak of a pang of pity, to spare for them? It was in the flicker of fancy, no doubt, that as I hung about the great topmost terrace in especial, and then again took my way through the high gaunt corridors and the square and bare alcoved and recessed saloons, all overscored with such a dim waste of those painted, those delicate and capricious decorations which the loggie of the Vatican promptly borrowed from the ruins of the Palatine, or from whatever other revealed and inspiring ancientries, and which make ghostly confession here of that descent, I gave the rein to my sense of the sinister too, of that vague after-taste as of evil things that lurks so often, for a suspicious sensibility, wherever the terrible game of the life of the Renaissance was played as the Italians played it; wherever the huge tesselated chessboard seems to stretch about us, swept bare, almost always violently swept bare, of its chiselled and shifting figures, of every value and degree, but with this echoing desolation itself representing the long gasp, as it were, of overstrained time, the great after-hush that follows on things too wonderful or dreadful.

I am putting here, however, my cart before my horse, for the hour just glanced at was but a final tag to a day of much brighter curiosity, and which seemed to take its baptism, as we passed through prodigious perched and huddled, adorably scattered and animated and even crowded Tivoli, from the universal happy spray of the drumming Anio waterfalls, all set in their permanent rainbows and Sibylline temples and classic allusions and Byronic quotations; a wondrous romantic jumble of such things and quite others—heterogeneous inns and clamorous *guingettes* and factories grabbing at the torrent, to say nothing of innumerable guides and donkeys and white-tied, swallow-tailed waiters dashing out of grottos and from under cataracts, and of the air, on the part of the whole population, of standing about, in the most characteristic *contadino* manner, to pounce on you and take you somewhere, snatch you from somebody else, shout something at you, the aqueous and other uproar permitting, and then charge you for it, your innocence aiding. I'm afraid our run the rest of the way to Subiaco remains with me but as an after-sense of that exhilaration, in spite of our rising admirably higher, all the while, and plunging constantly deeper into splendid solitary gravities, supreme romantic solemnities and sublimities, of landscape. The Benedictine convent, which clings to certain more or less vertiginous ledges and slopes of a vast precipitous gorge, constitutes, with the whole perfection of its setting, the very ideal of the tradition of that *extraordinary in the romantic* handed down to us, as the most attaching and inviting spell of Italy, by all the old academic literature of travel and art of the Salvator Rosas and Claudes. This is the main tribute I may pay in a few words to an impression of which a sort of divine rightness of oddity, a pictorial felicity that was almost not of this world, but of a higher degree of distinction altogether, affected me as the leading note; yet about the whole exquisite complexity of which I can't pretend to be informing.

All the elements of the scene melted for me together; even from the pause for luncheon on a grassy wayside knoll, over heaven knows what admirable preparatory headlong slopes and ravines and iridescent distances, under spreading chestnuts and in the high air that was cool and sweet, to the final pedestrian climb of sinuous mountain-paths that the shining limestone and the strong green of shrub and herbage made as white as silver. There the miraculous home of St. Benedict awaited us in the form of a builded and pictured-over maze of chapels and shrines, cells and corridors, stupefying rock-chambers and caves, places all at an extraordinary variety of different levels and with labyrinthine intercommunications; there the spirit of the centuries sat like some invisible icy presence that only permits you to stare and wonder. I stared, I wondered, I went up and down and in and out and lost myself in the fantastic fable of the innumerable hard facts themselves; and whenever I could, above all, I peeped out of small windows and hung over chance terraces for the love of the general outer picture, the splendid fashion in which the fretted mountains of marble, as they might have been, round about, seemed to inlay themselves, for the effect of the "distinction" I speak of, with vegetations of dark emerald. There above all—or at least in what such aspects did further for the prodigy of the Convent, whatever that prodigy might do for *them*—was, to a life-long victim of Italy, almost verily as never before, the operation of the old love-philtre; there were the inexhaustible sources of interest and charm.

These mystic fountains broke out for me elsewhere, again and again, I rejoice to say—and perhaps more particularly, to be frank about it, where the ground about them was pressed with due emphasis of appeal by the firm wheels of the great winged car. I motored, under invitation and protection, repeatedly back into the sense of the other years, that sense of the "old" and comparatively idle Rome of my particular infatuated prime which I was living to see superseded, and this even when the fond vista bristled with innumerable "signs of the times," unmistakable features of the new era, that, by I scarce know what perverse law, succeeded in ministering to a happy effect. Some of these false notes proceed simply from the immense growth of every sort of facilitation—so that people are much more free than of old to come and go and do, to inquire and explore, to pervade and generally "infest"; with a consequent loss, for the fastidious individual, of his blest earlier sense, not infrequent, of having the occasion and the impression, as he used complacently to say, all to himself. We none of us had anything quite all to ourselves during an afternoon at Ostia, on a beautiful June Sunday; it was a different affair, rather, from the long, the comparatively slow and quite unpeopled drive that I was to remember having last taken early in the autumn thirty years before, and which occupied

the day—with the aid of a hamper from once supreme old
Spillman, the provider for picnics to a vanished world (since I
suspect the antique ideal of "a picnic in the Campagna," the
fondest conception of a happy day, has lost generally much of its
glamour). Our idyllic afternoon, at any rate, left no chord of
sensibility that could possibly have been in question untouched
—not even that of tea on the shore at Fiumincino, after we had
spent an hour among the ruins of Ostia and seen our car ferried
across the Tiber, almost saffron-coloured here and swirling
towards its mouth, on a boat that was little more than a big
rustic raft and that yet bravely resisted the prodigious weight.
What shall I say, in the way of the particular, of the general
felicity before me, for the sweetness of the hour to which the
incident just named, with its strange and amusing juxtapositions
of the patriarchally primitive and the insolently supersubtle, the
earliest and the latest efforts of restless science, were almost
immediately to succeed?

We had but skirted the old gold-and-brown walls of Castel
Fusano, where the massive Chigi tower and the immemorial
stone-pines and the afternoon sky and the desolate sweetness
and concentrated rarity of the picture all kept their appointment,
to fond memory, with that especial form of Roman faith, the
fine æsthetic conscience in things, that is never, never broken.
We had wound through tangled lanes and met handsome sallow
country-folk lounging at leisure, as became the Sunday, and ever
so pleasantly and garishly clothed, if not quite consistently
costumed, as just on purpose to feed our wanton optimism;
and then we had addressed ourselves with a soft superficiality to
the open, the exquisite little Ostian reliquary, an exhibition of
stony vaguenesses half straightened out. The ruins of the ancient
port of Rome, the still recoverable identity of streets and habitations and other forms of civil life, are a not inconsiderable handful, though making of the place at best a very small sister to
Pompeii; but a soft superficiality is ever the refuge of my shy

sense before any ghost of informed reconstitution, and I plead my surrender to it with the less shame that I believe I "enjoy" such scenes even on such futile pretexts as much as it can be appointed them by the invidious spirit of History to *be* enjoyed. It may be said, of course, that enjoyment, question-begging term at best, isn't in these austere connections designated—but rather some principle of appreciation that can at least give a coherent account of itself. On that basis then—as I could, I profess, *but* revel in the looseness of my apprehension, so wide it seemed to fling the gates of vision and divination—I won't pretend to dot, as it were, too many of the i's of my incompetence. I was competent only to have been abjectly interested. On reflection, moreover, I see that no impression of over-much company invaded the picture till the point was exactly reached for its contributing thoroughly to character and amusement; across at Fiumincino, which the age of the bicycle has made, in a small way, the handy Gravesend or Coney Island of Rome, the cafés and *birrerie* were at high pressure, and the bustle all motley and friendly beside the melancholy river, where the waterside life itself had twenty quaint and vivid notes and where a few upstanding objects, ancient or modern, looked eminent and interesting against the delicate Roman sky that dropped down and down to the far-spreading marshes of malaria. Besides which "company" is ever intensely gregarious, hanging heavily together and easily outwitted; so that we had but to proceed a scant distance further and meet the tideless Mediterranean, where it tumbled in a trifle breezily on the sands, to be all to ourselves with our tea-basket, quite as in the good old fashion—only in truth with the advantage that the contemporary tea-basket is so much improved.

I jumble my memories as a tribute to the whole idyll—I give the golden light in which they come back to me for what it is worth; worth, I mean, as allowing that the possibilities of charm of the Witch of the Seven Hills, as we used to call her in

magazines, haven't all been vulgarised away. It was precisely
there, on such an occasion and in such a place, that this might
seem signally to have happened; whereas in fact the mild
suburban riot, in which the so gay but so light potations before
the array of little houses of entertainment were what struck one
as really making most for mildness, was brushed over with a
fabled grace, was harmonious, felicitous, distinguished, quite
after the fashion of some thoroughly trained chorus or phalanx
of opera or ballet. Bicycles were stacked up by the hundred;
the youth of Rome are ardent cyclists, with a great taste for
flashing about in more or less denuded or costumed athletic
and romantic bands and guilds, and on our return cityward,
toward evening, along the right bank of the river, the road
swarmed with the patient wheels and bent backs of these budding
cives Romani quite to the effect of its finer interest. Such at
least, I felt, could only be one's acceptance of almost any feature
of a scene bathed in that extraordinarily august air that the
waning Roman day is so insidiously capable of taking on when
any other element of style happens at all to contribute. Weren't
they present, these other elements, in the great classic lines and
folds, the fine academic or historic attitudes of the darkening
land itself as it hung about the old highway, varying its vague
accidents, but achieving always perfect "composition"? I
shamelessly add that cockneyfied impression, at all events, to
what I have called my jumble; Rome, to which we all swept
on together in the wondrous glowing medium, *saved* everything,
spreading afar her wide wing and applying after all but her
supposed grand gift of the secret of salvation. We kept on
and on into the great dim rather sordidly papal streets that
approach the quarter of St. Peter's; to the accompaniment,
finally, of that markedly felt provocation of fond wonder which
had never failed to lie in wait for me under any question of a
renewed glimpse of the huge unvisited rear of the basilica.
There was no renewed glimpse just then, in the gloaming;

P

but the region I speak of had been for me, in fact, during the previous weeks, less unvisited than ever before, so that I had come to count an occasional walk round and about it as quite of the essence of the convenient small change with which the heterogeneous City may still keep paying you. These frequentations in the company of a sculptor friend had been incidental to our reaching a small artistic foundry of fine metal, an odd and interesting little establishment placed, as who should say in the case of such a mere left-over scrap of a large loose margin, nowhere : it lurked so unsuspectedly, that is, among the various queer things that Rome comprehensively refers to as " behind St. Peter's."

We had passed then, on the occasion of our several pilgrimages, in beneath the great flying, or at least straddling buttresses to the left of the mighty façade, where you enter that great idle precinct of fine dense pavement and averted and sacrificed grandeur, the reverse of the monstrous medal of the front. Here the architectural monster rears its back and shoulders on an equal scale and this whole unregarded world of colossal consistent symmetry and hidden high finish gives you the measure of the vast total treasure of items and features. The outward face of all sorts of inward majesties of utility and ornament here above all correspondingly reproduces itself; the expanses of golden travertine—the freshness of tone, the cleanness of surface, in the sunny air, being extraordinary—climb and soar and spread under the crushing weight of a scheme carried out in every ponderous particular. Never was such a show of *wasted* art, of pomp for pomp's sake, as where all the chapels bulge and all the windows, each one a separate constructional masterpiece, tower above almost grass-grown vacancy ; with the full and immediate effect, of course, of reading us a lesson on the value of lawful pride. The pride is the pride of indifference as to whether a greatness so founded be gaped at in all its features or not. My friend and I were alone to gape at them most often while, for the unfailing impression of them, on our way to watch the casting of our figure, we extended our circuit of the place. To which I may add, as another example of that tentative, that appealing twitch of the garment of Roman association of which one kept renewing one's consciousness, the half-hour at the little foundry itself was all charming—with its quite shabby and belittered and ramshackle recall of the old Roman "art-life" of one's early dreams. Everything was somehow in the picture, the rickety sheds, the loose paraphernalia, the sunny, grassy yard where a goat was browsing; then the queer interior gloom of the pits, frilled with little overlooking scaffoldings and bridges, for the sinking fireward of the image that was to take on hardness; and all the pleasantness and quickness, the beguiling refinement, of the three or four light fine "hands" of whom the staff consisted and into whose type and tone one liked to read, with whatever harmless extravagance, so many signs that a lively sense of stiff processes, even in humble life, could still leave untouched the traditional rare feeling for the artistic. How delightful such an occupation in such a general setting—those of my friend, I at such moments irrepressibly moralised; and how one might after such a fashion endlessly go and come and ask nothing better; or if better, only so to the extent of another impression I was to owe to him : that of an evening meal spread, in the warm still darkness that made no candle flicker, on the wide high space of an old loggia that overhung, in one quarter, the great obelisked Square preceding one of the Gates, and in the other the Tiber and the far Trastevere and more things than I can say—above all, as it were, the whole backward past, the mild confused romance of the Rome one had loved and of which one was exactly taking leave under protection of the friendly lanterned and garlanded feast and the commanding, all-embracing roof-garden. It was indeed a reconciling, it was an altogether penetrating, last hour.

1909.

A CHAIN OF CITIES

ONE day in midwinter, some years since, during a journey from Rome to Florence perforce too rapid to allow much wayside sacrifice to curiosity, I waited for the train at Narni. There was time to stroll far enough from the station to have a look at the famous old bridge of Augustus, broken short off in mid-Tiber. While I stood admiring the measure of impression was made to overflow by the gratuitous grace of a white-cowled monk who came trudging up the -road that wound to the gate of the town. Narni stood, in its own presented felicity, on a hill a good space away, boxed in behind its perfect grey wall, and the monk, to oblige me, crept slowly along and disappeared within the aperture. Everything was distinct in the clear air, and the view exactly as like the bit of background by an Umbrian master as it ideally should have been. The winter is bare and brown enough in southern Italy and the earth reduced to more of a mere anatomy than among ourselves, for whom the very *crânerie* of its exposed state, naked and unashamed, gives it much of the robust serenity, not of a fleshless skeleton, but of a fine nude statue. In these regions, at any rate, the tone of the air, for the eye, during the brief desolation, has often an extraordinary charm : nature still smiles as with the deputed and provisional charity of colour and light, the duty of not ceasing to cheer man's heart. Her whole behaviour, at the time, cast such a spell on the broken bridge, the little walled town and the trudging friar, that I turned away with the impatient vow and the fond vision of how I would take the journey again and pause to my heart's content at Narni, at Spoleto, at Assisi, at Perugia, at Cortona, at Arezzo. But we have generally to clip our vows a little when we come to fulfil them; and so it befell that when my blest springtime arrived I had to begin as resignedly as possible, yet with comparative meagreness, at Assisi.

I suppose enjoyment would have a simple zest which it often lacks if we always did things at the moment we want to, for it's mostly when we can't that we're thoroughly sure we *would*, and we can answer too little for moods in the future conditional. Winter at least seemed to me to have put something into these seats of antiquity that the May sun had more or less melted away—a desirable strength of tone, a depth upon depth of queerness and quaintness. Assisi had been in the January twilight, after my mere snatch at Narni, a vignette out of some brown old missal. But you'll have to be a fearless explorer now to find of a fine spring day any such cluster of curious objects as doesn't seem made to match before anything else Mr. Baedeker's polyglot estimate of its chief recommendations. This great man was at Assisi in force, and a brand-new inn for his accommodation has just been opened cheek by jowl with the church of St. Francis. I don't know that even the dire discomfort of this harbourage makes it seem less impertinent; but I confess I sought its protection, and the great view seemed hardly less beautiful from my window that from the gallery of the convent. This view embraces the whole wide reach of Umbria, which becomes as twilight deepens a purple counterfeit of the misty sea. The visitor's first errand is with the church; and it's fair furthermore to admit that when he has crossed that threshold the position and quality of his hotel cease for the time to be matters of moment. This twofold temple of St. Francis is one of the very sacred places of Italy, and it would be hard to breathe anywhere an air more heavy with holiness. Such seems especially the case if you happen thus to have come from Rome, where everything ecclesiastical is, in aspect, so very much of this world—so florid, so elegant, so full of accommodations and excrescences.   The mere site here makes for authority, and they were brave builders who laid the foundation-stones. The thing rises straight from a steep mountain-side and plunges forward on its great substructure of arches even as a crowned headland may frown over the main.   Before it stretches a long, a grassy piazza, at the end of which you look up a small grey street, to see it first climb a little way the rest of the hill and then pause and leave a broad green slope, crested, high in the air, with a ruined castle.   When I say before it I mean before the upper church ; for by way of doing something supremely handsome and impressive the sturdy architects of the thirteenth century piled temple upon temple and bequeathed a double version of their idea.   One may imagine them to have intended perhaps an architectural image of the relation between heart and head.   Entering the lower church at the bottom of the great flight of steps which leads from the upper door, you seem to push at least into the very heart of Catholicism.

For the first minutes after leaving the clearer gloom you catch nothing but a vista of low black columns closed by the great fantastic cage surrounding the altar, which is thus placed, by your impression, in a sort of gorgeous cavern.   Gradually you distinguish details, become accustomed to the penetrating chill, and even manage to make out a few frescoes ; but the general effect remains splendidly sombre and subterranean.   The vaulted roof is very low and the pillars dwarfish, though immense in girth, as befits pillars supporting substantially a cathedral. The tone of the place is a triumph of mystery, the richest harmony of lurking shadows and dusky corners, all relieved by scattered images and scintillations.   There was little light but what came through the windows of the choir over which the red curtains had been dropped and were beginning to glow with the downward sun.   The choir was guarded by a screen behind which a dozen venerable voices droned vespers; but over the top of the screen came the heavy radiance and played among the ornaments of the high fence round the shrine, casting the shadow of the whole elaborate mass forward into the obscured nave. The darkness of vaults and side-chapels is overwrought with vague frescoes, most of them by Giotto and his school, out of which confused richness the terribly distinct little faces characteristic of these artists stare at you with a solemn formalism. Some are faded and injured, and many so ill-lighted and ill-placed that you can only glance at them with decent conjecture; the great group, however—four paintings by Giotto on the ceiling above the altar—may be examined with some success. Like everything of that grim and beautiful master they deserve examination; but with the effect ever of carrying one's appreciation in and in, as it were, rather than of carrying it out and out, off and off, as happens for us with those artists who have been helped by the process of "evolution" to grow wings. This one, "going in" for emphasis at any price, stamps hard, as who should say, on the very spot of his idea—thanks to which fact he has a concentration that has never been surpassed. He was in other words, in proportion to his means, a genius supremely expressive; he makes the very shade of an intended meaning or a represented attitude so unmistakable that his figures affect us at moments as creatures all too suddenly, too alarmingly, too menacingly met. Meagre, primitive, undeveloped, he yet is immeasurably strong; he even suggests that if he had lived the due span of years later Michael Angelo might have found a rival. Not that he is given, however, to complicated postures or superhuman flights. The something strange that troubles and haunts us in his work spring rather from a kind of fierce familiarity.

It is part of the weaith of the lower church that it contains an admirable primitive fresco by an artist of genius rarely encountered, Pietro Cavallini, pupil of Giotto. This represents the Crucifixion ; the three crosses rising into a sky spotted with the winged heads of angels while a dense crowd presses below. You will nowhere see anything more direfully lugubrious, or more approaching for direct force, though not of course for amplitude of style, Tintoretto's great renderings of the scene in Venice. The abject anguish of the crucified and the straddling authority and brutality of the mounted guards in the foreground are contrasted in a fashion worthy of a great dramatist. But the most poignant touch is the tragic grimaces of the little angelic heads that fall like hailstones through the dark air. It is genuine realistic weeping, the act of irrepressible " crying," that the painter has depicted, and the effect is pitiful at the same time as grotesque. There are many more frescoes besides ; all the chapels on one side are lined with them, but these are chiefly interesting in their general impressiveness—as they people the dim recesses with startling presences, with apparitions out of scale. Before leaving the place I lingered long near the door, for I was sure I shouldn't soon again enjoy such a feast of scenic composition. The opposite end glowed with subdued colour ; the middle portion was vague and thick and brown, with two or three scattered worshippers looming through the obscurity ; while, all the way down, the polished pavement, its uneven slabs glittering dimly in the obstructed light, was of the very essence of expensive picture. It is certainly desirable, if one takes the lower church of Saint Francis to represent the human heart, that one should find a few bright places there. But if the general effect is of brightness terrorised and smothered, is the symbol less valid ? For the contracted, prejudiced, passionate heart let it stand.

One thing at all events we can say, that we should rejoice to boast as capacious, symmetrical and well-ordered a head as the upper sanctuary. Thanks to these merits, in spite of a brave array of Giottesque work which has the advantage of being easily seen, it lacks the great character of its counterpart. The frescoes, which are admirable, represent certain leading events in the life of Saint Francis, and suddenly remind you, by one of those anomalies that are half the secret of the consummate *mise-en-scène* of Catholicism, that the apostle of beggary, the saint whose only tenement in life was the ragged robe which barely covered him, is the hero of this massive structure. Church upon church, nothing less will adequately shroud his consecrated clay. The great reality of Giotto's designs adds to the helpless wonderment with which we feel the passionate pluck of the Hero, the sense of being separated from it by an impassable gulf, the reflection on all that has come and gone to make morality at that vertiginous pitch impossible. There are no such high places of humility left to climb to. An observant friend who has lived long in Italy lately declared to me, however, that she detested the name of this moralist, deeming him chief propagator of the Italian vice most trying to the would-be lover of the people, the want of personal self-respect. There is a solidarity in the use of soap, and every cringing beggar, idler, liar and pilferer flourished for her under the shadow of the great Franciscan indifference to it. She was possibly right; at Rome, at Naples, I might have admitted she was right; but at Assisi, face to face with Giotto's vivid chronicle, we admire too much in its main subject the exquisite play of that subject's genius—we don't remit to him, and this for very envy, a single throb of his consciousness. It took in, that human, that divine embrace, everything *but* soap.

I should find it hard to give an orderly account of my next adventures or impressions at Assisi, which couldn't well be anything more than mere romantic *flânerie*. One may easily plead as the final result of a meditation at the shrine of Saint Francis a great and even an amused charity. This state of mind led me slowly up and down for a couple of hours through the steep little streets, and at last stretched itself on the grass with me in the shadow of the great ruined castle that decorates so grandly the eminence above the town. I remember edging along the sunless side of the small mouldy houses and pausing very often to look at nothing in particular. It was all very hot, very hushed, very resignedly but very persistently old. A wheeled vehicle in such a place is an event, and the *forestiero's* interrogative tread in the blank sonorous lanes has the privilege of bringing the inhabitants to their doorways. Some of the better houses, however, achieve a sombre stillness that protests against the least curiosity as to what may happen in any such century as this. You wonder, as you pass, what lingering old-world social types vegetate there, but you won't find out; albeit that in one very silent little street I had a glimpse of an open door which I have not forgotten. A long-haired peddler who must have been a Jew, and who yet carried without prejudice a burden of mass-books and rosaries, was offering his wares to a stout old priest. The priest had opened the door rather stingily and appeared half-heartedly to dismiss him. But the peddler held up something I couldn't see; the priest wavered with a timorous concession to profane curiosity and then furtively pulled the agent of sophistication, or whatever it might be, into the house. I should have liked to enter with that worthy.

I saw later some gentlemen of Assisi who also seemed bored enough to have found entertainment in his tray. They were at the door of the café on the Piazza, and were so thankful to me for asking them the way to the cathedral that, answering all in chorus, they lighted up with smiles as sympathetic as if I had done them a favour. Of that type were my mild, my delicate adventures. The Piazza has a fine old portico of an ancient Temple of Minerva—six fluted columns and a pediment, of beautiful proportions, but sadly battered and decayed. Goethe, I believe, found it much more interesting than the mighty mediæval church, and Goethe, as a cicerone, doubtless could have persuaded one that it was so; but in the humble society of Murray we shall most of us find a richer sense in the later monument. I found quaint old meanings enough in the dark yellow façade of the small cathedral as I sat on a stone bench by the oblong green stretched before it. This is a pleasing piece of Italian Gothic and, like several of its companions at Assisi, has an elegant wheel window and a number of grotesque little carvings of creatures human and bestial. If with Goethe I were to balance anything against the attractions of the double church I should choose the ruined castle on the hill above the town. I had been having glimpses of it all the afternoon at the end of steep street-vistas, and promising myself half-an-hour beside its grey walls at sunset. The sun was very late setting, and my half-hour became a long lounge in the lee of an abutment which arrested the gentle uproar of the wind. The castle is a splendid piece of ruin, perched on the summit of the mountain to whose slope Assisi clings and dropping a pair of stony arms to enclose the little town in its embrace. The city wall, in other words, straggles up the steep green hill and meets the crumbling skeleton of the fortress. On the side off from the town the mountain plunges into a deep ravine, the opposite face of which is formed by the powerful undraped shoulder of Monte Subasio, a fierce reflector of the sun. Gorge and mountain are wild enough, but their frown expires in the teeming softness of the great vale of Umbria. To lie aloft there on the grass, with silver-grey ramparts at one's back and the warm rushing wind in one's ears, and watch the beautiful plain mellow into the tones of twilight, was as exquisite a form of repose as ever fell to a tired tourist's lot.

Perugia too has an ancient stronghold, which one must speak of in earnest as that unconscious humourist the classic American traveller is supposed invariably to speak of the Colosseum : it will be a very handsome building when it's finished. Even Perugia is going the way of all Italy—straightening out her streets, preparing her ruins, laying her venerable ghosts. The castle is being completely *remis à neuf*—a Massachusetts schoolhouse couldn't cultivate a "smarter" ideal. There are shops in the basement and fresh putty on all the windows ; so that the only thing proper to a castle it has kept is its magnificent position and range, which you may enjoy from the broad platform where the Perugini assemble at eventide. Perugia is chiefly known to fame as the city of Raphael's master ; but it has a still higher claim to renown and ought to figure in the gazetteer of fond memory as the little City of the infinite View. The small dusky, crooked place tries by a hundred prompt pretensions, immediate contortions, rich mantling flushes and other ingenuities, to waylay your attention and keep it at home ; but your consciousness, alert and uneasy from the first moment, is all abroad even when your back is turned to the vast alternative or when fifty house-walls conceal it, and you are forever rushing up by-streets and peeping round corners in the hope of another glimpse or reach of it. As it stretches away before you in that eminent indifference to limits which is at the same time at every step an eminent homage to style, it is altogether too free and fair for compasses and terms. You can only say, and rest upon it, that you prefer it to any other visible fruit of position or claimed empire of the eye that you are anywhere likely to enjoy.

For it is such a wondrous mixture of blooming plain and gleaming river and wavily-multitudinous mountain vaguely dotted with pale grey cities, that, placed as you are, roughly speaking, in the centre of Italy, you all but span the divine peninsula from sea to sea. Up the long vista of the Tiber you look—almost to Rome ; past Assisi, Spello, Foligno, Spoleto, all perched on their respective heights and shining through the violet haze. To the north, to the east, to the west, you see a hundred variations of the prospect, of which I have kept no record. Two notes only I have made : one—though who hasn't made it over and over again ?—on the exquisite elegance of mountain forms in this endless play of the excrescence, it being exactly as if there were variation of sex in the upheaved mass, with the effect here mainly of contour and curve and complexion determined in the feminine sense. It further came home to me that the command of such an outlook on the world goes far, surely, to give authority and centrality and experience, those of the great seats of dominion, even to so scant a cluster of attesting objects as here. It must deepen the civic consciousness and take off the edge of ennui. It performs this kindly office, at any rate, for the traveller who may overstay his curiosity as to Perugino and the Etruscan relics. It continually solicits his wonder and praise—it reinforces the historic page. I spent a week in the place, and when it was gone I had had enough of Perugino, but hadn't had enough of the View.

I should perhaps do the reader a service by telling him just how a week at Perugia may be spent. His first care must be to ignore the very dream of haste, walking everywhere very slowly and very much at random, and to impute an esoteric sense to almost anything his eye may happen to encounter. Almost everything in fact lends itself to the historic, the romantic, the æsthetic fallacy—almost everything has an antique queerness and richness that ekes out the reduced state ; that of a grim and battered old adventuress, the heroine of many shames and scandals, surviving to an extraordinary age and a considerable penury, but with ancient gifts of princes and other forms of the wages of sin to show, and the most beautiful garden of all the world to sit and doze and count her beads in and remember. He must hang a great deal about the huge Palazzo Pubblico, which indeed is very well worth any acquaintance you may scrape with it. It masses itself gloomily above the narrow street to an immense elevation, and leads up the eye along a cliff-like surface of rugged wall, mottled with old scars and new repairs, to the loggia dizzily perched on its cornice. He must repeat his visit to the Etruscan Gate, by whose immemorial composition he must indeed linger long to resolve it back into the elements originally attending it.   He must uncap to the irrecoverable, the inimitable style of the statue of Pope Julius III. before the cathedral, remembering that Hawthorne fabled his Miriam, in an air of romance from which we are well-nigh as far to-day as from the building of Etruscan gates, to have given rendezvous to Kenyon at its base.   Its material is a vivid green bronze, and the mantle and tiara are covered with a delicate embroidery worthy of a silversmith.

Then our leisurely friend must bestow on Perugino's frescoes in the Exchange, and on his pictures in the University, all the placid contemplation they deserve.   He must go to the theatre every evening, in an orchestra-chair at twenty-two soldi, and enjoy the curious didacticism of Amore senza Stima, Severità e Debolezza, La Società Equivoca, and other popular specimens of contemporaneous Italian comedy—unless indeed the last-named be not the edifying title applied, for peninsular use, to " Le Demi-Monde " of the younger Dumas.   I shall be very much surprised if, at the end of a week of this varied entertainment, he hasn't learnt how to live, not exactly in, but with, Perugia.   His strolls will abound in small accidents and mercies of vision, but of which a dozen pencil-strokes would be a better memento than this poor word-sketching.   From the hill on which the town is planted radiate a dozen ravines, down whose sides the houses slide and scramble with an alarming indifference to the cohesion of their little rugged blocks of flinty red stone. You ramble really nowhither without emerging on some small court or terrace that throws your view across a gulf of tangled gardens or vineyards and over to a cluster of serried black dwellings which have to hollow in their backs to keep their balance on the opposite ledge.   On archways and street-staircases and dark alleys that bore through a density of massive basements, and curve and climb and plunge as they go, all to the truest mediæval tune, you may feast your fill.   These are the local, the architectural, the compositional commonplaces.   Some of the little streets in out-of-the-way corners are so rugged and brown and silent that you may imagine them passages long since hewn by the pick-axe in a deserted stone-quarry. The battered black houses, of the colour of buried things—things buried, that is, in accumulations of time, closer packed, even as such are, than spadefuls of earth—resemble exposed sections of natural rock; none the less so when, beyond some narrow gap, you catch the blue and silver of the sublime circle of landscape.

But I oughtn't to talk of mouldy alleys, or yet of azure distances, as if they formed the main appeal to taste in this accomplished little city. In the Sala del Cambio, where in ancient days the money-changers rattled their embossed coin and figured up their profits, you may enjoy one of the serenest æsthetic pleasures that the golden age of art anywhere offers us. Bank parlours, I believe, are always handsomely appointed, but are even those of Messrs. Rothschild such models of mural bravery as this little counting-house of a bygone fashion? The bravery is Perugino's own; for, invited clearly to do his best, he left it as a lesson to the ages, covering the four low walls and the vault with scriptural and mythological figures of extraordinary beauty. They are ranged in artless attitudes round the upper half of the room—the sybils, the prophets, the philosophers, the Greek and Roman heroes—looking down with broad serene faces, with small mild eyes and sweet mouths that commit them to nothing in particular unless to being comfortably and charmingly alive, at the incongruous proceedings of a Board of Brokers. Had finance a very high tone in those days, or were genius and faith then simply as frequent as capital and enterprise are among ourselves? The great distinction of the Sala del Cambio is that it has a friendly Yes for both these questions. There was a rigid transactional probity, it seems to say; there was also a high tide of inspiration. About the artist himself many things come up for us—more than I can attempt in their order; for he was not, I think, to an attentive observer, the mere smooth and entire and devout spirit we at first are inclined to take him for. He has that about him which leads us to wonder if he may not, after all, play a proper part enough here as the patron of the money-changers. He is the delight of a million of young ladies; but who knows whether we shouldn't find in his works, might we "go into" them a little, a trifle more of manner than of conviction and of system than of deep sincerity?

This, I allow, would put no great affront on them, and one speculates thus partly but because it's a pleasure to hang about him on any pretext, and partly because his immediate effect is to make us quite inordinately embrace the pretext of his lovely soul. His portrait, painted on the wall of the Sala (you may see it also in Rome and Florence) might at any rate serve for the likeness of Mr. Worldly-Wiseman in Bunyan's allegory. He was fond of his glass, I believe, and he made his art lucrative. This tradition is not refuted by his preserved face, and after some experience—or rather after a good deal, since you can't have a *little* of Perugino, who abounds wherever old masters congregate, so that one has constantly the sense of being "in" for all there is—you may find an echo of it in the uniform type of his creatures, their monotonous grace, their prodigious invariability. He may very well have wanted to produce figures of a substantial, yet at the same time of an impeccable innocence; but we feel that he had taught himself *how* even beyond his own belief in them, and had arrived at a process that acted at last mechanically. I confess at the same time that, so interpreted, the painter affects me as hardly less interesting, and one can't but become conscious of one's style when one's style has become, as it were, so conscious of one's, or at least of its own, fortune. If he was the inventor of a remarkably calculable *facture*, a calculation that never fails is in its way a grace of the first order, and there are things in this special appearance of perfection of practice that make him the forerunner of a mighty and more modern race. More than any of the early painters who strongly charm, you may take all his measure from a single specimen. The other samples infallibly match, reproduce unerringly the one type he had mastered, but which had the good fortune to be adorably fair, to seem to have dawned on a vision unsullied by the shadows of earth. Which truth, moreover, leaves Perugino all delightful as composer and draughtsman; he has in each of these characters a sort of spacious neatness which suggests that the whole conception has been washed clean by some spiritual chemistry the last thing before reaching the canvas; after which it has been applied to that surface with a rare economy of time and means. Giotto and Fra Angelico, beside him, are full of interesting waste and irrelevant passion. In the sacristy of the charming church of San Pietro—a museum of pictures and carvings—is a row of small heads of saints formerly covering the frame of the artist's Ascension, carried off by the French. It is almost miniature work, and here at least Perugino triumphs in sincerity, in apparent candour, as well as in touch. Two of the holy men are reading their breviaries, but with an air of infantine innocence quite consistent with their holding the book upside down.

Between Perugia and Cortona lies the large weedy water of Lake Thrasymene, turned into a witching word forever by Hannibal's recorded victory over Rome. Dim as such records have become to us and remote such realities, he is yet a passionless pilgrim who doesn't, as he passes, of a heavy summer's day, feel the air and the light and the very faintness of the breeze all charged and haunted with them, all interfused as with the wasted ache of experience and with the vague historic haze. Processions of indistinguishable ghosts bore me company to Cortona itself, most sturdily ancient of Italian towns. It must have been a seat of ancient knowledge even when Hannibal and Flaminius came to the shock of battle, and have looked down afar from its

grey ramparts on the contending swarm with something of the
philosophic composure suitable to a survivor of Pelasgic and
Etruscan revolutions.   These grey ramparts are in great part still
visible, and form the chief attraction of Cortona.   It is perched
on the very pinnacle of a mountain, and I wound and doubled
interminably over the face of the great hill, while the jumbled
roofs and towers of the arrogant little city still seemed nearer to
the sky than to the railway-station.   "Rather rough," Murray
pronounces the local inn ; and rough indeed it was ; there was
scarce a square foot of it that you would have cared to stroke
with your hand.   The landlord himself, however, was all
smoothness and the best fellow in the world ; he took me up
into a rickety old loggia on the tip-top of his establishment and
played showman as to half the kingdoms of the earth.   I was
free to decide at the same time whether my loss or my gain was
the greater for my seeing Cortona through the medium of a
festa.   On the one hand the museum was closed (and in a certain
sense the smaller and obscurer the town the more I like the
museum) ; the churches—an interesting note of manners and
morals—were impenetrably crowded, though, for that matter, so
was the café, where I found neither an empty stool nor the edge
of a table.   I missed a sight of the famous painted Muse, the
art-treasure of Cortona and supposedly the most precious, as it
falls little short of being the only, sample of the Greek painted
picture that has come down to us.   On the other hand, I saw—
but this is what I saw.

A part of the mountain-top is occupied by the church of
St. Margaret, and this was St. Margaret's day.   The houses
pause roundabout it and leave a grassy slope, planted here and
there with lean black cypresses.   The contadini from near and
far had congregated in force and were crowding into the church
or winding up the slope.   When I arrived they were all kneeling
or uncovered ; a bedizened procession, with banners and censers,
bearing abroad, I believe, the relics of the saint, was re-entering

the church. The scene made one of those pictures that Italy still brushes in for you with an incomparable hand and from an inexhaustible palette when you find her in the mood. The day was superb—the sky blazed overhead like a vault of deepest sapphire. The grave brown peasantry, with no great accent of costume, but with sundry small ones—decked, that is, in cheap fineries of scarlet and yellow—made a mass of motley colour in the high wind-stirred light. The procession halted in the pious hush, and the lovely land around and beneath us melted away, almost to either sea, in tones of azure scarcely less intense than the sky. Behind the church was an empty crumbling citadel, with half-a-dozen old women keeping the gate for coppers. Here were views and breezes and sun and shade and grassy corners to the heart's content, together with one couldn't say what huge seated mystic melancholy presence, the after-taste of everything the still open maw of time had consumed. I chose a spot that fairly combined all these advantages, a spot from which I seemed to look, as who should say, straight down the throat of the monster, no dark passage now, but with all the glorious day playing into it, and spent a good part of my stay at Cortona lying there at my length and observing the situation over the top of a volume that I must have brought in my pocket just for that especial wanton luxury of the resource provided and slighted. In the afternoon I came down and hustled awhile through the crowded little streets, and then strolled forth under the scorching sun and made the outer circuit of the wall. There I found tremendous uncemented blocks; they glared and twinkled in the powerful light, and I had to put on a blue eye-glass in order to throw into its proper perspective the vague Etruscan past, obtruded and magnified in such masses quite as with the effect of inadequately-withdrawn hands and feet in photographs.

I spent the next day at Arezzo, but I confess in very much the same uninvestigating fashion—taking in the "general impression," I dare say, at every pore, but rather systematically leaving the dust of the ages unfingered on the stored records : I should doubtless, in the poor time at my command, have fingered it to so little purpose. The seeker for the story of things has moreover, if he be worth his salt, a hundred insidious arts ; and in that case indeed—by which I mean when his sensibility has come duly to adjust itself—the story assaults him but from too many sides. He even feels at moments that he must sneak along on tiptoe in order not to have too much of it. Besides which the case all depends on the kind of use, the range of application, his tangled consciousness, or his intelligible genius, say, may come to recognize for it. At Arezzo, however this might be, one was far from Rome, one was well within genial Tuscany, and the historic, the romantic decoction seemed to reach one's lips in less stiff doses. There at once was the "general impression"—the exquisite sense of the scarce expressible Tuscan quality, which makes immediately, for the whole pitch of one's perception, a grateful, a not at all strenuous difference, attaches to almost any coherent group of objects, to any happy aspect of the scene, for a main note, some mild recall, through pleasant friendly colour, through settled ample form, through something homely and economic too at the very heart of "style," of an identity of temperament and habit with those of the divine little Florence that one originally knew. Adorable Italy in which, for the constant renewal of interest, of attention, of affection, these refinements of variety, these so harmoniously-grouped and individually-seasoned fruits of the great garden of history, keep presenting themselves ! It seemed to fall in with the cheerful Tuscan mildness for instance—sticking as I do to that ineffectual expression of the Tuscan charm, of the yellow-brown Tuscan dignity at large—that the ruined castle on the hill (with which agreeable feature Arezzo is no less furnished than Assisi and Cortona) had been converted into a great blooming, and I hope all profitable, podere or market-garden. I lounged away the half hours there under a spell as potent as the "wildest" forecast of propriety—propriety to all the particular conditions—could have figured it. I had seen Santa Maria della Pieve and its campanile of quaint colonnades, the stately, dusky cathedral—grass-plotted and residenced about almost after the fashion of an English "close"—and John of Pisa's elaborate marble shrine; I had seen the museum and its Etruscan vases and majolica platters. These were very well, but the old pacified citadel somehow, through a day of soft saturation, placed me most in relation. Beautiful hills surrounded it, cypresses cast straight shadows at its corners, while in the middle grew a wondrous Italian tangle of wheat and corn, vines and figs, peaches and cabbages, memories and images, anything and everything.

1873.

SIENA EARLY AND LATE

I

FLORENCE being oppressively hot and delivered over to the mosquitoes, the occasion seemed to favour that visit to Siena which I had more than once planned and missed. I arrived late in the evening, by the light of a magnificent moon, and while a couple of benignantly-mumbling old crones were making up my bed at the inn strolled forth in quest of a first impression. Five minutes brought me to where I might gather it unhindered as it bloomed in the white moonshine. The great Piazza of Siena is famous, and though in this day of multiplied photographs and blunted surprises and profaned revelations none of the world's wonders can pretend, like Wordsworth's phantom of delight, really to "startle and waylay," yet as I stepped upon the waiting scene from under a dark archway I was conscious of no loss of the edge of a precious presented sensibility. The waiting scene, as I have called it, was in the shape of a shallow horse-shoe—as the untravelled reader who has turned over his travelled friends' portfolios will respectfully remember ; or, better, of a bow in which the high wide face of the Palazzo Pubblico forms the cord and everything else the arc. It was void of any human presence that could figure to me the current year ; so that, the moonshine assisting, I had half-an-hour's infinite vision of mediæval Italy. The Piazza being built on the side of a hill—or rather, as I believe science affirms, in the cup of a volcanic crater—the vast pavement converges downwards in slanting radiations of stone, the spokes of a great wheel, to a point directly before the Palazzo, which may mark the hub, though it is nothing more ornamental than the mouth of a drain. The great monument stands on the lower side and might seem, in spite of its goodly mass and its embattled cornice, to be rather defiantly out-countenanced by vast private constructions occupying the opposite eminence. This *might* be, without the extraordinary dignity of the architectural gesture with which the huge high-shouldered pile asserts itself.

On the firm edge of the palace, from bracketed base to grey-capped summit against the sky, there grows a tall slim tower which soars and soars till it has given notice of the city's greatness over the blue mountains that mark the horizon. It rises as slender and straight as a pennoned lance planted on the steel-shod toe of a mounted knight, and keeps all to itself in the blue air, far above the changing fashions of the market, the proud consciousness or rare arrogance once built into it. This beautiful tower, the finest thing in Siena and, in its rigid fashion, as permanently fine thus as a really handsome nose on a face of no matter what accumulated age, figures there still as a Declaration of Independence beside which such an affair as ours, thrown off at Philadelphia, appears to have scarce done more than helplessly give way to time. Our Independence has become a dependence on a thousand such dreadful things as the incorrupt declaration of Siena strikes us as looking for ever straight over the level of. As it stood silvered by the moonlight, while my greeting lasted, it seemed to speak, all as from soul to soul, very much indeed as some ancient worthy of a lower order, buttonholing one on the coveted chance and at the quiet hour, might have done, of a state of things long and vulgarly superseded, but to the pride and power, the once prodigious vitality, of which who could expect any one effect to testify more incomparably, more indestructibly, quite, as it were, more immortally? The gigantic houses enclosing the rest of the Piazza took up the tale and mingled with it their burden. "We are very old and a trifle weary, but we were built strong and piled high, and we shall last for many an age. The present is cold and heedless, but we keep ourselves in heart by brooding over our store of memories and traditions. We are haunted houses in every creaking timber and aching stone." Such were the gossiping connections I established with Siena before I went to bed.

Since that night I have had a week's daylight knowledge of the surface of the subject at least, and don't know how I can better present it than simply as another and a vivider page of the lesson that the ever-hungry artist has only to *trust* old Italy for her to feed him at every single step from her hand—and if not with one sort of sweetly-stale grain from that wondrous mill of history which during so many ages ground finer than any other on earth, why then always with something else. Siena has at any rate "preserved appearances"—kept the greatest number of them, that is, unaltered for the eye—about as consistently as one can imagine the thing done. Other places perhaps may treat you to as drowsy an odour of antiquity, but few exhale it from so large an area. Lying massed within her walls on a dozen clustered hilltops, she shows you at every turn in how much greater a way she once lived; and if so much of the grand manner is extinct the receptacle of the ashes still solidly rounds itself. This heavy general stress of all her emphasis on the past is what she constantly keeps in your eyes and your ears, and if you be but a casual observer and admirer the generalised response is mainly what you give her. The casual observer, however beguiled, is mostly not very learned, not over-equipped in advance with data; he hasn't specialised, his notions are necessarily vague, the chords of his imagination, for all his good-will, are inevitably muffled and weak. But such as it is, his received, his welcome impression serves his turn so far as the life of sensibility goes, and reminds him from time to time

that even the lore of German doctors is but the shadow of
satisfied curiosity. I have been living at the inn, walking about
the streets, sitting in the Piazza; these are the simple terms of
my experience. But streets and inns in Italy are the vehicles
of half one's knowledge; if one has no fancy for their lessons
one may burn one's note-book. In Siena everything is Sienese.
The inn has an English sign over the door—a little battered
plate with a rusty representation of the lion and the unicorn;
but advance hopefully into the mouldy stone alley which serves
as vestibule and you will find local colour enough. The landlord, I was told, had been servant in an English family, and I
was curious to see how he met the probable argument of the
casual Anglo-Saxon after the latter's first twelve hours in his
establishment. As he failed to appear I asked the waiter if he
weren't at home. "Oh," said the latter, "he's a *piccolo grasso
vecchiotto* who doesn't like to move." I'm afraid this little fat
old man has simply a bad conscience. It's no small burden for
one who likes the Italians—as who doesn't, under this restric-
tion?—to have so much indifference even to rudimentary
purifying processes to dispose of. What is the real philosophy
of dirty habits, and are foul surfaces merely superficial? If
unclean manners have in truth the moral meaning which I
suspect in them we must love Italy better than consistency.
This a number of us are prepared to do, but while we are
making the sacrifice it is as well we should be aware.

We may plead moreover for these impecunious heirs of the
past that even if it were easy to be clean in the midst of their
mouldering heritage it would be difficult to appear so. At the
risk of seeming to flaunt the silly superstition of restless renovation for the sake of renovation, which is but the challenge of the
infinitely precious principle of duration, one is still moved to say
that the prime result of one's contemplative strolls in the dusky
alleys of such a place is an ineffable sense of disrepair. Everything is cracking, peeling, fading, crumbling, rotting. No young

Sienese eyes rest upon anything youthful; they open into a world battered and befouled with long use. Everything has passed its meridian except the brilliant façade of the cathedral, which is being diligently retouched and restored, and a few private palaces whose broad fronts seem to have been lately furbished and polished. Siena was long ago mellowed to the pictorial tone; the operation of time is·now to deposit shabbiness upon shabbiness. But it's for the most part a patient, sturdy, sympathetic shabbiness, which soothes rather than irritates the nerves, and has in many cases doubtless as long a career to run as most of our pert and shallow freshnesses. It projects at all events a deeper shadow into the constant twilight of the narrow streets—that vague historic dusk, as I may call it, in which one walks and wonders. These streets are hardly more than sinuous flagged alleys, into which the huge black houses, between their almost meeting cornices, suffer a meagre light to filter down over rough-hewn stone, past windows often of graceful Gothic form, and great pendent iron rings and twisted sockets for torches. Scattered over their many-headed hill, they suffer the roadway often to incline to the perpendicular, becoming so impracticable for vehicles that the sound of wheels is only a trifle less anomalous than it would be in Venice. But all day long there comes up to my window an incessant shuffling of feet and clangour of voices. The weather is very warm for the season, all the world is out of doors, and the Tuscan tongue (which in Siena is reputed to have a classic purity) wags in every imaginable key. It doesn't rest even at night, and I am often an uninvited guest at concerts and *conversazioni* at two o'clock in the morning. The concerts are sometimes charming. I not only don't curse my wakefulness, but go to my window to listen. Three men come carolling by, trolling and quavering with voices of delightful sweetness, or a lonely troubadour in his shirt-sleeves draws such artful lovenotes from his clear, fresh tenor, that I seem for the moment to be behind the scenes at the opera, watching some Rubini or Mario go " on " and waiting for the round of applause. In the intervals a couple of friends or enemies stop—Italians always make their points in conversation by pulling up, letting you walk on a few paces, to turn and find them standing with finger on nose and engaging your interrogative eye—they pause, by a happy instinct, directly under my window, and dispute their point or tell their story or make their confidence. One scarce is sure which it may be ; everything has such an explosive promptness, such a redundancy of inflection and action. But everything for that matter takes on such dramatic life as *our* lame colloquies never know—so that almost any uttered communications here become an acted play, improvised, mimicked, proportioned and rounded, carried bravely to its *dénoûment*. The speaker seems actually to establish his stage and face his foot-lights, to create by a gesture a little scenic circumscription about him ; he rushes to and fro and shouts and stamps and postures, he ranges through every phase of his inspiration. I noted the other evening a striking instance of the spontaneity of the Italian gesture, in the person of a small Sienese of I hardly know what exact age—the age of inarticulate sounds and the experimental use of a spoon. It was a Sunday evening, and this little man had accompanied his parents to the café. The Caffè Greco at Siena is a most delightful institution ; you get a capital *demi-tasse* for three sous, and an excellent ice for eight, and while you consume these easy luxuries you may buy from a little hunchback the local weekly periodical, the *Vita Nuova*, for three centimes (the two centimes left from your sou, if you are under the spell of this magical frugality, will do to give the waiter). My young friend was sitting on his father's knee and helping himself to the half of a strawberry-ice with which his mamma had presented him. He had so many misadventures with his spoon that this lady at length confiscated it, there being nothing left of the ice but a little crimson liquid which he might dispose of by the common instinct of childhood. But he was no friend, it appeared, to such freedoms ; he was a perfect little gentleman and he resented its being expected of him that he should drink down his remnant. He protested therefore, and it was the manner of his protest that struck me. He didn't cry audibly, though he made a very wry face. It was no stupid squall, and yet he was too young to speak. It was a penetrating concord of inarticulately pleading, accusing sounds, accompanied by gestures of the most exquisite propriety. These were perfectly mature ; he did everything that a man of forty would have done if he had been pouring out a flood of sonorous eloquence. He shrugged his shoulders and wrinkled his eyebrows, tossed out his hands and folded his arms, obtruded his chin and bobbed about his head—and at last, I am happy to say, recovered his spoon. If I had had a solid little silver one I would have presented it to him as a testimonial to a perfect, though as yet unconscious, artist.

My actual tribute to him, however, has diverted me from what I had in mind — a much weightier matter — the great private palaces which are the massive majestic syllables, sentences, periods, of the strange message the place addresses to us. They are extraordinarily spacious and numerous, and one wonders what part they can play in the meagre economy of the actual city. The Siena of to-day is a mere shrunken semblance of the rabid little republic which in the thirteenth century waged triumphant war with Florence, cultivated the arts with splendour, planned a cathedral (though it had ultimately to curtail the design) of proportions almost unequalled, and contained a population of two hundred thousand souls. Many of these dusky piles still bear the names of the old mediæval magnates the vague mild occupancy of whose descendants has the effect of armour of proof worn over " pot " hats and tweed jackets and trousers. Half-a-dozen of them are as high as the Strozzi and Riccardi palaces in Florence ; they couldn't well be higher. The very essence of the romantic and the scenic is in the way these colossal dwellings are packed together in their steep streets, in the depths of their little enclosed, agglomerated city. When we, in our day and country, raise a structure of half the mass and dignity, we leave a great space about it in the manner of a pause after a showy speech. But when a Sienese countess, as things are here, is doing her hair near the window, she is a wonderfully near neighbour to the cavalier opposite, who is being shaved by his valet. Possibly the countess doesn't object to a certain chosen publicity at her toilet; what does an Italian gentleman assure me but that the aristocracy make very free with each other? Some of the palaces are shown, but only when the occupants are at home, and now they are in *villeggiatura*. Their villeggiatura lasts eight months of the year, the waiter at the inn informs me, and they spend little more than the carnival in the city. The gossip of an inn-waiter ought perhaps to be beneath the dignity of even such thin history as this; but I confess that when, as a story-seeker always and ever, I have come in from my strolls with an irritated sense of the dumbness of stones and mortar, it has been to listen with avidity, over my dinner, to the proffered confidences of the worthy man who stands by with a napkin. His talk is really very fine, and he prides himself greatly on his cultivated tone, to which he calls my attention. He has very little good to say about the Sienese nobility. They are " proprio d'origine egoista "—whatever that may be—and there are many who can't write their names. This may be calumny; but I doubt whether the most blameless of them all could have spoken more delicately of a lady of peculiar personal appearance who had been dining near me. "She's too fat," I grossly said on her leaving the room. The waiter shook his head with a little sniff: " È troppo materiale." This lady and her companion were the party whom, thinking I might relish a little company—I had been dining alone for a week—he glee-fully announced to me as newly arrived Americans. They were

Americans, I found, who wore, pinned to their heads in permanence, the black lace veil or mantilla, conveyed their beans to their mouth with a knife, and spoke a strange raucous Spanish. They were in fine compatriots from Montevideo. The genius of old Siena, however, would make little of any stress of such distinctions; one representative of a far-off social platitude being about as much in order as another as he stands before the great loggia of the Casino di Nobili, the club of the best society. The nobility, which is very numerous and very rich, is still, says the apparently competent native I began by quoting, perfectly feudal and uplifted and separate. Morally and intellectually, behind the walls of its palaces, the fourteenth century, it's thrilling to think, hasn't ceased to hang on. There is no bourgeoisie to speak of; immediately after the aristocracy come the poor people, who are very poor indeed. My friend's account of these matters made me wish more than ever, as a lover of the preserved social specimen, of type at almost any price, that one weren't, a helpless victim of the historic sense, reduced simply to staring at black stones and peeping up stately staircases; and that when one had examined the street-face of the palace, Murray in hand, one might walk up to the great drawing-room, make one's bow to the master and mistress, the old abbé and the young count, and invite them to favour one with a sketch of their social philosophy or a few first-hand family anecdotes.

The dusky labyrinth of the streets, we must in default of such initiations content ourselves with noting, is interrupted by two great candid spaces: the fan-shaped piazza, of which I just now said a word, and the smaller square in which the cathedral erects its walls of many-coloured marble. Of course since paying the great piazza my compliments by moonlight I have strolled through it often at sunnier and shadier hours. The market is held there, and wherever Italians buy and sell, wherever they count and chaffer —as indeed you hear them do right and left, at almost any moment, as you take your way among them—the pulse of life beats fast. It has been doing so on the spot just named, I suppose, for the last five hundred years, and during that time the cost of eggs and earthen pots has been gradually but inexorably increasing. The buyers 'nevertheless wrestle over their purchases as lustily as so many fourteenth-century burghers suddenly waking up in horror to current prices. You have but to walk aside, however, into the Palazzo Pubblico really to feel yourself a thrifty old mediævalist. The state affairs of the Republic were formerly transacted here, but it now gives shelter to modern law-courts and other prosy business. I was marched through a number of vaulted halls and chambers, which, in the intervals of the administrative sessions held in them, are peopled only by the great mouldering archaic frescoes—anything but inanimate these even in their present ruin—that cover the walls and ceiling. The chief painters of the Sienese school lent a hand in producing the works I name, and you may complete there the connoisseurship in which, possibly, you will have embarked at the Academy. I say " possibly " to be very judicial, my own observation having led me no great length. I have rather than otherwise cherished the thought that the Sienese school suffers one's eagerness peacefully to slumber—benignantly abstains in fact from whipping up a languid curiosity and a tepid faith. " A formidable rival to the Florentine," says some book—I forget which—into which I recently glanced. Not a bit of it thereupon boldly say I ; the Florentines may rest on their laurels and the lounger on his lounge. The early painters of the two groups have indeed much in common ; but the Florentines had the good fortune to see their efforts gathered up and applied by a few pre-eminent spirits, such as never came to the rescue of the groping Sienese. Fra Angelico and Ghirlandaio said all their feebler *confrères* dreamt of and a great deal more beside, but the inspiration of Simone Memmi and Ambrogio Lorenzetti and Sano di Pietro has a painful air of never efflorescing into a maximum.

Sodoma and Beccafumi are to my taste a rather abortive maximum. But one should speak of them all gently—and I do, from my soul; for their labour, by their lights, has wrought a precious heritage of still-living colour and rich figure-peopled shadow for the echoing chambers of their old civic fortress. The faded frescoes cover the walls like quaintly-storied tapestries; in one way or another they cast their spell. If one owes a large debt of pleasure to pictorial art one comes to think tenderly and easily of its whole evolution, as of the conscious experience of a single mysterious, striving spirit, and one shrinks from saying rude things about any particular phase of it, just as one would from referring without precautions to some error or lapse in the life of a person one esteemed. You don't care to remind a grizzled veteran of his defeats, and why should we linger in Siena to talk about Beccafumi? I by no means go so far as to say, with an amateur with whom I have just been discussing the matter, that "Sodoma is a precious poor painter and Beccafumi no painter at all"; but, opportunity being limited, I am willing to let the remark about Beccafumi pass for true. With regard to Sodoma, I remember seeing four years ago in the choir of the Cathedral of Pisa a certain small dusky specimen of the painter—an Abraham and Isaac, if I am not mistaken—which was charged with a gloomy grace. One rarely meets him in general collections, and I had never done so till the other day. He was not prolific, apparently; he had however his own elegance, and his rarity is a part of it.

Here in Siena are a couple of dozen scattered frescoes and three or four canvases; his masterpiece, among others, an harmonious Descent from the Cross. I wouldn't give a fig for the equilibrium of the figures or the ladders; but while it lasts the scene is all intensely solemn and graceful and sweet—too sweet for so bitter a subject. Sodoma's women are strangely sweet; an imaginative sense of morbid appealing attitude—as notably in the sentimental, the pathetic, but the none the less pleasant, "Swooning of Saint Catherine," the great Sienese heroine, at San Domenico—seems to me the author's finest accomplishment. His frescoes have all the same almost appealing evasion of difficulty, and a kind of mild melancholy which I am inclined to think the sincerest part of them, for it strikes me as practically the artist's depressed suspicion of his own want of force. Once he determined, however, that if he couldn't be strong he would make capital of his weakness, and painted the Christ bound to the Column, of the Academy. Here he got much nearer and I have no doubt mixed his colours with his tears; but the result can't be better described than by saying that it is, pictorially, the first of the modern Christs. Unfortunately it hasn't been the last.

The main strength of Sienese art went possibly into the erection of the Cathedral, and yet even here the strength is not of the greatest strain. If, however, there are more interesting temples in Italy, there are few more richly and variously scenic and splendid, the comparative meagreness of the architectural idea being overlaid by a marvellous wealth of ingenious detail. Opposite the church—with the dull old archbishop's palace on one side and a dismantled residence of the late Grand Duke of Tuscany on the other—is an ancient hospital with a big stone bench running all along its front. Here I have sat awhile every morning for a week, like a philosophic convalescent, watching the florid façade of the cathedral glitter against the deep blue sky. It has been lavishly restored of late years, and the fresh white marble of the densely clustered pinnacles and statues and beasts and flowers flashes in the sunshine like a mosaic of jewels. There is more of this goldsmith's work in stone than I can remember or describe; it is piled up over three great doors with immense margins of exquisite decorative sculpture—still in the ancient cream-coloured marble—and beneath three sharp pediments embossed with images relieved against red marble and tipped with golden mosaics. It is in the highest degree fantastic

and luxuriant—it is on the whole very lovely. As a triumph of
the many-hued it prepares you for the interior, where the same
parti-coloured splendour is endlessly at play—a confident complication of harmonies and contrasts and of the minor structural
refinements and braveries. The internal surface is mainly
wrought in alternate courses of black and white marble ; but as
the latter has been dimmed by the centuries to a fine mild brown
the place is all a concert of relieved and dispersed glooms. Save
for Pinturicchio's brilliant frescoes in the Sacristy there are no
pictures to speak of ; but the pavement is covered with many
elaborate designs in black and white mosaic after cartoons by
Beccafumi. The patient skill of these compositions makes them
a rare piece of decoration ; yet even here the friend whom
I lately quoted rejects this over-ripe fruit of the Sienese school.
The designs are nonsensical, he declares, and all his admiration
is for the cunning artisans who have imitated the hatchings and
shadings and hair-strokes of the pencil by the finest curves of
inserted black stone. But the true romance of handiwork at
Siena is to be seen in the wondrous stalls of the choir, under
the coloured light of the great wheel-window. Wood-carving
has ever been a cherished craft of the place, and the best masters
of the art during the fifteenth century lavished themselves on
this prodigious task. It is the frost-work on one's window-
panes interpreted in polished oak. It would be hard to find,
doubtless, a more moving illustration of the peculiar patience,
the sacred candour, of the great time. Into such artistry as
this the author seems to put more of his personal substance
than into any other ; he has to wrestle not only with his subject,
but with his material. He is richly fortunate when his subject
is charming—when his devices, inventions and fantasies spring
lightly to his hand ; for in the material itself, after age and use
have ripened and polished and darkened it to the richness of
ebony and to a greater warmth there is something surpassingly

delectable and venerable.   Wander behind the altar at Siena
when the chanting is over and the incense has faded, and look
well at the stalls of the Barili.

1873.

II

I leave the impression noted in the foregoing pages to tell
its own small story, but have it on my conscience to wonder, in
this connection, quite candidly and publicly and by way of due
penance, at the scantness of such first-fruits of my sensibility.
I was to see Siena repeatedly in the years to follow, I was to
know her better, and I would say that I was to do her an ampler
justice didn't that remark seem to reflect a little on my earlier
poor judgment. This judgment strikes me to-day as having
fallen short—true as it may be that I find ever a value, or at
least an interest, even in the moods and humours and lapses of
any brooding, musing or fantasticating observer to whom the
finer sense of things is *on the whole* not closed.   If he has on a
given occasion nodded or stumbled or strayed, this fact by itself
speaks to me of him—speaks to me, that is, of his faculty and
his idiosyncrasies, and I care nothing for the application of his
faculty unless it be, first of all, in itself interesting.   Which
may serve as my reply to any objection here breaking out—on
the ground that if a spectator's languors are evidence, of a sort,
about that personage, they are scarce evidence about the case
before him, at least if the case be important.   I let my perhaps
rather weak expression of the sense of Siena stand, at any rate—
for the sake of what I myself read into it ; but I should like to
amplify it by other memories, and would do so eagerly if I
might here enjoy the space.   The difficulty for these rectifica-
tions is that if the early vision has failed of competence or of
full felicity, if initiation has thus been slow, so, with renewals

and extensions, so, with the larger experience, one hindrance is
exchanged for another. There is quite such a possibility as
having lived into a relation too much to be able to make a
statement of it.

I remember on one occasion arriving very late of a summer
night, after an almost unbroken run from London, and the note
of that approach——I was the only person alighting at the station
below the great hill of the little fortress city, under whose at
once frowning and gaping gate I must have passed, in the warm
darkness and the absolute stillness, very much after the felt
fashion of a person of importance about to be enormously
incarcerated——gives me, for preservation thus belated, the pitch,
as I may call it, at various times, though always at one season,
of an almost systematised æsthetic use of the place. It wasn't
to be denied that the immensely better "accommodations" insti-
tuted by the multiplying, though alas more bustling, years had
to be recognised as supplying a basis, comparatively prosaic if
one would, to that luxury. No sooner have I written which
words, however, than I find myself adding that one "wouldn't,"
that one doesn't——doesn't, that is, consent now to regard the
then "new" hotel (pretty old indeed by this time) as anything
but an aid to a free play of perception. The strong and rank
old Arme d'Inghilterra, in the darker street, had passed away;
but its ancient rival the Aquila Nera put forth claims to
modernisation, and the Grand Hotel, the still fresher flower
of modernity near the gate by which you enter from the
station, takes on to my present remembrance a mellowness as
of all sorts of comfort, cleanliness and kindness. The particular
facts, those of the visit I began here by alluding to and those of
still others, at all events, inveterately made in June or early in
July, enter together into a fusion as of hot golden-brown objects
seen through the practicable crevices of shutters drawn upon
high, cool, darkened rooms where the scheme of the scene
involved longish days of quiet work, with late afternoon

emergence and contemplation waiting on the better or the worse conscience. I thus associate the compact world of the admirable hilltop, the world of a predominant golden-brown, with a general invocation of sensibility and fancy, and think of myself as going forth into the lingering light of summer evenings all attuned to intensity of the idea of compositional beauty, or in other words, freely speaking, to the question of colour, to intensity of picture. To communicate with Siena in this charming way was thus, I admit, to have no great margin for the prosecution of inquiries, but I am not sure that it wasn't, little by little, to feel the whole combination of elements better than by a more exemplary method, and this from beginning to end of the scale.

More of the elements indeed, for memory, hang about the days that were ushered in by that straight flight from the north than about any other series—if partly, doubtless, but because of my having then stayed longest. I specify it at all events for fond reminiscence as the year, the only year, at which I was present at the Palio, the earlier one, the series of furious horse-races between elected representatives of different quarters of the town taking place toward the end of June, as the second and still more characteristic exhibition of the same sort is appointed to the month of August; a spectacle that I am far from speaking of as the finest flower of my old and perhaps even a little faded cluster of impressions, but which smudges that special sojourn as with the big thumb-mark of a slightly soiled and decidedly ensanguined hand. For really, after all, the great loud gaudy romp or heated frolic, simulating ferocity if not achieving it, that is the annual pride of the town, was not intrinsically, to my view, extraordinarily impressive—in spite of its bristling with all due testimony to the passionate Italian clutch of any pretext for costume and attitude and utterance, for mumming and masquerading and raucously representing; the vast cheap vividness rather somehow refines itself, and the swarm and hubbub of the immense square melt, to the uplifted sense of a very high-placed balcony of the overhanging Chigi palace, where everything was superseded but the intenser passage, across the ages, of the great Renaissance tradition of architecture and the infinite sweetness of the waning golden day. The Palio, indubitably, was *criard*—and the more so for quite monopolising, at Siena, the note of crudity; and much of it demanded doubtless of one's patience a due respect for the long local continuity of such things; it drops into its humoured position, however, in any retrospective command of the many brave aspects of the prodigious place. Not that I am pretending here, even for rectification, to take these at all in turn; I only go on a little with my rueful glance at the marked gaps left in my original report of sympathies entertained.

I bow my head for instance to the mystery of my not having mentioned that the coolest and freshest flower of the day was ever that of one's constant renewal of a charmed homage to Pinturicchio, coolest and freshest and signally youngest and most matutinal (as distinguished from merely primitive or crepuscular) of painters, in the library or sacristy of the Cathedral. Did I *always* find time before work to spend half-an-hour of immersion, under that splendid roof, in the clearest and tenderest, the very cleanest and "straightest," as it masters our envious credulity, of all storied fresco-worlds? This wondrous apartment, a monument in itself to the ancient pride and power of the Church, and which contains an unsurpassed treasure of gloriously illuminated missals, psalters and other vast parchment folios, almost each of whose successive leaves gives the impression of rubies, sapphires and emeralds set in gold and practically embedded in the page, offers thus to view, after a fashion splendidly sustained, a pictorial record of the career of Pope Pius II., Æneas Sylvius of the Siena Piccolomini (who gave him for an immediate successor a second of their name), most profanely literary of Pontiffs and last of would-be Crusaders,

whose adventures and achievements under Pinturicchio's brush
smooth themselves out for us very much to the tune of the
" stories " told by some fine old man of the world, at the restful
end of his life, to the cluster of his grandchildren.   The end of
Æneas Sylvius was not restful ; he died at Ancona in troublous
times, preaching war, and attempting to make it, against the
then terrific Turk ; but over no great worldly personal legend,
among those of men of arduous affairs, arches a fairer, lighter
or more pacific memorial vault than the shining Libreria of
Siena.   I seem to remember having it and its unfrequented
enclosing precinct so often all to myself that I must indeed
mostly have resorted to it for a prompt benediction on the day.
Like no other strong solicitation, among artistic appeals to which
one may compare it up and down the whole wonderful country,
is the felt neighbouring presence of the overwrought Cathedral
in its little proud possessive town : you may so often feel by the
week at a time that it stands there really for your own personal
enjoyment, your romantic convenience, your small wanton
æsthetic use.   In such a light shines for me, at all events,
under such an accumulation and complication of tone flushes
and darkens and richly recedes for me, across the years, the
treasure-house of many-coloured marbles in the untrodden, the
drowsy, empty Sienese square.   One could positively do, in the
free exercise of any responsible fancy or luxurious taste, what
one would with it.

But that proposition holds true, after all, for almost any mild
pastime of the incurable student of loose meanings and stray
relics and odd references and dim analogies in an Italian hill-city
bronzed and seasoned by the ages.   I ought perhaps, for justification of the right to talk, to have plunged into the Siena
archives of which, on one occasion, a kindly custodian gave me,
in rather dusty and stuffy conditions, as the incident vaguely
comes back to me, a glimpse that was like a moment's stand at
the mouth of a deep, dark mine.   I didn't descend into the pit ;

I did, instead of this, a much idler and easier thing : I simply went every afternoon, my stint of work over, I like to recall, for a musing stroll upon the Lizza—the Lizza which had its own unpretentious but quite insidious art of meeting the lover of old stories half-way. The great and subtle thing, if you are not a strenuous specialist, in places of a heavily charged historic consciousness, is to profit by the sense of that consciousness— or in other words to cultivate a relation with the oracle—after the fashion that suits yourself ; so that if the general after-taste of experience, experience at large, the fine distilled essence of the matter, seems to breathe, in such a case, from the very stones and to make a thick strong liquor of the very air, you may thus gather as you pass what is most to your purpose ; which is more the indestructible mixture of lived things, with its concentrated lingering odour, than any interminable list of numbered chapters and verses. Chapters and verses, literally scanned, refuse coincidence, mostly, with the divisional proprieties of your own pile of manuscript—which is but another way of saying, in short, that if the Lizza is a mere fortified promontory of the great Sienese hill, serving at once as a stronghold for the present military garrison and as a planted and benched and band-standed walk and recreation-ground for the citizens, so I could never, toward close of day, either have enough of it or yet feel the vaguest saunterings there to be vain. They were vague with the qualification always of that finer massing, as one wandered off, of the bronzed and seasoned element, the huge rock pedestal, the bravery of walls and gates and towers and palaces and loudly asserted dominion ; and then of that pervaded or mildly infested air in which one feels the experience of the ages, of which I just spoke, to be exquisitely in solution ; and lastly of the wide, strange, sad, beautiful horizon, a rim of far mountains that always pictured, for the leaner on old rubbed and smoothed parapets at the sunset hour, a country not exactly blighted or deserted, but that had had its life, on an immense scale, and had gone, with all its memories and relics, into rather austere, in fact into almost grim and misanthropic, retirement. This was a manner and a mood, at any rate, in all the land, that favoured in the late afternoons the divinest landscape blues and purples—not to speak of its favouring still more my practical contention that the whole guarded headland in question, with the immense ramparts of golden brown and red that dropped into vineyards and orchards and cornfields and all the rustic elegance of the Tuscan *podere*, was knitting for me a chain of unforgettable hours; to the justice of which claim let these divagations testify.

It wasn't, however, that one mightn't without disloyalty to that scheme of profit seek impressions further afield—though indeed I may best say of such a matter as the long pilgrimage to the pictured convent of Monte Oliveto that it but played on the same fine chords as the overhanging, the far-gazing Lizza. What it came to was that one simply put to the friendly test, as it were, the mood and manner of the country. This remembrance is precious, but the demonstration of that sense as of a great heaving region stilled by some final shock and returning thoughtfully, in fact tragically, on itself, couldn't have been more pointed. The long-drawn rural road I refer to, stretching over hill and dale and to which I devoted the whole of the longest day of the year—I was in a small single-horse conveyance, of which I had already made appreciative use, and with a driver as disposed as myself ever to sacrifice speed to contemplation— is doubtless familiar now with the rush of the motor-car; the thought of whose free dealings with the solitude of Monte Oliveto makes me a little ruefully reconsider, I confess, the spirit in which I have elsewhere in these pages, on behalf of the lust, the landscape lust, of the eyes, acknowledged our general increasing debt to that vehicle. For that we met nothing whatever, as I seem at this distance of time to recall, while we gently trotted and trotted through the splendid summer hours and a dry desolation that yet somehow smiled and smiled, was part of the charm and the intimacy of the whole impression—the impression that culminated at last, before the great cloistered square, lonely, bleak and stricken, in the almost aching vision, more frequent in the Italy of to-day than anywhere in the world, of the uncalculated waste of a myriad forms of piety, forces of labour, beautiful fruits of genius. However, one gaped above all things for the impression, and what one mainly asked was that it should be strong of its kind. That was the case, I think I couldn't but feel, at every moment of the couple of hours I spent in the vast, cold, empty shell, out of which the Benedictine brotherhood sheltered there for ages had lately been turned by the strong arm of a secular State. There was but one good brother left, a very lean and tough survivor, a dusky, elderly, friendly Abbate, of an indescribable type and a perfect manner, of whom I think I felt immediately thereafter that I should have liked to say much, but as to whom I must have yielded to the fact that ingenious and vivid commemoration was even then in store for him. Literary portraiture had marked him for its own, and in the short story of *Un Saint*, one of the most finished of contemporary French *nouvelles*, the art and the sympathy of Monsieur Paul Bourget preserve his interesting image. He figures in the beautiful tale, the Abbate of the desolate cloister and of those comparatively quiet years, as a clean, clear type of sainthood; a circumstance this in itself to cause a fond analyst of other than "Latin" race (model and painter in this case having their Latinism so strongly in common) almost endlessly to meditate. Oh, the unutterable differences in any scheme or estimate of physiognomic values, in any range of sensibility to expressional association, among observers of different, of inevitably more or less opposed, traditional and "racial" points of view! One had heard convinced Latins— or at least I had!—speak of situations of trust and intimacy in which they couldn't have endured near them a Protestant or, as who should say for instance, an Anglo-Saxon; but I was to remember my own private attempt to measure such a change of sensibility as might have permitted the prolonged close approach of the dear dingy, half-starved, very possibly all heroic, and quite ideally urbane Abbate. The depth upon depth of things, the cloud upon cloud of associations, on one side and the other, that would have had to change first !

To which I may add nevertheless that since one ever supremely invoked intensity of impression and abundance of character, I feasted my fill of it at Monte Oliveto, and that for that matter this would have constituted my sole refreshment in the vast icy void of the blighted refectory if I hadn't bethought myself of bringing with me a scrap of food, too scantly apportioned, I recollect—very scantly indeed, since my *cocchiere* was to share with me—by my purveyor at Siena. Our tragic—even if so tenderly tragic—entertainer had nothing to give us; but the immemorial cold of the enormous monastic interior in which we smilingly fasted would doubtless not have had for me without that such a wealth of reference. I was to have " liked " the whole adventure, so I must somehow have liked that; by which remark I am recalled to the special treasure of the desecrated temple, those extraordinarily strong and brave frescoes of Luca Signorelli and Sodoma that adorn, in admirable condition, several stretches of cloister wall. These creations in a manner took care of themselves; aided by the blue of the sky above the cloister-court they glowed, they insistently lived; I remember the frigid prowl through all the rest of the bareness, including that of the big dishonoured church and that even of the Abbate's abysmally resigned testimony to his mere human and personal situation; and then, with such a force of contrast and effect of relief, the great sheltered sun-flares and colour-patches of scenic composition and design where a couple of hands centuries ago turned to dust had so wrought the defiant miracle of life and beauty that the effect is of a garden blooming among ruins. Discredited somehow, since they all would, the destroyers themselves, the ancient piety, the general spirit and intention, but still bright and assured and sublime—practically, enviably immortal—the other, the still subtler, the all æsthetic good faith.

1909.

THE AUTUMN IN FLORENCE

FLORENCE too has its "season," not less than Rome, and I have been rejoicing for the past six weeks in the fact that this comparatively crowded parenthesis hasn't yet been opened. Coming here in the first days of October I found the summer still in almost unmenaced possession, and ever since, till within a day or two, the weight of its hand has been sensible. Properly enough, as the city of flowers, Florence mingles the elements most artfully in the spring—during the divine crescendo of March and April, the weeks when six months of steady shiver have still not shaken New York and Boston free of the long Polar reach. But the very quality of the decline of the year as we at present here feel it suits peculiarly the mood in which an undiscourageable gatherer of the sense of things, or taster at least of "charm," moves through these many-memoried streets and galleries and churches. Old things, old places, old people, or at least old races, ever strike us as giving out their secrets most freely in such moist, grey, melancholy days as have formed the complexion of the past fortnight. With Christmas arrives the opera, the only opera worth speaking of—which indeed often means in Florence the only opera worth talking through; the gaiety, the gossip, the reminders in fine of the cosmopolite and watering-place character to which the city of the Medici long ago began to bend her antique temper. Meanwhile it is pleasant enough for the tasters of charm, as I say, and for the makers of invidious distinctions, that the Americans haven't all arrived, however many may be on their way, and that the weather has a monotonous overcast softness in which, apparently, aimless contemplation grows less and less ashamed. There is no crush along the Cascine, as on the sunny days of winter, and the Arno, wandering away toward the mountains in the haze, seems as shy of being looked at as a good picture in a bad light. No light, to my eyes, nevertheless, could be better than this, which reaches us, all strained and filtered and refined, exquisitely coloured and even a bit conspicuously sophisticated, through the heavy air of the past that hangs about the place forever.

I first knew Florence early enough, I am happy to say, to have heard the change for the worse, the taint of the modern order, bitterly lamented by old haunters, admirers, lovers— those qualified to present a picture of the conditions prevailing under the good old Grand-Dukes, the two last of their line in especial, that, for its blest reflection of sweetness and mild- ness and cheapness and ease, of every immediate boon in life to be enjoyed quite for nothing, could but draw tears from belated listeners. Some of these survivors from the golden age—just the beauty of which indeed was in the gold, of sorts, that it poured into your lap, and not in the least in its own importunity on that head—have needfully lingered on, have seen the ancient walls pulled down and the compact and belted mass of which the Piazza della Signoria was the immemorial centre expand, under the treatment of enterprising syndics, into an ungirdled organism of the type, as they viciously say, of Chicago; one of those places of which, as their grace of a cir- cumference is nowhere, the dignity of a centre can no longer be predicated. Florence loses itself to-day in dusty boulevards and smart *beaux quartiers*, such as Napoleon III. and Baron Haussmann were to set the fashion of to a too mediæval Europe—with the effect of some precious page of antique text swallowed up in a marginal commentary that smacks of the style of the newspaper. So much for what has happened on this side of that line of demarcation which, by an odd law,

makes us, with our preference for what we are pleased to call
the picturesque, object to such occurrences even *as* occurrences.
The real truth is that objections are too vain, and that he would
be too rude a critic here, just now, who shouldn't be in the
humour to take the thick with the thin and to try at least to
read something of the old soul into the new forms.

There is something to be said moreover for your liking a
city (once it's a question of your actively circulating) to pretend to comfort you more by its extent than by its limits; in
addition to which Florence was anciently, was in her palmy
days peculiarly, a daughter of change and movement and
variety, of shifting moods, policies and *régimes*—just as the
Florentine character, as we have it to-day, is a character that
takes all things easily for having seen so many come and go.
It saw the national capital, a few years since, arrive and sit
down by the Arno, and took no further thought than sufficed
for the day; then it saw the odd visitor depart and whistled
her cheerfully on her way to Rome. The new boulevards of
the Sindaco Peruzzi come, it may be said, but they don't go;
which, after all, it isn't from the æsthetic point of view strictly
necessary they should. A part of the essential amiability of
Florence, of her genius for making you take to your favour
on easy terms everything that in any way belongs to her, is
that she has already flung an element of her grace over all
their undried mortar and plaster. Such modern arrangements
as the Piazza d'Azeglio and the *viale* or Avenue of the Princess Margaret please not a little, I think—for what they are!—
and do so even in a degree, by some fine local privilege, just
because they are Florentine. The afternoon lights rest on them
as if to thank them for not being worse, and their vistas are
liberal where they look toward the hills. They carry you close
to these admirable elevations, which hang over Florence on all
sides, and if in the foreground your sense is a trifle perplexed
by the white pavements dotted here and there with a policeman

or a nursemaid, you have only to reach beyond and see Fiesole turn to violet, on its ample eminence, from the effect of the opposite sunset.

Facing again then to Florence proper you have local colour enough and to spare—which you enjoy the more, doubtless, from standing off to get your light and your point of view. The elder streets abutting on all this newness bore away into the heart of the city in narrow, dusky perspectives that quite refine, in certain places, by an art of their own, on the romantic appeal.   There are temporal and other accidents thanks to which, as you pause to look down them and to penetrate the deepening shadows that accompany their retreat, they resemble little corridors leading out from the past, mystical like the ladder in Jacob's dream ; so that when you see a single figure advance and draw nearer you are half afraid to wait till it arrives—it must be too much of the nature of a ghost, a messenger from an underworld.   However this may be, a place paved with such great mosaics of slabs and lined with palaces of so massive a tradition, structures which, in their large dependence on pure proportion for interest and beauty, repro-duce more than other modern styles the simple nobleness of Greek architecture, must ever have placed dignity first in the scale of invoked effect and laid up no great treasure of that ragged picturesqueness—the picturesqueness of large poverty— on which we feast our idle eyes at Rome and Naples.   Except in the unfinished fronts of the churches, which, however, un-fortunately, are mere ugly blankness, one finds less of the poetry of ancient over-use, or in other words less romantic southern shabbiness, than in most Italian cities.   At two or three points, none the less, this sinister grace exists in perfection—just such perfection as so often proves that what is literally hideous may be constructively delightful and what is intrinsically tragic play on the finest chords of appreciation.   On the north side of the Arno, between Ponte Vecchio and Ponte Santa Trinità, is a row of immemorial houses that back on the river, in whose yellow flood they bathe their sore old feet. Anything more battered and befouled, more cracked and disjointed, dirtier, drearier, poorer, it would be impossible to conceive. They look as if fifty years ago the liquid mud had risen over their chimneys and then subsided again and left them coated forever with its unsightly slime. And yet forsooth, because the river is yellow, and the light is yellow, and here and there, else-where, some mellow mouldering surface, some hint of colour, some accident of atmosphere, takes up the foolish tale and repeats the note—because, in short, it is Florence, it is Italy, and the fond appraiser, the infatuated alien, may have had in his eyes, at birth and afterwards, the micaceous sparkle of brown-stone fronts no more interesting than so much sand-paper, these miserable dwellings, instead of suggesting mental invocations to an enterprising board of health, simply create their own standard of felicity and shamelessly live in it. Lately, during the misty autumn nights, the moon has shone on them faintly and refined their shabbiness away into some-thing ineffably strange and spectral. The turbid stream sweeps along without a sound, and the pale tenements hang above it like a vague miasmatic exhalation. The dimmest back-scene at the opera, when the tenor is singing his sweetest, seems hardly to belong to a world more detached from responsibility.

What it is that infuses so rich an interest into the general charm is difficult to say in a few words; yet as we wander hither and thither in quest of sacred canvas and immortal bronze and stone we still feel the genius of the place hang about. Two industrious English ladies, the Misses Horner, have lately pub-lished a couple of volumes of " Walks " by the Arno-side, and their work is a long enumeration of great artistic deeds. These things remain for the most part in sound preservation, and, as the weeks go by and you spend a constant portion of your days among them the sense of one of the happiest periods of human

Taste—to put it only at that—settles upon your spirit. It was
not long; it lasted, in its splendour, for less than a century;
but it has stored away in the palaces and churches of Florence
a heritage of beauty that these three enjoying centuries since
haven't yet exhausted. This forms a clear intellectual atmosphere into which you may turn aside from the modern world
and fill your lungs as with the breath of a forgotten creed.
The memorials of the past here address us moreover with a
friendliness, win us by we scarcely know what sociability, what
equal amenity, that we scarce find matched in other great æsthetically endowed communities and periods. Venice, with her old
palaces cracking under the weight of their treasures, is, in her
influence, insupportably sad; Athens, with her maimed marbles
and dishonoured memories, transmutes the consciousness of
sensitive observers, I am told, into a chronic heartache; but in
one's impression of old Florence the abiding felicity, the sense
of saving sanity, of something sound and human, predominates,
offering you a medium still conceivable for life. The reason of
this is partly, no doubt, the "sympathetic" nature, the temperate joy, of Florentine art in general—putting the sole Dante,
greatest of literary artists, aside; partly the tenderness of time,
in its lapse, which, save in a few cases, has been as sparing of
injury as if it knew that when it should have dimmed and
corroded these charming things it would have nothing so sweet
again for its tooth to feed on. If the beautiful Ghirlandaios
and Lippis are fading this generation will never know it. The
large Fra Angelico in the Academy is as clear and keen as if the
good old monk stood there wiping his brushes; the colours
seem to *sing*, as it were, like new-fledged birds in June.
Nothing is more characteristic of early Tuscan art than the
high-reliefs of Luca della Robbia; yet there isn't one of them
that, except for the unique mixture of freshness with its wisdom,
of candour with its expertness, mightn't have been modelled
yesterday.

But perhaps the best image of the absence of stale melancholy or wasted splendour, of the positive presence of what I have called temperate joy, in the Florentine impression and genius, is the bell-tower of Giotto, which rises beside the Cathedral. No beholder of it will have forgotten how straight and slender it stands there, how strangely rich in the common street, plated with coloured marble patterns, and yet so far from simple or severe in design that we easily wonder how its author, the painter of exclusively and portentously grave little pictures, should have fashioned a building which in the way of elaborate elegance, of the true play of taste, leaves a jealous modern criticism nothing to miss. Nothing can be imagined at once more lightly and more pointedly fanciful; it might have been handed over to the city, as it stands, by some Oriental genie tired of too much detail. Yet for all that suggestion it seems of no particular time—not grey and hoary like a Gothic steeple, not cracked and despoiled like a Greek temple; its marbles shining so little less freshly than when they were laid together, and the sunset lighting up its cornice with such a friendly radiance, that you come at last to regard it simply as the graceful, indestructible soul of the place made visible. The Cathedral, externally, for all its solemn hugeness, strikes the same note of would-be reasoned elegance and cheer; it has conventional grandeur, of course, but a grandeur so frank and ingenuous even in its *parti-pris*. It has seen so much, and outlived so much, and served so many sad purposes, and yet remains in aspect so full of the fine Tuscan geniality, the feeling for life, one may almost say the feeling for amusement, that inspired it. Its vast many-coloured marble walls become at any rate, with this, the friendliest note of all Florence; there is an unfailing charm in walking past them while they lift their great acres of geometrical mosaic higher in the air than you have time or other occasion to look. You greet them from the deep street as you greet the side of a mountain when you move in the gorge—not twisting back your head to keep looking at the top, but content with the minor accidents, the nestling hollows and soft cloud-shadows, the general protection of the valley.

Florence is richer in pictures than we really know till we have begun to look for them in outlying corners. Then, here and there, one comes upon lurking values and hidden gems that it quite seems one might as a good New Yorker quietly "bag" for the so aspiring Museum of that city without their being missed. The Pitti Palace is of course a collection of master-pieces; they jostle each other in their splendour, they perhaps even, in their merciless multitude, rather fatigue our admiration. The Uffizi is almost as fine a show, and together with that long serpentine artery which crosses the Arno and connects them, making you ask yourself, whichever way you take it, what goal can be grand enough to crown such a journey, they form the great central treasure-chamber of the town. But I have been neglecting them of late for love of the Academy, where there are fewer copyists and tourists, above all fewer pictorial lions, those whose roar is heard from afar and who strike us as expecting overmuch to have it their own way in the jungle. The pictures at the Academy are all, rather, doves—the whole impression is less pompously tropical. Selection still leaves one too much to say, but I noted here, on my last occasion, an enchanting Botti-celli so obscurely hung, in one of the smaller rooms, that I scarce knew whether most to enjoy or to resent its relegation. Placed, in a mean black frame, where you wouldn't have looked for a masterpiece, it yet gave out to a good glass every characteristic of one. Representing as it does the walk of Tobias with the angel, there are really parts of it that an angel might have painted; but I doubt whether it is observed by half-a-dozen persons a year. That was my excuse for my wanting to know, on the spot, though doubtless all sophistically, what dishonour, could the transfer be artfully accomplished, a strong American light and a brave gilded frame would, comparatively speaking, do it. There and then it would shine with the intense authority that we claim for the fairest things—would exhale its wondrous beauty as a sovereign example. What it comes to is that this master is the most interesting of a great band—the only Florentine save Leonardo and Michael in whom the impulse was original and the invention rare. His imagination is of things strange, subtle and complicated—things it at first strikes us that we moderns have reason to know, and that it has taken us all the ages to learn; so that we permit ourselves to wonder how a "primitive" could come by them. We soon enough reflect, however, that we ourselves have come by them almost only *through* him, exquisite spirit that he was, and that when we enjoy, or at least when we encounter, in our William Morrises, in our Rossettis and Burne-Joneses, the note of the haunted or over-charged consciousness, we are but treated, with other matters, to repeated doses of diluted Botticelli. He practically set with his own hand almost all the copies to almost all our so-called pre-Raphaelites, earlier and later, near and remote.

Let us at the same time, none the less, never fail of response to the great Florentine geniality at large. Fra Angelico, Filippo Lippi, Ghirlandaio, were not "subtly" imaginative, were not even riotously so; but what other three were ever more gladly observant, more vividly and richly true? If there should some time be a weeding out of the world's possessions the best works of the early Florentines will certainly be counted among the flowers. With the ripest performances of the Venetians—by which I don't mean the over-ripe—we can but take them for the most valuable things in the history of art. Heaven forbid we should be narrowed down to a cruel choice; but if it came to a question of keeping or losing between half-a-dozen Raphaels and half-a-dozen things it would be a joy to pick out at the Academy, I fear that, for myself, the memory of the Trans-figuration, or indeed of the other Roman relics of the painter wouldn't save the Raphaels. And yet this was so far from the opinion of a patient artist whom I saw the other day copying the finest of Ghirlandaios—a beautiful Adoration of the Kings at the Hospital of the Innocenti.   Here was another sample of the buried art-wealth of Florence.   It hangs in an obscure chapel, far aloft, behind an altar, and though now and then a stray tourist wanders in and puzzles awhile over the vaguely-glowing forms, the picture is never really seen and enjoyed.   I found an aged Frenchman of modest mien perched on a little platform beneath it, behind a great hedge of altar-candlesticks, with an admirable copy all completed.   The difficulties of his task had been well-nigh insuperable, and his performance seemed to me a real feat of magic.   He could scarcely move or turn, and could find room for his canvas but by rolling it together and painting a small piece at a time, so that he never enjoyed a view of his *ensemble*.   The original is gorgeous with colour and bewildering with decorative detail, but not a gleam of the painter's crimson was wanting, not a curl in his gold arabesques. It seemed to me that if I had copied a Ghirlandaio in such conditions I would at least maintain for my own credit that he was the first painter in the world.   " Very good of its kind," said the weary old man with a shrug of reply for my raptures ; " but oh how far short of Raphael ! "   However that may be, if the reader chances to observe this consummate copy in the so commendable Museum devoted in Paris to such works, let him stop before it with a due reverence ; it is one of the patient things of art.   Seeing it wrought there, in its dusky nook, under such scant convenience, I found no bar in the painter's foreignness to a thrilled sense that the old art-life of Florence isn't yet extinct. It still at least works spells and almost miracles.

1873.

FLORENTINE NOTES

I

YESTERDAY that languid organism known as the Florentine Carnival put on a momentary semblance of vigour, and decreed a general *corso* through the town. The spectacle was not brilliant, but it suggested some natural reflections. I encountered the line of carriages in the square before Santa Croce, of which they were making the circuit. They rolled solemnly by, with their inmates frowning forth at each other in apparent wrath at not finding each other more worth while. There were no masks, no costumes, no decorations, no throwing of flowers or sweetmeats. It was as if each carriageful had privately and not very heroically resolved not to be at costs, and was rather discomfited at finding that it was getting no better entertainment than it gave. The middle of the piazza was filled with little tables, with shouting mountebanks, mostly disguised in battered bonnets and crinolines, offering chances in raffles for plucked fowls and kerosene lamps. I have never thought the huge marble statue of Dante, which overlooks the scene, a work of the last refinement; but, as it stood there on its high pedestal, chin in hand, frowning down on all this cheap foolery, it seemed to have a great moral intention. The carriages followed a prescribed course—through Via Ghibellina, Via del Proconsolo, past the Badia and the Bargello, beneath the great tessellated cliffs of the Cathedral, through Via Tornabuoni and out into ten minutes' sunshine beside the Arno. Much of all this is the gravest and stateliest part of Florence, a quarter of supreme dignity, and there was an almost ludicrous incongruity in seeing Pleasure leading her train through these dusky historic streets. It was most uncomfortably cold, and in the absence of masks many a fair nose was fantastically tipped with purple. But as the carriages crept solemnly along they seemed to keep a funeral march—to follow an antique custom, an exploded faith, to its tomb. The Carnival is dead, and these good people who had come abroad to make merry were funeral mutes and grave-diggers. Last winter in Rome it showed but a galvanised life, yet compared with this humble exhibition it was operatic. At Rome indeed it was too operatic. The knights on horseback there were a bevy of circus-riders, and I'm sure half the mad revellers repaired every night to the Capitol for their twelve sous a day.

I have just been reading over the Letters of the Président de Brosses. A hundred years ago, in Venice, the Carnival lasted six months; and at Rome for many weeks each year one was free, under cover of a mask, to perpetrate the most fantastic follies and cultivate the most remunerative vices. It's very well to read the President's notes, which have indeed a singular interest; but they make us ask ourselves why we should expect the Italians to persist in manners and practices which we our-selves, if we had responsibilities in the matter, should find intolerable. The Florentines at any rate spend no more money nor faith on the carnivalesque. And yet this truth has a qualifi-cation; for what struck me in the whole spectacle yesterday, and prompted these observations, was not at all the more or less of costume of the occupants of the carriages, but the obstinate survival of the merrymaking instinct in the people at large. There could be no better example of it than that so dim a shadow of entertainment should keep all Florence standing and strolling, densely packed for hours, in the cold streets. There was nothing to see that mightn't be seen on the Cascine any fine day in the year—nothing but a name, a tradition, a pretext for sweet staring idleness. The faculty of making much of common things and converting small occasions into great pleasures is, to a son of communities strenuous as ours are strenuous, the most salient characteristic of the so-called Latin civilisations. It charms him and vexes him, according to his mood ; and for the most part it represents a moral gulf between his own temperamental and indeed spiritual sense of race, and that of Frenchmen and Italians, far wider than the watery leagues that a steamer may annihilate. But I think his mood is wisest when he accepts the "foreign" easy surrender to *all* the senses as the sign of an unconscious philosophy of life, instilled by the experience of centuries—the philosophy of people who have lived long and much, who have discovered no short cuts to happiness and no effective circumvention of effort, and so have come to regard the average lot as a ponderous fact that absolutely calls for a certain amount of sitting on the lighter tray of the scales. Florence yesterday then took its holiday in a natural, placid fashion that seemed to make its own temper an affair quite independent of the splendour of the compensation decreed on a higher line to the weariness of its legs. That the *corso* was stupid or lively was the shame or the glory of the powers "above"— the fates, the gods, the *forestieri*, the town-councilmen, the rich or the stingy. Common Florence, on the narrow footways, pressed against the houses, obeyed a natural need in looking about complacently, patiently, gently, and never pushing, nor trampling, nor swearing, nor staggering. This liberal margin for festivals in Italy gives the masses a more than man-of-the-world urbanity in taking their pleasure.

Meanwhile it occurs to me that by a remote New England fireside an unsophisticated young person of either sex is reading in an old volume of travels or an old romantic tale some account of these anniversaries and appointed revels as old Catholic lands offer them to view. Across the page swims a vision of sculptured

palace-fronts draped in crimson and gold and shining in a
southern sun; of a motley train of maskers sweeping on in
voluptuous confusion and pelting each other with nosegays
and love-letters. Into the quiet room, quenching the rhythm
of the Connecticut clock, floats an uproar of delighted voices,
a medley of stirring foreign sounds, an echo of far-heard music
of a strangely alien cadence. But the dusk is falling, and the
unsophisticated young person closes the book wearily and wanders
to the window. The dusk is falling on the beaten snow. Down
the road is a white wooden meeting-house, looking grey among
the drifts. The young person surveys the prospect awhile, and
then wanders back and stares at the fire. The Carnival of
Venice, of Florence, of Rome; colour and costume, romance
and rapture! The young person gazes in the firelight at the
flickering chiaroscuro of the future, discerns at last the glowing
phantasm of opportunity, and determines with a wild heart-beat
to go and see it all—twenty years hence!

II

A couple of days since, driving to Fiesole, we came back
by the castle of Vincigliata. The afternoon was lovely; and,
though there is as yet (February 10th) no visible revival of
vegetation, the air was full of a vague vernal perfume, and the
warm colours of the hills and the yellow western sunlight
flooding the plain seemed to contain the promise of Nature's
return to grace. It's true that above the distant pale blue gorge
of Vallombrosa the mountain-line was tipped with snow; but
the liberated soul of Spring was nevertheless at large. The
view from Fiesole seems vaster and richer with each visit. The
hollow in which Florence lies, and which from below seems deep
and contracted, opens out into an immense and generous valley
and leads away the eye into a hundred gradations of distance.
The place itself showed, amid its chequered fields and gardens,

with as many towers and spires as a chess-board half cleared. The domes and towers were washed over with a faint blue mist. The scattered columns of smoke, interfused with the sinking sunlight, hung over them like streamers and pennons of silver gauze; and the Arno, twisting and curling and glittering here and there, was a serpent cross-striped with silver.

Vincigliata is a product of the millions, the leisure and the eccentricity, I suppose people say, of an English gentleman—Mr. Temple Leader, whose name should be commemorated. You reach the castle from Fiesole by a narrow road, returning toward Florence by a romantic twist through the hills and passing nothing on its way save thin plantations of cypress and cedar. Upward of twenty years ago, I believe, this gentleman took a fancy to the crumbling shell of a mediæval fortress on a breezy hilltop overlooking the Val d'Arno and forthwith bought it and began to "restore" it. I know nothing of what the original ruin may have cost; but in the dusky courts and chambers of the present elaborate structure this impassioned archæologist must have buried a fortune. He has, however, the compensation of feeling that he has erected a monument which, if it is never to stand a feudal siege, may encounter at least some critical overhauling. It is a disinterested work of art and really a triumph of æsthetic culture. The author has reproduced with minute accuracy a sturdy home-fortress of the fourteenth century, and has kept throughout such rigid terms with his model that the result is literally uninhabitable to degenerate moderns. It is simply a massive facsimile, an elegant museum of archaic images, mainly but most amusingly counterfeit, perched on a spur of the Apennines. The place is most politely shown. There is a charming cloister, painted with extremely clever "quaint" frescoes, celebrating the deeds of the founders of the castle—a cloister that is everything delightful a cloister should be except truly venerable and employable. There is a beautiful castle court, with the embattled tower climbing into the blue far above it, and a spacious loggia with rugged medallions and mild-hued Luca della Robbias fastened unevenly into the walls. But the apartments are the great success, and each of them as good a "reconstruction" as a tale of Walter Scott; or, to speak frankly, a much better one. They are all low-beamed and vaulted, stone-paved, decorated in grave colours and lighted, from narrow, deeply recessed windows, through small leaden-ringed plates of opaque glass.

The details are infinitely ingenious and elaborately grim, and the indoor atmosphere of mediævalism most forcibly revived. No compromising fact of domiciliary darkness and cold is spared us, no producing condition of mediæval manners not glanced at. There are oaken benches round the room, of about six inches in depth and gaunt fauteuils of wrought leather, illustrating the suppressed transitions which, as George Eliot says, unite all contrasts—offering a visible link between the modern conceptions of torture and of luxury. There are fireplaces nowhere but in the kitchen, where a couple of sentry-boxes are inserted on either side of the great hooded chimney-piece, into which people might creep and take their turn at being toasted and smoked. One may doubt whether this dearth of the hearthstone could have raged on such a scale, but it's a happy stroke in the representation of an Italian dwelling of any period. It shows how the graceful fiction that Italy is all "meridional" flourished for some time before being refuted by grumbling tourists. And yet amid this cold comfort you feel the incongruous presence of a constant intuitive regard for beauty. The shapely spring of the vaulted ceilings; the richly figured walls, coarse and hard in substance as they are; the charming shapes of the great platters and flagons in the deep recesses of the quaintly carved black dressers; the wandering hand of ornament, as it were, playing here and there for its own diversion in unlighted corners—such things redress, to our fond credulity, with all sorts of grace, the balance of the picture.

And yet, somehow, with what dim, unillumined vision one fancies even such inmates as those conscious of finer needs than the mere supply of blows and beef and beer would meet passing their heavy eyes over such slender household beguilements! These crepuscular chambers at Vincigliata are a mystery and a challenge; they seem the mere propounding of an answerless riddle. You long, as you wander through them, turning up your coat-collar and wondering whether ghosts can catch bronchitis, to answer it with some positive notion of what people so encaged and situated "did," how they looked and talked and carried themselves, how they took their pains and pleasures, how they counted off the hours. Deadly ennui seems to ooze out of the stones and hang in clouds in the brown corners. No wonder men relished a fight and panted for a fray. "Skullsmashers" were sweet, ears ringing with pain and ribs cracking in a tussle were soothing music, compared with the cruel quietude of the dim-windowed castle. When they came back they could only have slept a good deal and eased their dislocated bones on those meagre oaken ledges. Then they woke up and turned about to the table and ate their portion of roasted sheep. They shouted at each other across the board and flung the wooden plates at the serving-men. They jostled and hustled and hooted and bragged; and then, after gorging and boozing and easing their doublets, they squared their, elbows one by one on the greasy table and buried their scarred foreheads and dreamed of a good gallop after flying foes. And the women? They must have been strangely simple—simpler far than any moral archæologist can show us in a learned restoration. Of course, their simplicity had its graces and devices; but one thinks with a sigh that, as the poor things turned away with patient looks from the viewless windows to the same, same looming figures on the dusky walls, they hadn't even the consolation of knowing that just this attitude and movement, set off by their peaked coifs, their falling sleeves and heavily-twisted trains, would sow the seed of yearning envy—of sorts—on the part of later generations.

There are moods in which one feels the impulse to enter a tacit protest against too gross an appetite for pure æsthetics in this starving and sinning world. One turns half away, musingly, from certain beautiful useless things. But the healthier state of mind surely is to lay no tax on any really intelligent manifestation of the curious and exquisite. Intelligence hangs together essentially, all along the line; it only needs time to make, as we say, its connections. The massive *pastiche* of Vincigliata has no superficial use; but, even if it were less complete, less successful, less brilliant, I should feel a reflective kindness for it. So disinterested and so expensive a toy is its own justification; it belongs to the heroics of dilettantism.

III

One grows to feel the collection of pictures at the Pitti Palace splendid rather than interesting. After walking through it once or twice you catch the key in which it is pitched—you know what you are likely not to find on closer examination; none of the works of the uncompromising period, nothing from the half-groping geniuses of the early time, those whose colouring was sometimes harsh and their outlines sometimes angular. Vague to me the principle on which the pictures were originally gathered and of the æsthetic creed of the princes who chiefly selected them. A princely creed I should roughly call it—the creed of people who believed in things presenting a fine face to society; who esteemed showy results rather than curious processes, and would have hardly cared more to admit into their collection a work by one of the laborious precursors of the full efflorescence than to see a bucket and broom left standing in a state saloon. The gallery contains in literal fact some eight or ten paintings of the early Tuscan School—notably two admirable specimens of Filippo

Lippi and one of the frequent circular pictures of the great
Botticelli—a Madonna, chilled with tragic prescience, laying a
pale cheek against that of a blighted Infant. Such a melancholy
mother as this of Botticelli would have strangled her baby in its
cradle to rescue it from the future. But of Botticelli there is
much to say. One of the Filippo Lippis is perhaps his masterpiece—a Madonna in a small rose-garden (such a "flowery
close" as Mr. William Morris loves to haunt), leaning over an
Infant who kicks his little human heels on the grass while half-
a-dozen curly-pated angels gather about him, looking back over
their shoulders with the candour of children in *tableaux vivants*,
and one of them drops an armful of gathered roses one by one
upon the baby. The delightful earthly innocence of these winged
youngsters is quite inexpressible. Their heads are twisted about
toward the spectator as if they were playing at leap-frog and were
expecting a companion to come and take a jump. Never did
"young" art, never did subjective freshness, attempt with greater
success to represent those phases. But these three fine works are
hung over the tops of doors in a dark back room—the bucket
and broom are thrust behind a curtain. It seems to me, nevertheless, that a fine Filippo Lippi is good enough company for an
Allori or a Cigoli, and that that too deeply sentient Virgin of
Botticelli might happily balance the flower-like irresponsibility
of Raphael's "Madonna of the Chair."

Taking the Pitti collection, however, simply for what it
pretends to be, it gives us the very flower of the sumptuous,
the courtly, the grand-ducal. It is chiefly official art, as one
may say, but it presents the fine side of the type—the brilliancy,
the facility, the amplitude, the sovereignty of good taste. I
agree on the whole with a nameless companion and with what he
lately remarked about his own humour on these matters ; that,
having been on his first acquaintance with pictures nothing if not
critical, and held the lesson incomplete and the opportunity
slighted if he left a gallery without a headache, he had come,

as he grew older, to regard them more as the grandest of all pleasantries and less as the most strenuous of all lessons, and to remind himself that, after all, it is the privilege of art to make us friendly to the human mind and not to make us suspicious of it. We do in fact as we grow older unstring the critical bow a little and strike a truce with invidious comparisons. We work off the juvenile impulse to heated partisanship and discover that one spontaneous producer isn't different enough from another to keep the all-knowing Fates from smiling over our loves and our aversions. We perceive a certain human solidarity in all cultivated effort, and are conscious of a growing accommodation of judgment—an easier disposition, the fruit of experience, to take the joke for what it is worth as it passes. We have in short less of a quarrel with the masters we don't dèlight in, and less of an impulse to pin all our faith on those in whom, in more zealous days, we fancied that we made out peculiar meanings. The meanings no longer seem quite so peculiar. Since then we have arrived at a few in the depths of our own genius that are not sensibly less striking.

And yet it must be added that all this depends vastly on one's mood—as a traveller's impressions do, generally, to a degree which those who give them to the world would do well more explicitly to declare. We have our hours of expansion and those of contraction, and yet while we follow the traveller's trade we go about gazing and judging with unadjusted confidence. We can't suspend judgment; we must take our notes, and the notes are florid or crabbed, as the case may be. A short time ago I spent a week in an ancient city on a hill-top, in the humour, for which I was not to blame, which produces crabbed notes. I knew it at the time, but couldn't help it. I went through all the motions of liberal appreciation; I uncapped in all the churches and on the massive ramparts stared all the views fairly out of countenance; but my imagination, which I suppose at bottom had very good reasons of its own and knew perfectly what it was about, refused to project into the dark old town and upon the yellow hills that sympathetic glow which forms half the substance of our genial impressions. So it is that in museums and palaces we are alternate radicals and conservatives. On some days we ask but to be somewhat sensibly affected; on others, Ruskin-haunted, to be spiritually steadied. After a long absence from the Pitti Palace I went back there the other morning and transferred myself from chair to chair in the great golden-roofed saloons—the chairs are all gilded and covered with faded silk—in the humour to be diverted at any price. I needn't mention the things that diverted me; I yawn now when I think of some of them. But an artist, for instance, to whom my kindlier judgment has made permanent concessions is that charming Andrea del Sarto. When I first knew him, in my cold youth, I used to say without mincing that I didn't like him. *Cet âge est sans pitié.* The fine sympathetic, melancholy, pleasing painter! He has a dozen faults, and if you insist pedantically on your rights the conclusive word you use about him will be the word weak. But if you are a generous soul you will utter it low—low as the mild grave tone of his own sought harmonies. He is monotonous, narrow, incomplete; he has but a dozen different figures and but two or three ways of distributing them; he seems able to utter but half his thought, and his canvases lack apparently some final return on the whole matter—some process which his impulse failed him before he could bestow. And yet in spite of these limitations his genius is both itself of the great pattern and lighted by the air of a great period. Three gifts he had largely: an instinctive, unaffected, unerring grace; a large and rich, and yet a sort of withdrawn and indifferent, sobriety; and best of all, as well as rarest of all, an indescribable property of relatedness as to the moral world. Whether he was aware of the connection or not, or in what measure, I cannot say; but he gives, so to speak, the taste of it. Before his handsome vague-browed Madonnas; the

T

mild, robust young saints who kneel in his foregrounds and look round at you with a conscious anxiety which seems to say that, though in the picture, they are not of it, but of your own sentient life of commingled love and weariness; the stately apostles, with comely heads and harmonious draperies, who gaze up at the high-seated Virgin like early astronomers at a newly seen star—there comes to you the brush of the dark wing of an inward life. A shadow falls for the moment, and in it you feel the chill of moral suffering. Did the Lippis suffer, father or son? Did Raphael suffer? Did Titian? Did Rubens suffer? Perish the thought—it wouldn't be fair to *us* that they should have had everything. And I note in our poor second-rate Andrea an element of interest lacking to a number of stronger talents.

Interspersed with him at the Pitti hang the stronger and the weaker in splendid abundance. Raphael is there, strong in por-traiture — easy, various, bountiful genius that he was — and (strong here isn't the word, but) happy beyond the common dream in his beautiful "Madonna of the Chair." The general instinct of posterity seems to have been to treat this lovely picture as a semi-sacred, an almost miraculous, manifestation. People stand in a worshipful silence before it, as they would before a taper-studded shrine. If we suspend in imagination on the right of it the solid realistic, unidealised portrait of Leo the Tenth (which hangs in another room) and transport to the left the fresco of the School of Athens from the Vatican, and then reflect that these were three separate fancies of a single youthful, amiable genius we recognise that such a producing consciousness must have been a "treat." My companion already quoted has a phrase that he "doesn't care for Raphael," but confesses, when pressed, that he was a most remarkable young man. Titian has a dozen portraits of unequal interest. I never par-ticularly noticed till lately—it is very ill hung—that portentous image of the Emperor Charles the Fifth. He was a burlier, more imposing personage than his usual legend figures, and in his great puffed sleeves and gold chains and full-skirted over-dress he seems to tell of a tread that might sometimes have been inconveniently resonant. But the *purpose* to have his way and work his will is there—the great stomach for divine right, the old monarchical temperament. The great Titian, in portraiture, however, remains that formidable young man in black, with the small compact head, the delicate nose and the irascible blue eye. Who was he? What was he? "*Ritratto virile*" is all the catalogue is able to call the picture. "Virile!" Rather! you vulgarly exclaim. You may weave what romance you please about it, but a romance your dream must be. Handsome, clever, defiant, passionate, dangerous, it was not his own fault if he hadn't adventures and to spare. He was a gentleman and a warrior, and his adventures balanced between camp and court. I imagine him the young orphan of a noble house, about to come into mortgaged estates. One wouldn't have cared to be his guardian, bound to paternal admonitions once a month over his precocious transactions with the Jews or his scandalous abduction from her convent of such and such a noble maiden.

The Pitti Gallery contains none of Titian's golden-toned groups; but it boasts a lovely composition by Paul Veronese, the dealer in silver hues—a Baptism of Christ. W—— named it to me the other day as the picture he most enjoyed, and surely painting seems here to have proposed to itself to discredit and annihilate—and even on the occasion of such a subject—everything but the loveliness of life. The picture bedims and enfeebles its neighbours. We ask ourselves whether painting as such can go further. It is simply that here at last the art stands complete. The early Tuscans, as well as Leonardo, as Raphael, as Michael, saw the great spectacle that surrounded them in beautiful sharp-edged elements and parts. The great Venetians felt its indissoluble unity and recognised that form and colour and earth and air were equal members of every possible subject ; and beneath their magical touch the hard outlines melted together and the blank intervals bloomed with meaning. In this beautiful Paul Veronese of the Pitti everything is part of the charm—the atmosphere as well as the figures, the look of radiant morning in the white-streaked sky as well as the living human limbs, the cloth of Venetian purple about the loins of the Christ as well as the noble humility of his attitude. The relation to Nature of the other Italian schools differs from that of the Venetian as courtship — even ardent courtship — differs from marriage.

IV

I went the other day to the secularised Convent of San Marco, paid my franc at the profane little wicket which creaks away at the door—no less than six custodians, apparently, are needed to turn it, as if it may have a recusant conscience—passed along the bright, still cloister and paid my respects to Fra Angelico's Crucifixion, in that dusky chamber in the basement. I looked long ; one can hardly do otherwise. The fresco deals with the pathetic on the grand scale, and after taking in its beauty you feel as little at liberty to go away abruptly as you would to leave church during the sermon. You may be as little of a formal Christian as Fra Angelico was much of one; you yet feel admonished by spiritual decency to let so yearning a view of the Christian story work its utmost will on you. The three crosses rise high against a strange completely crimson sky, which deepens mysteriously the tragic expression of the scene, though I remain perforce vague as to whether this lurid background be a fine intended piece of symbolism or an effective accident of time. In the first case the extravagance quite triumphs. Between the crosses, under no great rigour of composition, are scattered the most exemplary saints—kneeling, praying, weeping, pitying, worshipping. The swoon of the

Madonna is depicted at the left, and this gives the holy presences, in respect to the case, the strangest historical or actual air. Everything is so real that you feel a vague impatience and almost ask yourself how it was that amid the army of his consecrated servants our Lord was permitted to suffer. On reflection you see that the painter's design, so far as coherent, has been simply to offer an immense representation of Pity, and all with such concentrated truth that his colours here seem dissolved in tears that drop and drop, however softly, through all time. Of this single yearning consciousness the figures are admirably expressive. No later painter learned to render with deeper force than Fra Angelico the one state of the spirit he could conceive —a passionate pious tenderness. Immured in his quiet convent, he apparently never received an intelligible impression of evil ; and his conception of human life was a perpetual sense of sacredly loving and being loved. But how, immured in his quiet convent, away from the streets and the studios, did he become that genuine, finished, perfectly professional painter ? No one is less of a mere mawkish amateur. His range was broad, from this really heroic fresco to the little trumpeting seraphs, in their opaline robes, enamelled, as it were, on the gold margins of his pictures.

I sat out the sermon and departed, I hope, with the gentle preacher's blessing. I went into the smaller refectory, near by, to refresh my memory of the beautiful Last Supper of Domenico Ghirlandaio. It would be putting things coarsely to say that I adjourned thus from a sermon to a comedy, though Ghirlandaio's theme, as contrasted with the blessed Angelico's, was the dramatic, spectacular side of human life. How keenly he observed it and how richly he rendered it, the world about him of colour and costume, of handsome heads and pictorial groupings ! In his admirable school there is no painter one enjoys—*pace* Ruskin— more sociably and irresponsibly. Lippo Lippi is simpler, quainter, more frankly expressive ; but we retain before him a remnant of the sympathetic discomfort provoked by the masters whose conceptions were still a trifle too large for their means. The pictorial vision in their minds seems to stretch and strain their undeveloped skill almost to a sense of pain. In Ghirlandaio the skill and the imagination are equal, and he gives us a delightful impression of enjoying his own resources. Of all the painters of his time he affects us least as positively not of ours. He enjoyed a crimson mantle spreading and tumbling in curious folds and embroidered with needlework of gold, just as he enjoyed a handsome well-rounded head, with vigorous dusky locks, profiled in courteous adoration. He enjoyed in short the various reality of things, and had the good fortune to live in an age when reality flowered into a thousand amusing graces —to speak only of those. He was not especially addicted to giving spiritual hints; and yet how hard and meagre they seem, the professed and finished realists of our own day, with the spiritual *bonhomie* or candour that makes half Ghirlandaio's richness left out! The Last Supper at San Marco is an excellent example of the natural reverence of an artist of that time with whom reverence was not, as one may say, a specialty. The main idea with him has been the variety, the material bravery and positively social charm of the scene, which finds expression, with irrepressible generosity, in the accessories of the background. Instinctively he imagines an opulent garden—imagines it with a good faith which quite tides him over the reflection that Christ and his disciples were poor men and unused to sit at meat in palaces. Great full-fruited orange-trees peep over the wall before which the table is spread, strange birds fly through the air, while a peacock perches on the edge of the partition and looks down on the sacred repast. It is striking that, without any at all intense religious purpose, the figures, in their varied naturalness, have a dignity and sweetness of attitude that admits of numberless reverential constructions. I should call all this the happy tact of a robust faith.

On the staircase leading up to the little painted cells of the Beato Angelico, however, I suddenly faltered and paused. Somehow I had grown averse to the intenser zeal of the Monk of Fiesole. I wanted no more of him that day. I wanted no more macerated friars and spear-gashed sides. Ghirlandaio's elegant way of telling his story had put me in the humour for something more largely intelligent, more profanely pleasing. I departed, walked across the square, and found it in the Academy, standing in a particular spot and looking up at a particular high-hung picture. It is difficult to speak adequately, perhaps even intelligibly, of Sandro Botticelli. An accomplished critic—Mr. Pater, in his *Studies on the History of the Renaissance*—has lately paid him the tribute of an exquisite, a supreme, curiosity. He was rarity and distinction incarnate, and of all the multitudinous masters of his group incomparably the most interesting, the one who detains and perplexes and fascinates us most. Exquisitely fine his imagination—infinitely audacious and adventurous his fancy. Alone among the painters of his time he strikes us as having invention. The glow and thrill of expanding observation—this was the feeling that sent his comrades to their easels; but Botticeili's moved him to reactions and emotions of which they knew nothing, caused his faculty to sport and wander and explore on its own account. These impulses have fruits often so ingenious and so lovely that it would be easy to talk nonsense about them. I hope it is not nonsense, however, to say that the picture to which I just alluded (the "Coronation of the Virgin," with a group of life-sized saints below and a garland of miniature angels above) is one of the supremely beautiful productions of the human mind. It is hung so high that you need a good glass to see it; to say nothing of the unprecedented delicacy of the work. The lower half is of moderate interest; but the dance of hand-clasped angels round the heavenly couple above has a beauty newly exhaled from the deepest sources of inspiration. Their perfect little hands are locked with ineffable elegance; their blowing robes are tossed into folds of which each line is a study; their charming feet have the relief of the most delicate sculpture. But, as I have already noted, of Botticelli there is much, too much to say—besides which Mr. Pater has said all. Only add thus to his inimitable grace of design that the exquisite pictorial force driving him goes a-Maying not on wanton errands of its own, but on those of some mystic superstition which trembles forever in his heart.

V

The more I look at the old Florentine domestic architecture the more I like it—that of the great examples at least; and if I ever am able to build myself a lordly pleasure-house I don't see how in conscience I can build it different from these. They are sombre and frowning, and look a trifle more as if they were meant to keep people out than to let them in; but what equally "important" type—if there be an equally important—is more expressive of domiciliary dignity and security and yet attests them with a finer æsthetic economy? They are impressively "handsome," and yet contrive to be so by the simplest means. I don't say at the smallest pecuniary cost—that's another matter. There is money buried in the thick walls and diffused through the echoing excess of space. The merchant nobles of the fifteenth century had deep and full pockets, I suppose, though the present bearers of their names are glad to let out their palaces in suites of apartments which are occupied by the commercial aristocracy of another republic. One is told of fine old mouldering chambers of which possession is to be enjoyed for a sum not worth mentioning. I am afraid that behind these so gravely harmonious fronts there is a good deal of dusky discomfort, and I speak now simply of the large serious faces themselves as you can see them from the street; see them ranged cheek to cheek in the grey historic light of Via dei Bardi, Via Maggio, Via degli Albizzi. The force of character, the familiar severity and majesty, depend on a few simple features: on the great iron-caged windows of the rough-hewn basement; on the noble stretch of space between the summit of one high, round-topped window and the bottom of that above; on the high-hung sculptured shield at the angle of the house; on the flat far-projecting roof; and, finally, on the magnificent tallness of the whole building, which so dwarfs our modern attempts at size. The finest of these Florentine palaces are, I imagine, the tallest habitations in Europe that are frankly and amply habitations— not mere shafts for machinery of the American grain-elevator pattern. Some of the creations of M. Haussmann in Paris may climb very nearly as high; but there is all the difference in the world between the impressiveness of a building which takes breath, as it were, some six or seven times, from storey to storey, and of one that erects itself to an equal height in three long-drawn pulsations. When a house is ten windows wide and the drawing-room floor is as high as a chapel it can afford but three floors. The spaciousness of some of those ancient drawing-rooms is that of a Russian steppe. The "family circle," gathered anywhere within speaking distance, must resemble a group of pilgrims encamped in the desert on a little oasis of carpet. Madame Gryzanowska, living at the top of a house in that dusky, tortuous old Borgo Pinti, initiated me the other evening most good-naturedly, lamp in hand, into the far-spreading mysteries of her apartment. Such quarters seem a translation into space of the old-fashioned idea of leisure. Leisure and "room" have been passing out of our manners together, but here and there, being of stouter structure, the latter lingers and survives.

Here and there, indeed, in this blessed Italy, reluctantly modern in spite alike of boasts and lamentations, it seems to have been preserved for curiosity's and fancy's sake, with a

vague, sweet odour of the embalmer's spices about it. I went
the other morning to the Corsini Palace. The proprietors
obviously are great people. One of the ornaments of Rome is
their great white-faced palace in the dark Trastevere and its
voluminous gallery, none the less delectable for the poorness of
the pictures. Here they have a palace on the Arno, with
another large, handsome, respectable and mainly uninteresting
collection. It contains indeed three or four fine examples of
early Florentines. It was not especially for the pictures that I
went, however; and certainly not for the pictures that I stayed.
I was under the same spell as the inveterate companion with
whom I walked the other day through the beautiful private
apartments of the Pitti Palace and who said : "I suppose I care
for nature, and I know there have been times when I have
thought it the greatest pleasure in life to lie under a tree and
gaze away at blue hills. But just now I had rather lie on that
faded sea-green satin sofa and gaze down through the open door
at that retreating vista of gilded, deserted, haunted chambers.
In other words I prefer a good 'interior' to a good landscape.
The impression has a greater intensity—the thing itself a more
complex animation. I like fine old rooms that have been occupied in a fine old way. I like the musty upholstery, the antiquated
knick-knacks, the view out of the tall deep-embrasured windows at
garden cypresses rocking against a grey sky. If you don't know
why I'm afraid I can't tell you." It seemed to me at the
Palazzo Corsini that I did know why. In places that have been
lived in so long and so much and in such a fine old way, as my
friend said—that is under social conditions so multifold and to
a comparatively starved and democratic sense so curious—the
past seems to have left a sensible deposit, an aroma, an atmosphere. This ghostly presence tells you no secrets, but it
prompts you to try and guess a few. What has been done
and said here through so many years, what has been ventured
or suffered, what has been dreamed or despaired of? Guess

the riddle if you can, or if you think it worth your ingenuity.   The rooms at Palazzo Corsini suggest indeed, and
seem to recall, but a monotony of peace and plenty.   One
of them imaged such a noble perfection of a home-scene that
I dawdled there until the old custodian came shuffling back
to see whether possibly I was trying to conceal a Caravaggio
about my person : a great crimson-draped drawing-room of the
amplest and yet most charming proportions ; walls hung with
large dark pictures, a great concave ceiling frescoed and moulded
with dusky richness, and half-a-dozen south windows looking
out on the Arno, whose swift yellow tide sends up the light in
a cheerful flicker.   I fear that in my appreciation of the particular effect so achieved I uttered a monstrous folly—some
momentary willingness to be maimed or crippled all my days if I
might pass them in such a place.   In fact half the pleasure of
inhabiting this spacious saloon would be that of using one's legs,
of strolling up and down past the windows, one by one, and
making desultory journeys from station to station and corner to
corner.   Near by is a colossal ball-room, domed and pilastered
like a Renaissance cathedral, and superabundantly decorated
with marble effigies, all yellow and grey with the years.

VI

In the Carthusian Monastery outside the Roman Gate,
mutilated and profaned though it is, one may still snuff up a
strong if stale redolence of old Catholicism and old Italy.   The
road to it is ugly, being encumbered with vulgar waggons and
fringed with tenements suggestive of an Irish-American suburb.
Your interest begins as you come in sight of the convent perched
on its little mountain and lifting against the sky, around the
bell-tower of its gorgeous chapel, a coronet of clustered cells.
You make your way into the lower gate, through a clamouring
press of deformed beggars who thrust at you their stumps of

limbs, and you climb the steep hillside through a shabby plantation which it is proper to fancy was better tended in the monkish time. The monks are not totally abolished, the government having the grace to await the natural extinction of the half-dozen old brothers who remain, and who shuffle doggedly about the cloisters, looking, with their white robes and their pale blank old faces, quite anticipatory ghosts of their future selves. A prosaic, profane old man in a coat and trousers serves you, however, as custodian. The melancholy friars have not even the privilege of doing you the honours of their dishonour. One must imagine the pathetic effect of their former silent pointings to this and that conventual treasure under stress of the feeling that such pointings were narrowly numbered. The convent is vast and irregular—it bristles with those picture-making arts and accidents which one notes as one lingers and passes, but which in Italy the overburdened memory learns to resolve into broadly general images. I rather deplore its position at the gates of a bustling city—it ought rather to be lodged in some lonely fold of the Apennines. And yet to look out from the shady porch of one of the quiet cells upon the teeming vale of the Arno and the clustered towers of Florence must have deepened the sense of monastic quietude.

The chapel, or rather the church, which is of great proportions and designed by Andrea Orcagna, the primitive painter, refines upon the consecrated type or even quite glorifies it. The massive cincture of black sculptured stalls, the dusky Gothic roof, the high-hung, deep-toned pictures and the superb pavement of verd-antique and dark red marble, polished into glassy lights, must throw the white-robed figures of the gathered friars into the highest romantic relief. All this luxury of worship has nowhere such value as in the chapels of monasteries, where we find it contrasted with the otherwise so ascetic economy of the worshippers. The paintings and gildings of their church, the gem-bright marbles and fantastic carvings, are really but the monastic tribute to sensuous delight—an imperious need for which the fond imagination of Rome has officiously opened the door.   One smiles when one thinks how largely a fine starved sense for the forbidden things of earth, if it makes the most of its opportunities, may gratify this need under cover of devotion.   Nothing is too base, too hard, too sordid for real humility, but nothing too elegant, too amiable, too caressing, caressed, caressable, for the exaltation of faith.   The meaner the convent cell the richer the convent chapel.   Out of poverty and solitude, inanition and cold, your honest friar may rise at his will into a Mahomet's Paradise of luxurious analogies.

There are further various dusky subterranean oratories where a number of bad pictures contend faintly with the friendly gloom.   Two or three of these funereal vaults, however, deserve mention.   In one of them, side by side, sculptured by Donatello in low relief, lie the white marble effigies of the three members of the Accaiuoli family who founded the convent in the thirteenth century.   In another, on his back, on the pavement, rests a grim old bishop of the same stout race by the same honest craftsman. Terribly grim he is, and scowling as if in his stony sleep he still dreamed of his hates and his hard ambitions.   Last and best, in another low chapel, with the trodden pavement for its bed, shines dimly a grand image of a later bishop—Leonardo Buonafede, who, dying in 1545, owes his monument to Francesco di San Gallo.   I have seen little from this artist's hand, but it was clearly of the cunningest.   His model here was a very sturdy old prelate, though I should say a very genial old man.   The sculptor has respected his monumental ugliness, but has suffused it with a singular homely charm—a look of confessed physical comfort in the privilege of paradise.   All these figures have an inimitable reality, and their lifelike marble seems such an incorruptible incarnation of the genius of the place that you begin to think of it as even more reckless than cruel on the part of the present public powers to have begun to pull the establishment down, morally speaking, about their ears. They are lying quiet yet awhile; but when the last old friar dies and the convent formally lapses, won't they rise on their stiff old legs and hobble out to the gates and thunder forth anathemas before which even a future and more enterprising régime may be disposed to pause?

Out of the great central cloister open the snug little detached dwellings of the absent fathers. When I said just now that the Certosa in Val d'Ema gives you a glimpse of old Italy I was thinking of this great pillared quadrangle, lying half in sun and half in shade, of its tangled garden-growth in the centre, surrounding the ancient customary well, and of the intense blue sky bending above it, to say nothing of the indispensable old white-robed monk who pokes about among the lettuce and parsley. We have seen such places before; we have visited them in that divinatory glance which strays away into space for a moment over the top of a suggestive book. I don't quite know whether it's more or less as one's fancy would have it that the monkish cells are no cells at all, but very tidy little *appartements complets*, consisting of a couple of chambers, a sitting-room and a spacious loggia, projecting out into space from the cliff-like wall of the monastery and sweeping from pole to pole the loveliest view in the world. It's poor work, however, taking notes on views, and I will let this one pass. The little chambers are terribly cold and musty now. Their odour and atmosphere are such as one used, as a child, to imagine those of the school-room during Saturday and Sunday.

VII

In the Roman streets, wherever you turn, the façade of a church in more or less degenerate flamboyance is the principal feature of the scene; and if, in the absence of purer motives, you are weary of æsthetic trudging over the corrugated surface of the

Seven Hills, a system of pavement in which small cobblestones anomalously endowed with angles and edges are alone employed, you may turn aside at your pleasure and take a reviving sniff at the pungency of incense. In Florence, one soon observes, the churches are relatively few and the dusky house-fronts more rarely interrupted by specimens of that extraordinary architecture which in Rome passes for sacred. In Florence, in other words, ecclesiasticism is less cheap a commodity and not dispensed in the same abundance at the street-corners. Heaven forbid, at the same time, that I should undervalue the Roman churches, which are for the most part treasure-houses of history, of curiosity, of promiscuous and associational interest. It is a fact, nevertheless, that, after Saint Peter's, I know but one really beautiful church by the Tiber, the enchanting basilica of Saint Mary Major. Many have structural character, some a great *allure*, but as a rule they all lack the dignity of the best of the Florentine temples. Here, the list being immeasurably shorter and the seed less scattered, the principal churches are all beautiful. And yet I went into the Annunziata the other day and sat there for half-an-hour because, forsooth, the gildings and the marbles and the frescoed dome and the great rococo shrine near the door, with its little black jewelled fetish, reminded me so poignantly of Rome. Such is the city properly styled eternal—since it is eternal, at least, as regards the consciousness of the individual. One loves it in its sophistications—though for that matter isn't it all rich and precious sophistication?—better than other places in their purity.

Coming out of the Annunziata you look past the bronze statue of the Grand Duke Ferdinand I. (whom Mr. Browning's heroine used to watch for—in the poem of "The Statue and the Bust"—from the red palace near by), and down a street vista of enchanting picturesqueness. The street is narrow and dusky and filled with misty shadows, and at its opposite end rises the vast bright-coloured side of the Cathedral. It stands up in very much the same mountainous fashion as the far-shining mass of the bigger prodigy at Milan, of which your first glimpse as you leave your hotel is generally through another such dark avenue ; only that, if we talk of mountains, the white walls of Milan must be likened to snow and ice from their base, while those of the Duomo of Florence may be the image of some mighty hillside enamelled with blooming flowers. The big bleak interior here has a naked majesty which, though it may fail of its effect at first, becomes after a while extraordinarily touching. Originally disconcerting, it soon inspired me with a passion. Externally, at any rate, it is one of the loveliest works of man's hands, and an overwhelming proof into the bargain that when elegance belittles grandeur you have simply had a bungling artist.

Santa Croce within not only triumphs here, but would triumph almost anywhere. " A trifle naked if you like," said my irrepressible companion, " but that's what I call architecture, just as I don't call bronze or marble clothes (save under urgent stress of portraiture) statuary." And indeed we are far enough away from the clustering odds and ends borrowed from every art and every province without which the ritually builded thing doesn't trust its spell to work in Rome. The vastness, the lightness, the open spring of the arches at Santa Croce, the beautiful shape of the high and narrow choir, the impression made as of mass without weight and the gravity yet reigning without gloom —these are my frequent delight, and the interest grows with acquaintance. The place is the great Florentine Valhalla, the final home or memorial harbour of the native illustrious dead, but that consideration of it would take me far. It must be confessed moreover that, between his coarsely-imagined statue out in front and his horrible monument in one of the aisles, the author of *The Divine Comedy*, for instance, is just hereabouts rather an extravagant figure. " Ungrateful Florence," declaims Byron. Ungrateful indeed—would she were more so ! the susceptible spirit of the great exile may be still aware enough to exclaim ;

in common, that is, with most of the other immortals sacrificed
on so very large a scale to current Florentine " plastic " facility.
In explanation of which remark, however, I must confine myself
to noting that, as almost all the old monuments at Santa Croce
are small, comparatively small, and interesting and exquisite, so
the modern, well nigh without exception, are disproportionately
vast and pompous, or in other words distressingly vague and vain.
The aptitude of hand, the compositional assurance, with which
such things are nevertheless turned out, constitutes an anomaly
replete with suggestion for an observer of the present state of the
arts on the soil and in the air that once befriended them, taking
them all together, as even the soil and the air of Greece scarce
availed to do. But on this head, I repeat, there would be too
much to say ; and I find myself checked by the same warning at
the threshold of the church in Florence really interesting beyond
Santa Croce, beyond all others. Such, of course, easily, is Santa
Maria Novella, where the chapels are lined and plated with
wonderful figured and peopled fresco-work even as most of those
in Rome with precious inanimate substances. These overscored
retreats of devotion, as dusky, some of them, as eremitic caves
swarming with importunate visions, have kept me divided all
winter between the love of Ghirlandaio and the fear of those
seeds of catarrh to which their mortal chill seems propitious till
far on into the spring. So I pause here just on the praise of that
delightful painter—as to the spirit of whose work the reflections
I have already made are but confirmed by these examples. In
the choir at Santa Maria Novella, where the incense swings and
the great chants resound, between the gorgeous coloured window
and the florid grand altar, he still " goes in," with all his might,
for the wicked, the amusing world, the world of faces and forms
and characters, of every sort of curious human and rare material
thing.

U

VIII

I had always felt the Boboli Gardens charming enough for me to "haunt" them; and yet such is the interest of Florence in every quarter that it took another *corso* of the same cheap pattern as the last to cause me yesterday to flee the crowded streets, passing under that archway of the Pitti Palace which might almost be the gate of an Etruscan city, so that I might spend the afternoon among the mouldy statues that compose with their screens of cypress, looking down at our clustered towers and our background of pale blue hills vaguely freckled with white villas. These pleasure-grounds of the austere Pitti pile, with its inconsequent charm of being so rough-hewn and yet somehow so elegantly balanced, plead with a voice all their own the general cause of the ample enclosed, planted, cultivated private preserve—preserve of tranquillity and beauty and immunity—in the heart of a city; a cause, I allow, for that matter, easy to plead anywhere, once the pretext is found, the large, quiet distributed town-garden, with the vague hum of big grudging boundaries all about it, but with everything worse excluded, being of course the most insolently-pleasant thing in the world. In addition to which, when the garden is in the Italian manner, with flowers rather remarkably omitted, as too flimsy and easy and cheap, and without lawns that are too smart, paths that are too often swept and shrubs that are too closely trimmed, though with a fanciful formalism giving style to its shabbiness, and here and there a dusky ilex-walk, and here and there a dried-up fountain, and everywhere a piece of mildewed sculpture staring at you from a green alcove, and just in the right place, above all, a grassy amphitheatre curtained behind with black cypresses and sloping downward in mossy marble steps—when, I say, the place possesses these attractions, and you lounge there of a soft Sunday afternoon, the racier spectacle of the streets having made your fellow-loungers few and left you to the deep stillness and the shady vistas that lead you wonder where, left you to the insidious irresistible mixture of nature and art, nothing too much of either, only a supreme happy resultant, a divine *tertium quid :* under these conditions, it need scarce be said, the revelation invoked descends upon you.

The Boboli Gardens are not large—you wonder how compact little Florence finds room for them within her walls. But they are scattered, to their extreme, their all-romantic advantage and felicity, over a group of steep undulations between the rugged and terraced palace and a still-surviving stretch of city wall, where the unevenness of the ground much adds to their apparent size. You may cultivate in them the fancy of their solemn and haunted character, of something faint and dim and even, if you like, tragic, in their prescribed, their functional smile ; as if they borrowed from the huge monument that overhangs them certain of its ponderous memories and regrets. This course is open to you, I mention, but it isn't enjoined, and will doubtless indeed not come up for you at all if it isn't your habit, cherished beyond any other, to spin your impressions to the last tenuity of fineness. Now that I bethink myself I must always have happened to wander here on grey and melancholy days. It remains none the less true that the place contains, thank goodness—or at least thank the grave, the infinitely-distinguished traditional *taste* of Florence—no cheerful, trivial object, neither parterres, nor pagodas, nor peacocks, nor swans. They have their famous amphitheatre already referred to, with its degrees or stone benches of a thoroughly aged and mottled complexion and its circular wall of evergreens behind, in which small cracked images and vases, things that, according to association, and with the law of the same quite indefinable, may make as much on one occasion for exquisite dignity as they may make on another for (to express it kindly) nothing at all. Something was once done in this charmed and forsaken circle—done or meant to be done ; what was it, dumb statues, who saw it with your blank eyes? Opposite stands the huge flat-roofed palace, putting forward two great rectangular arms and looking, with its closed windows and its foundations of almost unreduced rock, like some ghost of a sample of a ruder Babylon. In the wide court-like space between the wings is a fine old white marble fountain that never plays. Its dusty idleness completes the general air of abandonment. Chancing on such a cluster of objects in Italy—glancing at them in a certain light and a certain mood—I get (perhaps on too easy terms, you may think) a sense of *history* that takes away my breath. Generations of Medici have stood at these closed windows, embroidered and brocaded according to their period, and held *fêtes champêtres* and floral games on the greensward, beneath the mouldering hemicycle. And the Medici were great people! But what remains of it all now is a mere tone in the air, a faint sigh in the breeze, a vague expression in things, a passive—or call it rather, perhaps, to be fair, a shyly, pathetically responsive—accessibility to the yearning guess. Call it much or call it little, the ineffaceability of this deep stain of experience, it is the interest of old places and the bribe to the brooding analyst. Time has devoured the doers and their doings, but there still hangs about some effect of their passage. We can "lay out" parks on virgin soil, and cause them to bristle with the most expensive importations, but we unfortunately can't scatter abroad again this seed of the eventual human soul of a place—that comes but in its time and takes too long to grow. There is nothing like it when it *has* come.

TUSCAN CITIES

THE cities I refer to are Leghorn, Pisa, Lucca and Pistoia, among which I have been spending the last few days. The most striking fact as to Leghorn, it must be conceded at the outset, is that, being in Tuscany, it should be so scantily Tuscan. The traveller curious in local colour must content himself with the deep blue expanse of the Mediterranean. The streets, away from the docks, are modern, genteel and rectangular ; Liverpool might acknowledge them if it weren't for their clean-coloured, sun-bleached stucco. They are the offspring of the new industry which is death to the old idleness. Of interesting architecture, fruit of the old idleness or at least of the old leisure, Leghorn is singularly destitute. It has neither a church worth one's attention, nor a municipal palace, nor a museum, and it may claim the distinction, unique in Italy, of being the city of no pictures. In a shabby corner near the docks stands a statue of one of the elder Grand-Dukes of Tuscany, appealing to posterity on grounds now vague —chiefly that of having placed certain Moors under tribute. Four colossal negroes, in very bad bronze, are chained to the base of the monument, which forms with their assistance a sufficiently fantastic group ; but to patronise the arts is not the line of the Livornese, and for want of the slender annuity which would keep its precinct sacred this curious memorial is buried in dockyard rubbish. I must add that on the other hand there is a very well-conditioned and, in attitude and gesture, extremely natural and familiar statue of Cavour in one of the city squares, and in another a couple of effigies of recent Grand-Dukes, represented, that is dressed, or rather undressed, in the character of heroes of Plutarch. Leghorn is a city of magnificent spaces, and it was so long a journey from the sidewalk to the pedestal of these images that I never took the time to go and read the inscriptions. And in truth, vaguely, I bore the originals a grudge, and wished to know as little about them as possible; for it seemed to me that as *patres patriæ*, in their degree, they might have decreed that the great blank, ochre-faced piazza should be a trifle less ugly. There is a distinct amenity, however, in any experience of Italy almost anywhere, and I shall probably in the future not be above sparing a light regret to several of the hours of which the one I speak of was composed. I shall remember a large cool bourgeois villa in the garden of a noiseless suburb—a middle-aged Villa Franco (I owe it as a genial pleasant *pension* the tribute of recognition), roomy and stony, as an Italian villa should be. I shall remember that, as I sat in the garden and, looking up from my book, saw through a gap in the shrubbery the red house-tiles against the deep blue sky and the grey underside of the ilex-leaves turned up by the Mediterranean breeze, it was all still quite Tuscany, if Tuscany in the minor key.

If you should naturally desire, in such conditions, a higher intensity, you have but to proceed, by a very short journey, to Pisa—where, for that matter, you will seem to yourself to have hung about a good deal already, and from an early age. Few of us can have had a childhood so unblessed by contact with the arts as that one of its occasional diversions shan't have been a puzzled scrutiny of some alabaster model of the Leaning Tower under a glass cover in a back-parlour. Pisa and its monuments have, in other words, been industriously vulgarised, but it is astonishing how well they have survived the process. The charm of the place is in fact of a high order and but partially foreshadowed by the famous crookedness of its campanile. I felt it irresistibly and yet almost inexpressibly the other afternoon, as I made my way to the classic corner of the city through the warm drowsy air which nervous people come to inhale as a sedative. I was with an invalid companion who had had no sleep to speak of for a fortnight. "Ah! stop the carriage," she sighed, or yawned, as I could feel, deliciously, "in the shadow of this old slumbering palazzo, and let me sit here and close my eyes, and taste for an hour of oblivion." Once strolling over the grass, however, out of which the quartette of marble monuments rises, we awaked responsively enough to the present hour. Most people remember the happy remark of tasteful, old-fashioned Forsyth (who touched a hundred other points in his "Italy" scarce less happily) as to the fact that the four famous objects are "fortunate alike in their society and their solitude." It must be admitted that they are more fortunate in their society than we felt ourselves to be in ours; for the scene presented the animated appearance for which, on any fine spring day, all the choicest haunts of ancient quietude in Italy are becoming yearly more remarkable. There were clamorous beggars at all the sculptured portals, and bait for beggars, in abundance, trailing in and out of them under convoy of loquacious ciceroni. I forget just how I apportioned the responsibility of intrusion, for it was not long before fellow-tourists and fellow-countrymen became a vague, deadened, muffled presence, that of the dentist's last words when he is giving you ether. They suffered mystic disintegration in the dense, bright, tranquil air, so charged with its own messages. The Cathedral and its companions are fortunate indeed in everything—fortunate in the spacious angle of the grey old city-wall which folds about them in their sculptured elegance like a strong protecting arm; fortunate in the broad greensward which stretches from the marble base of Cathedral and cemetery to the rugged foot of the rampart; fortunate in the little vagabonds who dot the grass, plucking daisies and exchanging Italian cries; fortunate in the pale-gold tone to which time and the soft sea-damp have mellowed and darkened their marble plates; fortunate, above all, in an indescribable grace of grouping, half hazard, half design, which insures them, in one's memory of things admired, very much the same isolated corner that they occupy in the charming city.

Of the smaller cathedrals of Italy I know none I prefer to that of Pisa; none that, on a moderate scale, produces more the impression of a great church. It has without so modest a measurability, represents so clean and compact a mass, that you are startled when you cross the threshold at the apparent space it encloses. An architect of genius, for all that he works with colossal blocks and cumbrous pillars, is certainly the most cunning of conjurors. The front of the Duomo is a small pyramidal screen, covered with delicate carvings and chasings, distributed over a series of short columns upholding narrow arches. It might be a sought imitation of goldsmith's work in stone, and the area covered is apparently so small that extreme fineness has been prescribed. How it is therefore that on the inner side of this façade the wall should appear to rise to a splendid height and to support one end of a ceiling as remote in its gilded grandeur, one could almost fancy, as that of St. Peter's; how it is that the nave should stretch away in such solemn vastness, the shallow transepts emphasise the grand impression and the apse of the choir hollow itself out like a dusky cavern fretted with golden stalactites, is all matter for exposition by a keener architectural analyst than I. To sit somewhere against a pillar where the vista is large and the incidents cluster richly, and vaguely revolve these mysteries without answering them, is the best of one's usual enjoyment of a great church. It takes no deep sounding to conclude indeed that a gigantic Byzantine Christ in mosaic, on the concave roof of the choir, contributes largely to the particular impression here as of very old and choice and original and individual things. It has even more of stiff solemnity than is common to works of its school, and prompts to more wonder than ever on the nature of the human mind at a time when such unlovely shapes could satisfy its conception of holiness. Truly pathetic is the fate of these huge mosaic idols, thanks to the change that has overtaken our manner of acceptance of them. Strong the contrast between the original sublimity of their pretensions and the way in which they flatter that free sense of the grotesque which the modern imagination has smuggled even into the appreciation of religious forms. They were meant to yield scarcely to the Deity itself in grandeur, but the only part they play now is to stare helplessly at our critical, our æsthetic patronage of them. The spiritual refinement marking the hither end of a progress hadn't, however, to wait for *us* to signalise it; it found expression three centuries ago in the beautiful specimen of the painter Sodoma on the wall of the choir. This latter, a small Sacrifice of Isaac, is one of the best examples of its exquisite author, and perhaps, as chance has it, the most perfect opposition that could be found in the way of the range of taste to the effect of the great mosaic. There are many painters more powerful than Sodoma—painters who, like the author of the mosaic, attempted and compassed grandeur ; but none has a more persuasive grace, none more than he was to sift and chasten a conception till it should affect one with the sweetness of a perfectly distilled perfume.

Of the patient successive efforts of painting to arrive at the supreme refinement of such a work as the Sodoma the Campo Santo hard by offers a most interesting memorial. It presents a long, blank marble wall to the relative profaneness of the Cathedral close, but within it is a perfect treasure-house of art. This quadrangular defence surrounds an open court where weeds and wild roses are tangled together and a sunny stillness seems to rest consentingly, as if Nature had been won to consciousness of the precious relics committed to her. Something in the quality of the place recalls the collegiate cloisters of Oxford, but it must be added that this is the handsomest compliment to that seat of learning. The open arches of the quadrangles of Magdalen and Christ Church are not of mellow Carrara marble, nor do they offer to sight columns, slim and elegant, that seem to frame the unglazed windows of a cathedral. To be buried in the Campo Santo of Pisa, I may however further qualify, you need only be, or to have more or less anciently been, illustrious, and there is a liberal allowance both as to the character and degree of your fame. The most obtrusive object in one of the long vistas is a most complicated monument to Madame Catalani, the singer, recently erected by her possibly too-appreciative heirs. The wide pavement is a mosaic of sepulchral slabs, and the walls, below the base of the paling frescoes, are encrusted with inscriptions and encumbered with urns and antique sarcophagi. The place is at once a cemetery and a museum, and its especial charm is its strange mixture of the active and the passive, of art and rest, of life and death. Originally its walls were one vast continuity of closely pressed frescoes ; but now the great capricious scars and stains have come to outnumber the pictures, and the cemetery has grown to be a burial-place of pulverised masterpieces as well as of finished lives. The fragments of painting that remain are fortunately the best ; for one is safe in believing that a host of undimmed neighbours would distract but little from the two great works of Orcagna. Most people know the "Triumph of Death" and the "Last Judgment" from descriptions and engravings ; but to measure the possible good faith of imitative art one must stand there and see the painter's howling potentates dragged into hell in all the vividness of his bright hard colouring ; see his feudal courtiers, on their palfreys, hold their noses at what they are so fast coming to ; see his great Christ, in judgment, refuse forgiveness with a gesture commanding enough, really inhuman enough, to make virtue merciless forever. The charge that Michael Angelo borrowed his cursing Saviour from this great figure of Orcagna is more valid than most accusations of plagiarism; but of the two figures one at least could be spared. For direct, triumphant expressiveness these two superb frescoes have probably never been surpassed. The painter aims at no very delicate meanings, but he drives certain gross ones home so effectively that for a parallel to his process one must look to the art of the actor, the emphasising "point"-making mime. Some of his female figures are superb—they represent creatures of a formidable temperament.

There are charming women, however, on the other side of the cloister—in the beautiful frescoes of Benozzo Gozzoli. If Orcagna's work was appointed to survive the ravage of time it is a happy chance that it should be balanced by a group of performances of such a different temper. The contrast is the more striking that in subject the inspiration of both painters is strictly, even though superficially, theological. But Benozzo cares, in his theology, for nothing but the story, the scene and the drama—the chance to pile up palaces and spires in his backgrounds against pale blue skies cross-barred with pearly, fleecy clouds, and to scatter sculptured arches and shady trellises over the front, with every incident of human life going forward lightly and gracefully beneath them. Lightness and grace are the painter's great qualities, marking the hithermost limit of unconscious elegance, after which "style" and science and the wisdom of the serpent set in. His charm is natural fineness; a little more and we should have refinement—which is a very different thing. Like all *les délicats* of this world, as M. Renan calls them, Benozzo has suffered greatly. The space on the walls he originally covered with his Old Testament stories is immense; but his exquisite handiwork has peeled off by the acre, as one may almost say, and the latter compartments of the series are swallowed up in huge white scars, out of which a helpless head or hand peeps forth like those of creatures sinking into a quicksand. As for Pisa at large, although it is not exactly what one would call a mouldering city—for it has a certain well-aired cleanness and brightness, even in its supreme tranquillity—it affects the imagination very much in the same way as the Campo Santo. And, in truth, a city so ancient and deeply historic as Pisa is at every step but the burial-ground of a larger life than its present one. The wide empty streets, the goodly Tuscan palaces—which look as if about all of them there were a genteel private understanding, independent of placards, that they are to be let extremely cheap—the delicious relaxing air, the full-flowing yellow river, the lounging Pisani, smelling, metaphorically, their poppy-flowers, seemed to me all so many admonitions to resignation and oblivion. And this is what I mean by saying that the charm of Pisa (apart from its cluster of monuments) is a charm of a high order. The architecture has but a modest dignity; the lions are few; there are no fixed points for stopping and gaping. And yet the impression is profound; the charm is a moral charm. If I were ever to be incurably disappointed in life, if I had lost my health, my money, or my friends, if I were resigned forevermore to pitching my expectations in a minor key, I should go and invoke the Pisan peace. Its quietude would seem something more than a stillness—a hush. Pisa may be a dull place to live in, but it's an ideal place to wait for death.

Nothing could be more charming than the country between Pisa and Lucca—unless possibly the country between Lucca and Pistoia. If Pisa is dead Tuscany Lucca is Tuscany still living and enjoying, desiring and intending. The town is a charming mixture of antique " character " and modern inconsequence ; and not only the town, but the country—the blooming romantic country which you admire from the famous promenade on the city-wall. The wall is of superbly solid and intensely " toned " brickwork and of extraordinary breadth, and its summit, planted with goodly trees and swelling here and there into bastions and outworks and little open gardens, surrounds the city with a circular lounging-place of a splendid dignity. This well-kept, shady, ivy-grown rampart reminded me of certain mossy corners of England; but it looks away to a prospect of more than English loveliness—a broad green plain where the summer yields a double crop of grain, and a circle of bright blue mountains speckled with high-hung convents and profiled castles and nestling villas, and traversed by valleys of a deeper and duskier blue. In one of the deepest and shadiest of these recesses one of the most "sympathetic" of small watering-places is hidden away yet awhile longer from easy invasion—the Baths to which Lucca has lent its name. Lucca is pre-eminently a city of churches; ecclesiastical architecture being indeed the only one of the arts to which it seems to have given attention. There are curious bits of domestic architecture, but no great palaces, and no importunate frequency of pictures. The Cathedral, however, sums up the merits of its companions and is a singularly noble and interesting church. Its peculiar boast is a wonderful inlaid front, on which horses and hounds and hunted beasts are lavishly figured in black marble over a white ground. What I chiefly appreciated in the grey solemnity of the nave and transepts was the superb effect of certain second-story Gothic arches—those which rest on the pavement being Lombard. These arches are delicate and slender, like those of the cloister at Pisa, and they play their part in the dusky upper air with real sublimity.

At Pistoia there is of course a Cathedral, and there is nothing unexpected in its being, externally at least, highly impressive; in its having a grand campanile at its door, a gaudy baptistery, in alternate layers of black and white marble, across the way, and a stately civic palace on either side. But even had I the space to do otherwise I should prefer to speak less of the particular objects of interest in the place than of the pleasure I found it to lounge away in the empty streets the quiet hours of a warm afternoon. To say where I lingered longest would be to tell of a little square before the hospital, out of which you look up at the beautiful frieze in coloured earthenware by the brothers Della Robbia, which runs across the front of the building. It represents the seven orthodox offices of charity and, with its brilliant blues and yellows and its tender expressiveness, brightens up amazingly, to the sense and soul, this little grey corner of the mediæval city. Pistoia is still mediæval. How grass-grown it seemed, how drowsy, how full of idle vistas and melancholy nooks! If nothing was supremely wonderful, everything was delicious.

1874.

OTHER TUSCAN CITIES

I

I HAD scanted charming Pisa even as I had scanted great
Siena in my original small report of it, my scarce more
than stammering notes of years before; but even if there
had been meagreness of mere gaping vision — which
there in fact hadn't been—as well as insufficiency of public
tribute, the indignity would soon have ceased to weigh on my
conscience. For to this affection I was to return again still
oftener than to the strong call of Siena; my eventual frequentations of Pisa, all merely impressionistic and amateurish as they
might be—and I pretended, up and down the length of the
land, to none other—leave me at the hither end of time with
little more than a confused consciousness of exquisite *quality*
on the part of the small sweet scrap of a place of ancient glory;
a consciousness so pleadingly content to be general and vague
that I shrink from pulling it to pieces. The Republic of Pisa
fought with the Republic of Florence, through the ages, so
ferociously and all but invincibly that what is so pale and
languid in her to-day may well be the aspect of any civil or,
still more, military creature bled and bled and bled at the
"critical" time of its life. She has verily a just languor and
is touchingly anæmic; the past history, or at any rate the
present perfect acceptedness, of which condition hangs about
her with the last grace of weakness, making her state in this
particular the very secret of her irresistible appeal. I was to
find the appeal, again and again, one of the sweetest, tenderest,

even if not one of the fullest and richest impressions possible;
and if I went back whenever I could it was very much as one
doesn't indecently neglect a gentle invalid friend. The couch
of the invalid friend, beautifully, appealingly resigned, has been
wheeled, say, for the case, into the warm still garden, and your
visit but consists of your sitting beside it with kind, discreet,
testifying silences. Such is the figurative form under which
the once rugged enemy of Florence, stretched at her length
by the rarely troubled Arno, to-day presents herself; and I
find my analogy complete even to my sense of the mere mild
séance, the inevitably tacit communion or rather blank inter-
change, between motionless cripple and hardly more incurable
admirer.

The terms of my enjoyment of Pisa scarce departed from
that ideal—slow contemplative perambulations, rather late in
the day and after work done mostly in the particular decent
inn-room that was repeatedly my portion; where the sunny
flicker of the river played up from below to the very ceiling,
which, by the same sign, anciently and curiously raftered and
hanging over my table at a great height, had been colour-
pencilled into ornament as fine (for all practical purposes) as
the page of a missal. I add to this, for remembrance, an
inveteracy of evening idleness and of reiterated ices in front
of one of the quiet cafés—quiet as everything at Pisa is quiet,
or will certainly but in these latest days have ceased to be; one
in especial so beautifully, so mysteriously void of bustle that
almost always the neighbouring presence and admirable chatter
of some group of the local University students would fall upon
my ear, by the half-hour at a time, not less as a privilege,
frankly, than as a clear-cut image of the young Italian mind
and life, by which I lost nothing. I use such terms as "admirable " and " privilege," in this last most casual of connections—
which was moreover no connection at all but what my attention
made it—simply as an acknowledgment of the interest that

might play there through some inevitable thoughts. These were, for that matter, intensely in keeping with the ancient scene and air : they dealt with the exquisite difference between that tone and type of ingenuous adolescence—in the mere relation of charmed *audition*—and other forms of juvenility of whose mental and material accent one had elsewhere met the assault. Civilised, charmingly civilised, were my loquacious neighbours—as how hadn't they to be, one asked oneself, through the use of a medium of speech that is in itself a sovereign saturation ? *There* was the beautiful congruity of the happily-caught impression ; the fact of my young men's general Tuscanism of tongue, which related them so on the spot to the whole historic consensus of things. It wasn't dialect—as it of course easily might have been elsewhere, at Milan, at Turin, at Bologna, at Naples ; it was the clear Italian in which all the rest of the surrounding story was told, all the rest of the result of time recorded ; and it made them delightful, prattling, unconscious men of the particular little constituted and bequeathed world which everything else that was charged with old meanings and old beauty referred to— all the more that their talk was never by any chance of romping games or deeds of violence, but kept flowering, charmingly and incredibly, into eager ideas and literary opinions and philosophic discussions and, upon my honour, vital questions.

They have taken me too far, for so light a reminiscence ; but I claim for the loose web of my impressions at no point a heavier texture. Which comes back to what I was a moment ago saying—that just in proportion as you " feel " the morbid charm of Pisa you press on it gently, and this somehow even under stress of whatever respectful attention. I found this last impulse, at all events, so far as I was concerned, quite contentedly spend itself in a renewed sense of the simple large pacified felicity of such an afternoon aspect as that of the Lung' Arno, taken up or down its course ; whether to within

sight of small Santa Maria della Spina, the tiny, the delicate,
the exquisite Gothic chapel perched where the quay drops
straight, or, in the other direction, toward the melting perspective of the narrow local pleasure-ground, the rather thin
and careless bosky grace of which recedes, beside the stream
whose very turbidity pleases, to a middle distance of hot and
tangled and exuberant rural industry and a proper blue horizon
of Carrara mountains. The Pisan Lung' Arno is shorter and
less featured and framed than the Florentine, but it has the
fine accent of a marked curve and is quite as bravely Tuscan ;
witness the type of river-fronting palace which, in half-a-dozen
massive specimens, the last word of the anciently " handsome,"
are of the essence of the physiognomy of the place. In the
glow of which retrospective admission I ask myself how I came,
under my first flush, reflected in other pages, to fail of justice
to so much proud domestic architecture—in the very teeth
moreover of the fact that I was forever paying my compliments, in a wistful, wondering way, to the fine Palazzo Lan-
franchi, occupied in 1822 by the migratory Byron, and whither
Leigh Hunt, as commemorated in the latter's Autobiography,
came out to join him in an odd journalistic scheme.

Of course, however, I need scarcely add, the centre of my
daily revolution—quite thereby on the circumference—was the
great Company of Four in their sequestered corner ; objects of
regularly recurrent pious pilgrimage, if for no other purpose
than to see whether each would each time again so inimitably
carry itself as one of a group of wonderfully-worked old ivories.
Their charm of relation to each other and to everything else
that concerns them, that of the quartette of monuments, is
more or less inexpressible all round ; but not the least of it,
ever, is in their beautiful secret for taking at different hours
and seasons, in different states of the light, the sky, the wind,
the weather—in different states, even, it used verily to seem to
me, of an admirer's imagination or temper or nerves—different

complexional appearances, different shades and pallors, different glows and chills. I have seen them look almost viciously black, and I have seen them as clear and fair as pale gold. And these things, for the most part, off on the large grassy carpet spread for them, and with the elbow of the old city-wall, not elsewhere erect, respectfully but protectingly crooked about, to the tune of a usual unanimity save perhaps in the case of the Leaning Tower—so abnormal a member of any respectable family this structure at best that I always somehow fancied its three companions, the Cathedral, the Baptistery and the Campo Santo, capable of quiet common understandings, for the major or the minor effect, into which their odd fellow, no hint thrown out to him, was left to enter as he might. If one haunted the place one ended by yielding to the conceit that, beautifully though the others of the group may be said to behave about him, one sometimes caught them in the act of tacitly combining to ignore him—as if he had, after so long, begun to give on their nerves. Or is that absurdity but my shamefaced form of admission that, for all the wonder of him, he finally gave on mine? Frankly—I would put it at such moments—he becomes at last an optical bore or *bêtise*.

II

To Lucca I was not to return often—I was to return only once; when that compact and admirable little city, the very model of a small *pays de Cocagne*, overflowing with everything that makes for ease, for plenty, for beauty, for interest and good example, renewed for me, in the highest degree, its genial and robust appearance. The perfection of this renewal must indeed have been, at bottom, the ground of my rather hanging back from possible excess of acquaintance—with the instinct that so right and rich and rounded a little impression had better be left than endangered. I remember positively saying to myself the second time that no brown-and-gold Tuscan city, even, could *be* as happy as Lucca looked—save always, exactly, Lucca; so that, on the chance of any shade of human illusion in the case, I wouldn't, as a brooding analyst, go within fifty miles of it again. Just so, I fear I must confess, it was this mere face-value of the place that, when I went back, formed my sufficiency; I spent all my scant time—or the greater part, for I took a day to drive over to the Bagni—just gaping at its visible attitude. This may be described as that of simply sitting there, through the centuries, at the receipt of perfect felicity; on its splendid solid seat of russet masonry, that is— for its great republican ramparts of long ago still lock it tight— with its wide garden-land, its ancient appanage or hereditary domain, teeming and blooming with everything that is good and pleasant for man, all about, and with a ring of graceful and noble, yet comparatively unbeneficed uplands and mountains watching it, for very envy, across the plain, as a circle of bigger boys, in the playground, may watch a privileged or pampered smaller one munch a particularly fine apple. Half smothered thus in oil and wine and corn and all the fruits of the earth, Lucca seems fairly to laugh for good-humour, and it's as if one can't say more for her than that, thanks to her putting forward for you a temperament somehow still richer than her heritage, you forgive her at every turn her fortune. She smiles up at you her greeting as you dip into her wide lap, out of which you may select almost any rare morsel whatever. Looking back at my own choice indeed I see it must have suffered a certain embarrassment—that of the sense of too many things; for I scarce remember choosing at all, any more than I recall having had to go hungry. I turned into all the churches—taking care, however, to pause before one of them, though before which I now irrecoverably forget, for verification of Ruskin's so characteristically magnified rapture over the high and rather narrow and obscure hunting-frieze on its front—and in the Cathedral paid my respects at every turn to the greatest of Lucchesi, Matteo Civitale, wisest, sanest, homeliest, kindest of *quattro-cento* sculptors, to whose works the Duomo serves almost as a museum. But my nearest approach to anything so invidious as a discrimination or a preference, under the spell of so felt an equilibrium, must have been the act of engaging a carriage for the Baths.

That inconsequence once perpetrated, let me add, the impression was as right as any other—the impression of the drive through the huge general tangled and fruited *podere* of the countryside; that of the pair of jogging hours that bring the visitor to where the wideish gate of the valley of the Serchio opens. The question after this became quite other; the narrowing, though always more or less smiling gorge that draws you on and on is a different, a distinct proposition altogether, with its own individual grace of appeal and association. It is the association, exactly, that would even now, on this page, beckon me forward, or perhaps I should rather say backward—weren't more than a glance at it out of the question—to a view of that easier and not so inordinately remote past when " people spent the summer " in these perhaps slightly stuffy shades. I speak of that age, I think of it at least, as easier than ours, in spite of the fact that even as I made my pilgrimage the mark of modern change, the railway in construction, had begun to be distinct, though the automobile was still pretty far in the future. The relations and proportions of everything are of course now altered—I indeed, I confess, wince at the vision of the cloud of motor-dust that must in the fine season hang over the whole connection. That represents greater promptness of approach to the bosky depths of Ponte-a-Serraglio and the Bagni Caldi, but it throws back the other time, that of the old jogging relation, of the Tuscan grand-ducal " season " and the small cosmopolite sociability, into quite Arcadian air and the comparatively primitive scale. The " easier " Italy of our infatuated precursors there wears its glamour of facility not through any question of " the development of communications," but through the very absence of the dream of that boon, thanks to which every one (among the infatuated) lived on terms of so much closer intercourse with the general object of their passion. After we had crossed the Serchio that beautiful day we passed into the charming, the amiably tortuous, the thickly umbrageous, valley of the Lima, and then it was that I seemed fairly to remount the stream of time ; figuring to myself wistfully, at the small scattered centres of entertainment—modest inns, pensions and other places of convenience clustered where the friendly torrent is bridged or the forested slopes adjust themselves—what the summer days and the summer rambles and the summer dreams must have been, in the blest place, when "people" (by which I mean the contingent of beguiled barbarians) didn't know better, as we say, than to content themselves with such a mild substitute, such a soft, sweet and essentially elegant apology, for adventure. One wanted not simply to hang about a little, but really to live back, as surely one might have done by staying on, into the so romantically strong, if mechanically weak, Italy of the associations of one's youth. It was a pang to have to revert to the present even in the form of Lucca—which says everything.

III

If undeveloped communications were to become enough for me at those retrospective moments, I might have felt myself supplied to my taste, let me go on to say, at the hour of my making, with great resolution, an attempt on high-seated and quite grandly out-of-the way Volterra : a reminiscence associated with quite a different year and, I should perhaps sooner have bethought myself, with my fond experience of Pisa—inasmuch as it was during a pause under that bland and motionless wing that I seem to have had to organise in the darkness of a summer dawn my approach to the old Etruscan stronghold. The railway then existed, but I rose in the dim small hours to take my train; moreover, so far as that might too much savour of an incongruous facility, the fault was in due course quite adequately repaired by an apparent repudiation of any awareness of such false notes on the part of the town. I may not invite the reader to penetrate with me by so much as a step the boundless backward reach of history to which the more massive of the Etruscan gates of Volterra, the Porta all' Arco, forms the solidest of thresholds; since I perforce take no step myself, and am even exceptionally condemned here to impressionism unashamed. My errand was to spend a Sunday with an Italian friend, a native in fact of the place, master of a house there in which he offered me hospitality; who, also arriving from Florence the night before, had obligingly come on with me from Pisa, and whose consciousness of a due urbanity, already rather overstrained, and still well before noon, by the accumulation of our matutinal vicissitudes and other grounds for patience, met all ruefully at the station the supreme shock of an apparently great desolate world of volcanic hills, of blank, though "engineered," undulations, as the emergence of a road testified, unmitigated by the smallest sign of a wheeled vehicle. The station, in other words, looked out at that time (and I daresay the case hasn't strikingly altered) on a mere bare huge hill-country, by some remote mighty shoulder of which the goal of our pilgrimage, so questionably "served" by the railway, was hidden from view. Served as well by a belated omnibus, a four-in-hand of lame and lamentable quality, the place, I hasten to add, eventually put forth some show of being; after a complete practical recognition of which, let me at once further mention, all the other, the positive and sublime, connections of Volterra established themselves for me without my lifting a finger.

The small shrunken, but still lordly prehistoric city is perched, when once you have rather painfully zigzagged to within sight of it, very much as an eagle's eyrie, oversweeping

the land and the sea ; and to that type of position, the ideal of
the airy peak of vantage, with all accessories and minor features
a drop, a slide and a giddiness, its individual items and elements
strike you at first as instinctively conforming.   This impression
was doubtless after a little modified for me ; there were levels,
there were small stony practicable streets, there were walks and
strolls, outside the gates and roundabout the cyclopean wall, to
the far end of downward-tending protrusions and promontories,
natural buttresses and pleasant terrene headlands, friendly suburban spots (one would call them if the word had less detest-
able references) where games of bowls and overtrellised wine-
tables could put in their note ; in spite of which however my
friend's little house of hospitality, clean and charming and oh so
immemorially Tuscan, was as perpendicular and ladder-like as
so compact a residence could be ; it kept up for me beautifully
—as regards posture and air, though humanly and socially it
rather cooed like a dovecote—the illusion of the vertiginously
" balanced " eagle's nest.   The air, in truth, all the rest of that
splendid day, must have been the key to the promptly-produced
intensity of one's relation to every aspect of the charming
episode ; the light, cool, keen air of those delightful high places,
in Italy, that tonically correct the ardours of July, and which at
our actual altitude could but affect me as the very breath of the
grand local legend.   I might have " had " the little house, our
particular eagle's nest, for the summer, and even on such touching terms ; and I well remember the force of the temptation to
take it, if only other complications had permitted ; to spend the
series of weeks with that admirable *interesting* freshness in my
lungs : interesting, I especially note as the strong appropriate
medium in which a continuity with the irrecoverable but still
effective past had been so robustly preserved.   I couldn't yield,
alas, to the conceived felicity, which had half-a-dozen appealing
aspects ; I could only, while thus feeling how the atmospheric
medium itself made for a positively initiative exhilaration, enjoy

my illusion till the morrow. The exhilaration therefore supplies to memory the whole light in which, for the too brief time, I went about "seeing" Volterra; so that my glance at the seated splendour reduces itself, as I have said, to the merest impressionism; nothing more was to be looked for, on the stretched surface of consciousness, from one breezy wash of the brush. I find there the clean strong image simplified to the three or four unforgettable particulars of the vast rake of the view; with the Maremma, of evil fame, more or less immediately below, but with those islands of the sea, Corsica and Elba, the names of which are sharply associational beyond any others, dressing the far horizon in the grand manner, and the Ligurian coast-line melting northward into beauty and history galore; with colossal uncemented blocks of Etruscan gates and walls plunging you—and by their very interest—into a sweet surrender of any privilege of appreciation more crushing than your general synthetic stare; and with the rich and perfectly arranged museum, an unsurpassed exhibition of monumental treasure from Etruscan tombs, funereal urns mainly, reliquaries of an infinite power to move and charm us still, contributing to this same so resigned, but somehow at the same time so inspired, collapse of the historic imagination under too heavy a pressure, or abeyance of "private judgment" in too unequal a relation.

IV

I remember recovering private judgment indeed in the course of two or three days following the excursion I have just noted; which must have shaped themselves in some sort of consonance with the idea that as we were hereabouts in the very middle of dim Etruria a common self-respect prescribed our somehow profiting by the fact. This kindled in us the spirit of exploration, but with results of which I here attempt no record, so utterly does the whole impression swoon away, for present memory, into vagueness, confusion and intolerable heat. Our self-respect was of the common order, but the blaze of the July sun was, even for Tuscany, of the uncommon; so that the project of a trudging quest for Etruscan tombs in shadeless wastes yielded to its own temerity. There comes back to me nevertheless at the same time, from the mild misadventure, and quite as through this positive humility of failure, the sense of a supremely intimate revelation of Italy in undress, so to speak (the state, it seemed, in which one would most fondly, most ideally, enjoy her); Italy no longer in winter starch and sobriety, with winter manners and winter prices and winter excuses, all addressed to the *forestieri* and the philistines; but lolling at her length, with her graces all relaxed, and thereby only the more natural; the brilliant performer, in short, *en famille*, the curtain down and her salary stopped for the season—thanks to which she is by so much more the easy genius and the good creature as she is by so much less the advertised *prima donna*. She received us nowhere more sympathetically, that is with less ceremony or self-consciousness, I seem to recall, than at Montepulciano, for instance—where it was indeed that the recovery of private judg-ment I just referred to couldn't help taking place. What we were doing, or what we expected to do, at Montepulciano I keep no other trace of than is bound up in a present quite tender consciousness that I wouldn't for the world not have been there. I think my reason must have been largely just in the beauty of the name (for could any beauty be greater?), reinforced no doubt by the fame of the local vintage and the sense of how we should quaff it on the spot. Perhaps we quaffed it too constantly; since the romantic picture reduces itself for me but to two definite appearances; that of the more priggish discrimination so far reasserting itself as to advise me that Montepulciano was dirty, even remarkably dirty; and that of its being not much else be-sides but perched and brown and queer and crooked, and noble withal (which is what almost any Tuscan city more easily than not acquits herself of); all the while she may on such occasions figure, when one looks off from her to the end of dark street-vistas or catches glimpses through high arcades, some big battered, blistered, overladen, overmasted ship, swimming in a violet sea.

If I have lost the sense of what we were doing, that could at all suffer commemoration, at Montepulciano, so I sit helpless before the memory of small stewing Torrita, which we must somehow have expected to yield, under our confidence, a view of shy charms, but which didn't yield, to my recollection, even anything that could fairly be called a breakfast or a dinner. There may have been in the neighbourhood a rumour of Etruscan tombs; the neighbourhood, however, was vast, and that possibility not to be verified, in the conditions, save after due refreshment. Then it was, doubtless, that the question of refreshment so beckoned us, by a direct appeal, straight across country, from Perugia, that, casting consistency, if not to the winds, since alas there were none, but to the lifeless air, we made the sweltering best of our way (and it took, for the distance, a terrible time) to the Grand Hotel of that city. This course shines for me, in the retrospect, with a light even more shameless than that in which my rueful conscience then saw it; since we thus exchanged again, at a stroke, the tousled *bonne fille* of our vacational Tuscany for the formal and figged-out presence of Italy on her good behaviour. We had never seen her conform more to all the proprieties, we felt, than under this aspect of lavish hospitality to that now apparently quite inveterate swarm of pampered *forestieri*, English and Americans in especial, who, having had Roman palaces and villas deliciously to linger in, break the northward journey, when once they decide to take it, in the Umbrian paradise. They were, goodness knows, within their rights, and we profited, as any one may easily and cannily profit at that time, by the sophistications paraded for them; only I feel, as I pleasantly recover it all, that though we had arrived perhaps at the most poetical of watering-places we had lost our finer clue. (The difference from other days was immense, all the span of evolution from the ancient malodorous inn which somehow didn't matter, to that new type of polyglot caravanserai which everywhere insists on mattering—mattering, even in places where other interests abound, so much more than anything else.) That clue, the finer as I say, I would fain at any rate to-day pick up for its close attachment to another Tuscan city or two—for a felt pull from strange little San Gimignano delle belle Torre in especial; by which I mean from the memory of a summer Sunday spent there during a stay at Siena. But I have already superabounded, for mere love of my general present rubric—the real thickness of experience having a good deal evaporated, so that the Tiny Town of the Many Towers hangs before me, not to say, rather, far behind me, after the manner of an object directly meeting the wrong or diminishing lens of one's telescope.

It did everything, on the occasion of that pilgrimage, that it was expected to do, presenting itself more or less in the guise of some rare silvery shell, washed up by the sea of time, cracked and battered and dishonoured, with its mutilated marks of adjustment to the extinct type of creature it once harboured figuring against the sky as maimed gesticulating arms flourished in protest against fate. If the centuries, however, had pretty well cleaned out, vulgarly speaking, this amazing little fortress-town, it wasn't that a mere aching void was bequeathed us, I recognise as I consult a somewhat faded impression; the whole scene and occasion come back to me as the exhibition, on the contrary, of a stage rather crowded and agitated, of no small quantity of sound and fury, of concussions, discussions, vociferations, hurryings to and fro, that could scarce have reached a higher pitch in the old days of the siege and the sortie. San Gimignano affected me, to a certainty, as not dead, I mean, but as inspired with that strange and slightly sinister new life that is now, in case after case, up and down the peninsula, and even in presence of the dryest and most scattered bones, producing the miracle of resurrection. The effect is often—and I find it strikingly involved in this particular reminiscence—that of the buried hero himself positively waking up to show you his bones for a fee, and almost capering about in his appeal to your attention. What has become of the soul of San Gimignano who shall say? —but, of a genial modern Sunday, it is as if the heroic skeleton, risen from the dust, were in high activity, officious for your entertainment and your detention, clattering and changing plates at the informal friendly inn, personally conducting you to a sight of the admirable Santa Fina of Ghirlandaio, as I believe is supposed, in a dim chapel of the Collegiata church; the poor young saint, on her low bed, in a state of ecstatic vision (the angelic apparition is given), accompanied by a few figures and accessories of the most beautiful and touching truth. This image is what has most vividly remained with me, of the day I thus so ineffectually recover; the precious ill-set gem or domestic treasure of Santa Fina, and then the wonderful drive, at eventide, back to Siena: the progress through the darkening land that was like a dense fragrant garden, all fireflies and warm emanations and dimly-seen motionless festoons, extravagant vines and elegant branches intertwisted for miles, with couples and companies of young countryfolk almost as fondly united and raising their voices to the night as if superfluously to sing out at you that they were happy, and above all were Tuscan. On reflection, and to be just, I connect the slightly incongruous loudness that hung about me under the Beautiful Towers with the really too coarse competition for my favour among the young vetturini who lay in wait for my approach, and with an eye to my subsequent departure, on my quitting, at some unremembered spot, the morning train from Siena, from which point there was then still a drive. That onset was of a fine mediæval violence, but the subsiding echoes of it alone must have afterwards borne me company; mingled, at the worst, with certain reverberations of the animated rather than concentrated presence of sundry young sketchers and copyists of my own nationality, which element in the picture conveyed beyond anything else how thoroughly it was all to sit again henceforth in the eye of day. My final vision perhaps was of a sacred reliquary not so much rudely as familiarly and "humorously" torn open. The note had, with all its references, its own interest; but I never went again.

RAVENNA

I WRITE these lines on a cold Swiss mountain-top, shut in by an intense white mist from any glimpse of the under-world of lovely Italy; but as I jotted down the other day in the ancient capital of Honorius and Theodoric the few notes of which they are composed, I let the original date stand for local colour's sake. Its mere look, as I transcribe it, emits a grateful glow in the midst of the Alpine rawness, and gives a depressed imagination something tangible to grasp while awaiting the return of fine weather. For Ravenna was glowing, less than a week since, as I edged along the narrow strip of shadow binding one side of the empty, white streets. After a long, chill spring the summer this year descended upon Italy with a sudden jump and an ominous hot breath. I stole away from Florence in the night, and even on top of the Apennines, under the dull starlight and in the rushing train, one could but sit and pant perspiringly.

At Bologna I found a festa, or rather two festas, a civil and a religious, going on in mutual mistrust and disparagement. The civil, that of the Statuto, was the one fully national Italian holiday as by law established—the day that signalises everywhere over the land at once its achieved and hard-won unification; the religious was a jubilee of certain local churches. The latter is observed by the Bolognese parishes in couples, and comes round for each couple but once in ten years—an arrangement by which the faithful at large insure themselves a liberal recurrence of expensive processions. It wasn't my business to distinguish the sheep from the goats, the pious from the profane, the prayers from the scoffers; it was enough that, melting together under the scorching sun, they filled the admirably solid city with a flood of spectacular life. The combination at one point was really dramatic. While a long procession of priests and young virgins in white veils, bearing tapers, marshalled itself in one of the streets, a review of the King's troops went forward outside the town. On its return a large detachment of cavalry passed across the space where the incense was burning, the pictured banners swaying and the litany being droned, and checked the advance of the little ecclesiastical troop. The long vista of the street, between the porticoes, was festooned with garlands and scarlet and tinsel; the robes and crosses and canopies of the priests, the clouds of perfumed smoke and the white veils of the maidens, were resolved by the hot bright air into a gorgeous medley of colour, across which the mounted soldiers rattled and flashed as if it had been a conquering army trampling on an embassy of propitiation. It was, to tell the truth, the first time an Italian festa had really exhibited to my eyes the genial glow and the romantic particulars promised by song and story; and I confess that those eyes found more pleasure in it than they were to find an hour later in the picturesque on canvas as one observes it in the Pinacoteca. I found myself scowling most unmercifully at Guido and Domenichino.

For Ravenna, however, I had nothing but smiles—grave, reflective, philosophic smiles, I hasten to add, such as accord with the historic dignity, not to say the mortal sunny sadness, of the place. I arrived there in the evening, before, even at drowsy Ravenna, the festa of the Statuto had altogether put itself to bed. I immediately strolled forth from the inn, and found it sitting up awhile longer on the piazza, chiefly at the café door, listening to the band of the garrison by the light of a dozen or so of feeble tapers, fastened along the front of the palace of the Government. Before long, however, it had dispersed and departed, and I was left alone with the grey illumination and with an affable citizen whose testimony as to the manners and customs of Ravenna I had aspired to obtain. I had, borrowing confidence from prompt observation, suggested deferentially that it wasn't the liveliest place in the world, and my friend admitted that it was in fact not a seat of ardent life. But had I seen the Corso? Without seeing the Corso one didn't exhaust the possibilities. The Corso of Ravenna, of a hot summer night, had an air of surprising seclusion and repose. Here and there in an upper closed window glimmered a light; my companion's footsteps and my own were the only sounds; not a creature was within sight. The suffocating air helped me to believe for a moment that I walked in the Italy of Boccaccio, hand-in-hand with the plague, through a city which had lost half its population by pestilence and the other half by flight. I turned back into my inn profoundly satisfied. This at last was the old-world dulness of a prime distillation; this at last was antiquity, history, repose.

The impression was largely confirmed and enriched on the following day; but it was obliged at an early stage of my visit to give precedence to another—the lively perception, namely, of the thinness of my saturation with Gibbon and the other sources of legend. At Ravenna the waiter at the café and the coachman who drives you to the Pine-Forest allude to Galla Placidia and Justinian as to any attractive topic of the hour; wherever you turn you encounter some fond appeal to your historic presence of mind. For myself I could only attune my spirit vaguely to so ponderous a challenge, could only feel I was breathing an air of prodigious records and relics. I conned my guide-book and looked up at the great mosaics, and then fumbled at poor Murray again for some intenser light on the court of Justinian; but I can imagine that to a visitor more intimate with the originals of the various great almond-eyed mosaic portraits in the vaults of the churches these extremely curious works of

Y

art may have a really formidable interest. I found in the place at large, by daylight, the look of a vast straggling depopulated village. The streets with hardly an exception are grass-grown, and though I walked about all day I failed to encounter a single wheeled vehicle. I remember no shop but the little establishment of an urbane photographer, whose views of the Pineta, the great legendary pine-forest just without the town, gave me an irresistible desire to seek that refuge. There was no architecture to speak of; and though there are a great many large domiciles with aristocratic names they stand cracking and baking in the sun in no very comfortable fashion. The houses have for the most part an all but rustic rudeness; they are low and featureless and shabby, as well as interspersed with high garden walls over which the long arms of tangled vines hang motionless into the stagnant streets. Here and there in all this dreariness, in some particularly silent and grassy corner, rises an old brick church with a front more or less spoiled by cheap modernisation, and a strange cylindrical campanile pierced with small arched windows and extremely suggestive of the fifth century. These churches constitute the palpable interest of Ravenna, and their own principal interest, after thirteen centuries of well-intentioned spoliation, resides in their unequalled collection of early Christian mosaics. It is an interest simple, as who should say, almost to harshness, and leads one's attention along a straight and narrow way. There are older churches in Rome, and churches which, looked at as museums, are more variously and richly informing; but in Rome you stumble at every step on some curious pagan memorial, often beautiful enough to make your thoughts wander far from the strange stiff primitive Christian forms.

Ravenna, on the other hand, began with the Church, and all her monuments and relics are harmoniously rigid. By the middle of the first century she possessed an exemplary saint, Apollinaris, a disciple of Peter, to whom her two finest places of worship are dedicated. It was to one of these, jocosely entitled the " new,"

that I first directed my steps. I lingered outside awhile and
looked at the great red, barrel-shaped bell-towers, so rusty, so
crumbling, so archaic, and yet so resolute to ring in another
century or two, and then went in to the coolness, the shining
marble columns, the queer old sculptured slabs and sarcophagi
and the long mosaics that scintillated, under the roof, along the
wall of the nave. San Apollinare Nuovo, like most of its companions, is a magazine of early Christian odds and ends ; fragments
of yellow marble encrusted with quaint sculptured emblems of
primitive dogma ; great rough troughs, containing the bones of
old bishops ; episcopal chairs with the marble worn narrow by
centuries of pressure from the solid episcopal person ; slabs from
the fronts of old pulpits, covered with carven hieroglyphics of an
almost Egyptian abstruseness—lambs and stags and fishes and
beasts of theological affinities even less apparent. Upon all these
strange things the strange figures in the great mosaic panorama
look down, with coloured cheeks and staring eyes, lifelike enough
to speak to you and answer your wonderment and tell you in bad
Latin of the decadence that it was in such and such a fashion
they believed and worshipped. First, on each side, near the
door, are houses and ships and various old landmarks of Ravenna ;
then begins a long procession, on one side, of twenty-two white-
robed virgins and three obsequious magi, terminating in a throne
bearing the Madonna and Child, surrounded by four angels ; on
the other side, of an equal number of male saints (twenty-five,
that is) holding crowns in their hands and leading to a Saviour
enthroned between angels of singular expressiveness. What it is
these long slim seraphs express I cannot quite say, but they have
an odd, knowing, sidelong look out of the narrow ovals of their
eyes which, though not without sweetness, would certainly make
me murmur a defensive prayer or so were I to find myself alone
in the church towards dusk. All this work is of the latter part
of the sixth century and brilliantly preserved. The gold backgrounds twinkle as if they had been inserted yesterday, and here

and there a figure is executed almost too much in the modern manner to be interesting ; for the charm of mosaic work is, to my sense, confined altogether to the infancy of the art. The great Christ, in the series of which I speak, is quite an elaborate picture, and yet he retains enough of the orthodox stiffness to make him impressive in the simpler, elder sense. He is clad in a purple robe, even as an emperor, his hair and beard are artfully curled, his eyebrows arched, his complexion brilliant, his whole aspect such a one as the popular mind may have attributed to Honorius or Valentinian. It is all very Byzantine, and yet I found in it much of that interest which is inseparable, to a facile imagination, from all early representations of our Lord. Practically they are no more authentic than the more or less plausible inventions of Ary Scheffer and Holman Hunt ; in spite of which they borrow a certain value, factitious perhaps but irresistible, from the mere fact that they are twelve or thirteen centuries less distant from the original. It is something that this was the way the people in the sixth century imagined Jesus to have looked ; the image has suffered by so many the fewer accretions. The great purple-robed monarch on the wall of Ravenna is at least a very potent and positive Christ, and the only objection I have to make to him is that though in this character he must have had a full apportionment of divine foreknowledge he betrays no apprehension of Dr. Channing and M. Renan. If one's preference lies, for distinctness' sake, between the old plainness and the modern fantasy, one must admit that the plainness has here a very grand outline.

I spent the rest of the morning in charmed transition between the hot yellow streets and the cool grey interiors of the churches. The greyness everywhere was lighted up by the scintillation, on vault and entablature, of mosaics more or less archaic, but always brilliant and elaborate, and everywhere too by the same deep amaze of the fact that, while centuries had worn themselves away and empires risen and fallen, these little cubes of coloured glass had stuck in their allotted places and kept their freshness. I have no space for a list of the various shrines so distinguished, and, to tell the truth, my memory of them has already become a very generalised and undiscriminated record. The total aspect of the place, its sepulchral stillness, its absorbing perfume of evanescence and decay and mortality, confounds the distinctions and blurs the details. The Cathedral, which is vast and high, has been excessively modernised, and was being still more so by a lavish application of tinsel and cotton-velvet in preparation for the centenary feast of Saint Apollinaris, which befalls next month. Things on this occasion are to be done handsomely, and a fair Ravennese informed me that a single family had contributed three thousand francs towards a month's vesper-music. It seemed to me hereupon that I should like in the August twilight to wander into the quiet nave of San Apollinare, and look up at the great mosaics through the resonance of some fine chanting. I remember distinctly enough, however, the tall basilica of San Vitale, of octagonal shape, like an exchange or custom-house— modelled, I believe, upon Saint Sophia at Constantinople. It has a great span of height and a great solemnity, as well as a choir densely pictured over on arch and apse with mosaics of the time of Justinian. These are regular pictures, full of movement, gesture and perspective, and just enough sobered in hue by time to bring home their remoteness. In the middle of the church, under the great dome, sat an artist whom I envied, making at an effective angle a study of the choir and its broken lights, its decorated altar and its encrusted twinkling walls. The picture, when finished, will hang, I suppose, on the library wall of some person of taste; but even if it is much better than is probable— I didn't look at it—all his taste won't tell the owner, unless he has been there, in just what a soundless, mouldering, out-of-the-way corner of old Italy it was painted. An even better place for an artist fond of dusky architectural nooks, except that here the dusk is excessive and he would hardly be able to tell his green from his red, is the extraordinary little church of the Santi

Nazaro e Celso, otherwise known as the mausoleum of Galla
Placidia. This is perhaps on the whole the spot in Ravenna
where the impression is of most sovereign authority and most
thrilling force. It consists of a narrow low-browed cave, shaped
like a Latin cross, every inch of which except the floor is covered
with dense symbolic mosaics. Before you and on each side,
through the thick brown light, loom three enormous barbaric
sarcophagi, containing the remains of potentates of the Lower
Empire. It is as if history had burrowed under ground to escape
from research and you had fairly run it to earth. On the right
lie the ashes of the Emperor Honorius, and in the middle those
of his sister, Galla Placidia, a lady who, I believe, had great
adventures. On the other side rest the bones of Constantius III.
The place might be a small natural grotto lined with glimmering
mineral substances, and there is something quite tremendous in
being shut up so closely with these three imperial ghosts.
The shadow of the great Roman name broods upon the huge
sepulchres and abides forever within the narrow walls.

But still other memories hang about than those of primitive
bishops and degenerate emperors. Byron lived here and Dante
died here, and the tomb of the one poet and the dwelling of the
other are among the advertised appeals. The grave of Dante, it
must be said, is anything but Dantesque, and the whole precinct
is disposed with that odd vulgarity of taste which distinguishes
most modern Italian tributes to greatness. The author of *The
Divine Comedy* commemorated in stucco, even in a slumbering corner of Ravenna, is not "sympathetic." Fortunately of
all poets he least needs a monument, as he was pre-eminently
an architect in diction and built himself his temple of fame in
verses more solid than Cyclopean blocks. If Dante's tomb is
not Dantesque, so neither is Byron's house Byronic, being a
homely, shabby, two-storied dwelling, directly on the street, with
as little as possible of isolation and mystery. In Byron's time it
was an inn, and it is rather a curious reflection that " Cain " and

the " Vision of Judgment " should have been written at an hotel.
The fact supplies a commanding precedent for self-abstraction to
tourists at once sentimental and literary.   I must declare indeed
that my acquaintance with Ravenna considerably increased my
esteem for Byron and helped to renew my faith in the sincerity
of his inspiration.   A man so much *de son temps* as the author of
the above-named and other pieces can have spent two long years
in this stagnant city only by the help of taking a great deal of
disinterested pleasure in his own genius.   He had indeed a
notable pastime—the various churches are adorned with monuments of ancestral Guicciolis—but it is none the less obvious
that Ravenna, fifty years ago, would have been an intolerably
dull residence to a foreigner of distinction unequipped with
intellectual resources.   The hour one spends with Byron's
memory then is almost compassionate.   After all, one says to
one's self as one turns away from the grandiloquent little slab in
front of his house and looks down the deadly provincial vista of
the empty, sunny street, the author of so many superb stanzas
asked less from the world than he gave it.   One of his diversions
was to ride in the Pineta, which, beginning a couple of miles
from the city, extends some twenty-five miles along the sands of
the Adriatic.   I drove out to it for Byron's sake, and Dante's,
and Boccaccio's, all of whom have interwoven it with their
fictions, and for that of a possible whiff of coolness from the
sea.   Between the city and the forest, in the midst of malarious
rice-swamps, stands the finest of the Ravennese churches, the
stately temple of San Apollinare in Classe.   The Emperor
Augustus constructed hereabouts a harbour for fleets, which
the ages have choked up, and which survives only in the title of
this ancient church.   Its extreme loneliness makes it doubly
impressive.   They opened the great doors for me, and let a
shaft of heated air go wander up the beautiful nave between the
twenty-four lustrous, pearly columns of cipollino marble, and
mount the wide staircase of the choir and spend itself beneath

the mosaics of the vault. I passed a memorable half-hour sitting in this wave of tempered light, looking down the cool grey avenue of the nave, out of the open door, at the vivid green swamps, and listening to the melancholy stillness. I rambled for an hour in the Wood of Associations, between the tall smooth, silvery stems of the pines, and beside a creek which led me to the outer edge of the wood and a view of white sails, gleaming and gliding behind the sand-hills. It was infinitely, it was nobly "quaint," but, as the trees stand at wide intervals and bear far aloft in the blue air but a little parasol of foliage, I suppose that, of a glaring summer day, the forest itself was only the more characteristic of its clime and country for being perfectly shadeless.

1873.

THE SAINT'S AFTERNOON
AND OTHERS

BEFORE and above all was the sense that, with the narrow limits of past adventure, I had never yet had such an impression of what the summer could be in the south or the south in the summer; but I promptly found it, for the occasion, a good fortune that my terms of comparison were restricted. It was really something, at a time when the stride of the traveller had become as long as it was easy, when the seven-league boots positively hung, for frequent use, in the closet of the most sedentary, to have kept one's self so innocent of strange horizons that the Bay of Naples in June might still seem quite final. That picture struck me—a particular corner of it at least, and for many reasons—as the last word; and it is this last word that comes back to me, after a short interval, in a green, grey northern nook, and offers me again its warm, bright golden meaning before it also inevitably catches the chill. Too precious, surely, for us not to suffer it to help us as it may is the faculty of putting together again in an order the sharp minutes and hours that the wave of time has been as ready to pass over as the salt sea to wipe out the letters and words your stick has traced in the sand. Let me, at any rate, recover a sufficient number of such signs to make a sort of sense.

I

Far aloft on the great rock was pitched, as the first note, and indeed the highest, of the wondrous concert, the amazing creation of the friend who had offered me hospitality, and whom, more almost than I had ever envied any one anything, I envied the privilege of being able to reward a heated, artless pilgrim with a revelation of effects so incalculable. There was none but the loosest prefigurement as the creaking and puffing little boat, which had conveyed me only from Sorrento, drew closer beneath the prodigious island—beautiful, horrible and haunted—that does most, of all the happy elements and accidents, towards making the Bay of Naples, for the study of composition, a lesson in the grand style. There was only, above and below, through the blue of the air and sea, a great confused shining of hot cliffs and crags and buttresses, a loss, from nearness, of the splendid couchant outline and the more comprehensive mass, and an opportunity—oh, not lost, I assure you—to sit and meditate, even moralise, on the empty deck, while a happy brotherhood of American and German tourists, including, of course, many sisters, scrambled down into little waiting, rocking tubs and, after a few strokes, popped systematically into the small orifice of the Blue Grotto. There was an appreciable moment when they were all lost to view in that receptacle, the daily " psychological " moment during which it must so often befall the recalcitrant observer on the deserted deck to find himself aware of how delightful it might be if none of them should come out again. The charm, the fascination of the idea is not a little—though also not wholly—in the fact that, as the wave rises over the aperture, there is the most encouraging appearance that they perfectly may not. There it is. There is no more of them. It is a case to which nature has, by the neatest stroke and with the best taste in the world, just quietly attended.

Beautiful, horrible, haunted: that is the essence of what, about itself, Capri says to you—dip again into your Tacitus and see why ; and yet, while you roast a little under the awning and in the vaster shadow, it is not because the trail of Tiberius is ineffaceable that you are most uneasy. The trail of Germanicus in Italy to-day ramifies further and bites perhaps even deeper ; a proof of which is, precisely, that his eclipse in the Blue Grotto is inexorably brief, that here he is popping out again, bobbing enthusiastically back and scrambling triumphantly back. The spirit, in truth, of his effective appropriation of Capri has a broad-faced candour against which there is no standing up, supremely expressive as it is of the well-known "love that kills," of Germanicus's fatal susceptibility. If I were to let myself, however, incline to *that* aspect of the serious case of Capri I should embark on strange depths. The straightness and simplicity, the classic, synthetic directness of the German passion for Italy, make this passion probably the sentiment in the world that is in the act of supplying enjoyment in the largest, sweetest mouthfuls ; and there is something unsurpassably marked in the way that on this irresistible shore it has seated itself to ruminate and digest. It keeps the record in its own loud accents ; it breaks out in the folds of the hills and on the crests of the crags into every manner of symptom and warning. Huge advertisements and portents stare across the bay ; the acclivities bristle with breweries and " restorations " and with great ugly Gothic names. I hasten, of course, to add that some such general consciousness as this may well oppress, under any sky, at the century's end, the brooding tourist who makes himself a prey by staying anywhere, when the gong sounds, "behind." It is behind, in the track and the reaction, that he least makes out the end of it all, perceives that to visit any one's country for any one's sake is more and more to find some one quite other in possession. No one, least of all the brooder himself, is in his own.

II

I certainly, at any rate, felt the force of this truth when, on scaling the general rock with the eye of apprehension, I made out at a point much nearer its summit than its base the gleam of a dizzily-perched white sea-gazing front which I knew for my particular landmark and which promised so much that it would have been welcome to keep even no more than half. Let me instantly say that it kept still more than it promised, and by no means least in the way of leaving far below it the worst of the outbreak of restorations and breweries. There is a road at present to the upper village, with which till recently communication was all by rude steps cut in the rock and diminutive donkeys scrambling on the flints ; one of those fine flights of construction which the great road-making " Latin races " take, wherever they prevail, without advertisement or bombast ; and even while I followed along the face of the cliff its climbing consolidated ledge, I asked myself how I could think so well of it without consistently thinking better still of the temples of beer so obviously destined to enrich its terminus. The perfect answer to that was of course that the brooding tourist is never bound to be consistent. What happier law for him than this very one, precisely, when on at last alighting, high up in the blue air, to stare and gasp and almost disbelieve, he embraced little by little the beautiful truth particularly, on this occasion, reserved for himself, and took in the stupendous picture ? For here above all had the thought and the hand come from far away—even from *ultima Thule*, and yet were in possession triumphant and acclaimed. Well, all one could say was that the way they had felt their opportunity, the divine conditions of the place, spoke of the advantage of some such intellectual perspective as a remote original standpoint alone perhaps can give. If what had finally, with infinite patience, passion, labour, taste, got itself done there, was like some supreme reward of an old dream of Italy, something perfect after long delays, was it not verily in *ultima Thule* that the vow would have been piously enough made and the germ tenderly enough nursed? For a certain art of asking of Italy all she can give, you must doubtless either be a rare *raffiné* or a rare genius, a sophisticated Norseman or just a Gabriele d'Annunzio.

All she can give appeared to me, assuredly, for that day and the following, gathered up and enrolled there : in the wondrous cluster and dispersal of chambers, corners, courts, galleries, arbours, arcades, long white ambulatories and vertiginous points of view. The greatest charm of all perhaps was that, thanks to the particular conditions, she seemed to abound, to overflow, in directions in which I had never yet enjoyed the chance to find her so free. The indispensable thing was therefore, in observation, in reflection, to press the opportunity hard, to recognise that as the abundance was splendid, so, by the same stroke, it was immensely suggestive. It dropped into one's lap, naturally, at the end of an hour or two, the little white flower of its formula : the brooding tourist, in other words, could only continue to brood till he had made out in a measure, as I may say, what was so wonderfully the matter with him. He was simply then in the presence, more than ever yet, of the possible poetry of the personal and social life of the south, and the fun would depend much—as occasions are fleeting—on his arriving in time, in the interest of that imagination which is his only field of sport, at adequate new notations of it. The sense of all this, his obscure and special fun in the general bravery, mixed, on the morrow, with the long, human hum of the bright, hot day and filled up the golden cup with questions and answers. The feast of St. Antony, the patron of the upper town, was the one thing in the air, and of the private beauty of the place, there on the narrow shelf, in the shining, shaded loggias and above the blue gulfs, all comers were to be made free.

III

The church-feast of its saint is of course for Anacapri, as for any self-respecting Italian town, the great day of the year, and the smaller the small "country," in native parlance, as well as the simpler, accordingly, the life, the less the chance for leakage, on other pretexts, of the stored wine of loyalty. This pure fluid, it was easy to feel overnight, had not sensibly lowered its level; so that nothing indeed, when the hour came, could well exceed the outpouring. All up and down the Sorrentine promontory the early summer happens to be the time of the saints, and I had just been witness there of a week on every day of which one might have travelled, through kicked-up clouds and other demonstrations, to a different hot holiday. There had been no bland evening that, somewhere or other, in the hills or by the sea, the white dust and the red glow didn't rise to the dim stars. Dust, perspiration, illumination, conversation—these were the regular elements. "They're very civilised," a friend who knows them as well as they can be known had said to me of the people in general; "plenty of fireworks and plenty of talk—that's all they ever want." That they were "civilised"— on the side on which they were most to show—was therefore to be the word of the whole business, and nothing could have, in fact, had more interest than the meaning that for the thirty-six hours I read into it.

Seen from below and diminished by distance, Anacapri makes scarce a sign, and the road that leads to it is not traceable over the rock; but it sits at its ease on its high, wide table, of which it covers—and with picturesque southern culture as well—as much as it finds convenient. As much of it as possible was squeezed all the morning, for St. Antony, into the piazzetta before the church, and as much more into that edifice as the robust odour mainly prevailing there allowed room for. It was the odour that was in prime occupation, and one could only wonder how so many men, women and children could cram themselves into so much smell. It was surely the smell, thick and resisting, that was least successfully to be elbowed. Meanwhile the good saint, before he could move into the air, had, among the tapers and the tinsel, the opera-music and the pulpit poundings, bravely to snuff it up. The shade outside was hot, and the sun was hot; but we waited as densely for him to come out, or rather to come " on," as the pit at the opera waits for the great tenor. There were people from below and people from the mainland and people from Pomerania and a brass band from Naples. There were other figures at the end of longer strings—strings that, some of them indeed, had pretty well given way and were now but little snippets trailing in the dust. Oh, the queer sense of the good old Capri of artistic legend, of which the name itself was, in the more benighted years—years of the contadina and the pifferaro—a bright evocation! Oh, the echo, on the spot, of each romantic tale. Oh, the loafing painters, so bad and so happy, the conscious models, the vague personalities! The "beautiful Capri girl" was of course not missed, though not perhaps so beautiful as in her ancient glamour, which none the less didn't at all exclude the probable presence—with *his* legendary light quite undimmed—of the English lord in disguise who will at no distant date marry her. The whole thing was there; one held it in one's hand.

The saint comes out at last, borne aloft in long procession and under a high canopy: a rejoicing, staring, smiling saint, openly delighted with the one happy hour in the year on which he may take his own walk. Frocked and tonsured, but not at all macerated, he holds in his hand a small wax puppet of an infant Jesus and shows him to all their friends, to whom he nods and bows: to whom, in the dazzle of the sun he literally seems to grin and wink, while his litter sways and his banners flap and every one gaily greets him. The ribbons and draperies flutter, and the white veils of the marching maidens, the music blares and the guns go off and the chants resound, and it is all as holy and merry and noisy as possible. The procession—down to the delightful little tinselled and bare-bodied babies, miniature St. Antonys irrespective of sex, led or carried by proud papas or brown grandsires—includes so much of the population that you marvel there is such a muster to look on—like the charades given in a family in which every one wants to act. But it is all indeed in a manner one house, the little high-niched island community, and nobody therefore, even in the presence of the head of it, puts on an air of solemnity. Singular and suggestive before everything else is the absence of any approach to our notion of the posture of respect, and this among people whose manners in general struck one as so good and, in particular, as so cultivated. The office of the saint—of which the festa is but the annual reaffirmation—involves not the faintest attribute of remoteness or mystery.

While, with my friend, I waited for him, we went for cool-ness into the second church of the place, a considerable and bedizened structure, with the rare curiosity of a wondrous pic-tured pavement of majolica, the garden of Eden done in large coloured tiles or squares, with every beast, bird and river, and a brave *diminuendo*, in especial, from portal to altar, of perspec-tive, so that the animals and objects of the foreground are big and those of the successive distances differ with much propriety. Here in the sacred shade the old women were knitting, gossip-ing, yawning, shuffling about; here the children were romping and "larking"; here, in a manner, were the open parlour, the nursery, the kindergarten and the conversazione of the poor. This is everywhere the case by the southern sea. I remember near Sorrento a wayside chapel that seemed the scene of every function of domestic life, including cookery and others. The odd thing is that it all appears to interfere so little with that special civilised note—the note of manners—which is so

constantly touched.   It is barbarous to expectorate in the temple
of your faith, but that doubtless is an extreme case.   Is civilisation really measured by the number of things people do respect ?
There would seem to be much evidence against it.   The oldest
societies, the societies with most traditions, are naturally not the
least ironic, the least *blasées*, and the African tribes who take so
many things into account that they fear to quit their huts at
night are not the fine flower.

IV

Where, on the other hand, it was impossible not to feel to
the full all the charming *riguardi*—to use their own good word
—in which our friends *could* abound, was, that afternoon, in
the extraordinary temple of art and hospitality that had been
benignantly opened to me.   Hither, from three o'clock to seven,
all the world, from the small in particular to the smaller and
the smallest, might freely flock, and here, from the first hour to
the last, the huge straw-bellied flasks of purple wine were tilted
for all the thirsty.   They were many, the thirsty, they were
three hundred, they were unending ; but the draughts they
drank were neither countable nor counted.   This boon was
dispensed in a long, pillared portico, where everything was white
and light save the blue of the great bay as it played up from far
below or as you took it in, between shining columns, with your
elbows on the parapet.   Sorrento and Vesuvius were over against
you ; Naples furthest off, melted, in the middle of the picture,
into shimmering vagueness and innocence ; and the long arm of
Posilippo and the presence of the other islands, Procida, the
stricken Ischia, made themselves felt to the left.   The grand air
of it all was in one's very nostrils and seemed to come from
sources too numerous and too complex to name.   It was antiquity in solution, with every brown, mild figure, every note of
the old speech, every tilt of the great flask, every shadow cast

z

by every classic fragment, adding its touch to the impression.
What was the secret of the surprising amenity ?—to the essence
of which one got no nearer than simply by feeling afresh the old
story of the deep interfusion of the present with the past. You
had felt that often before, and all that could, at the most, help
you now was that, more than ever yet, the present appeared to
become again really classic, to sigh with strange elusive sounds
of Virgil and Theocritus. Heaven only knows how little they
would in truth have had to say to it, but we yield to these
visions as we must, and when the imagination fairly turns in its
pain almost any soft name is good enough to soothe it.

It threw such difficulties but a step back to say that the
secret of the amenity was " style "; for what in the world was
the secret of style, which you might have followed up and down
the abysmal old Italy for so many a year only to be still vainly
calling for it ? Everything, at any rate, that happy afternoon,
in that place of poetry, was bathed and blessed with it. The
castle of Barbarossa had been on the height behind ; the villa of
black Tiberius had overhung the immensity from the right ; the
white arcades and the cool chambers offered to every step some
sweet old " piece " of the past, some rounded porphyry pillar
supporting a bust, some shaft of pale alabaster upholding a
trellis, some mutilated marble image, some bronze that had
roughly resisted. Our host, if we came to that, had the secret ;
but he could only express it in grand practical ways. One of
them was precisely this wonderful " afternoon tea," in which
tea only—*that*, good as it is, has never the note of style—was
not to be found. The beauty and the poetry, at all events,
were clear enough, and the extraordinary uplifted distinction ;
but where, in all this, it may be asked, was the element of
" horror " that I have spoken of as sensible ?—what obsession
that was not charming could find a place in that splendid light,
out of which the long summer squeezes every secret and shadow ?
I'm afraid I'm driven to plead that these evils were exactly in

one's imagination, a predestined victim always of the cruel, the fatal historic sense. To make so much distinction, how much history had been needed!—so that the whole air still throbbed and ached with it, as with an accumulation of ghosts to whom the very climate was pitiless, condemning them to blanch for ever in the general glare and grandeur, offering them no dusky northern nook, no place at the friendly fireside, no shelter of legend or song.

V

My friend had, among many original relics, in one of his white galleries—and how he understood the effect and the "value" of whiteness!—two or three reproductions of the finest bronzes of the Naples museum, the work of a small band of brothers whom he had found himself justified in trusting to deal with their problem honourably and to bring forth something as different as possible from the usual compromise of commerce. They had brought forth, in especial, for him, a copy of the young resting, slightly-panting Mercury which it was a pure delight to live with, and they had come over from Naples on St. Antony's eve, as they had done the year before, to report themselves to their patron, to keep up good relations, to drink Capri wine and to join in the tarantella. They arrived late, while we were at supper; they received their welcome and their billet, and I am not sure it was not the conversation and the beautiful manners of these obscure young men that most fixed in my mind for the time the sense of the side of life that, all around, was to come out strongest. It would be artless, no doubt, to represent them as high types of innocence or even of energy—at the same time that, weighing them against *some* ruder folk of our own race, we might perhaps have made bold to place their share even of these qualities in the scale. It was an impression indeed never infrequent in Italy, of which I might, in these days, first have felt the force during a stay, just earlier, with a friend at Sorrento—a friend who had good-naturedly "had in," on his wondrous terrace, after dinner, for the pleasure of the gaping alien, the usual local quartette, violins, guitar and flute, the musical barber, the musical tailor, sadler, joiner, humblest sons of the people and exponents of Neapolitan song. Neapolitan song, as we know, has been blown well about the world, and it is late in the day to arrive with a ravished ear for it. That, however, was scarcely at all, for me, the question : the question, on the Sorrento terrace, so high up in the cool Capri night, was of the present outlook, in the world, for the races with whom it has been a tradition, in intercourse, positively to please.

The personal civilisation, for intercourse, of the musical barber and tailor, of the pleasant young craftsmen of my other friend's company, was something that could be trusted to make the brooding tourist brood afresh—to say more to him in fact, all the rest of the second occasion, than everything else put together. The happy address, the charming expression, the indistinctive discretion, the complete eclipse, in short, of vulgarity and brutality—these things easily became among these people the supremely suggestive note, begetting a hundred hopes and fears as to the place that, with the present general turn of affairs about the globe, is being kept for them. They are perhaps what the races politically feeble have still most to contribute—but what appears to be the happy prospect for the races politically feeble? And so the afternoon waned, among the mellow marbles and the pleasant folk—the purple wine flowed, the golden light faded, song and dance grew free and circulation slightly embarrassed. But the great impression remained and finally was exquisite. It was all purple wine, all art and song, and nobody a grain the worse. It was fireworks and conversation—the former, in the piazzetta, were to come later ; it was civilisation and amenity. I took in the greater picture, but I lost nothing else ; and I talked with the contadini about antique sculpture.   No, nobody was a grain the worse ; and I had plenty to think of.   So it was I was quickened to remember that we others, we of my own country, as a race politically *not* weak, had —by what I had somewhere just heard—opened " three hundred ' saloons' " at Manilla.

VI

The "other" afternoons I here pass on to—and I may include in them, for that matter, various mornings scarce less charmingly sacred to memory—were occasions of another and a later year ; a brief but all felicitous impression of Naples itself, and of the approach to it from Rome, as well as of the return to Rome by a different wonderful way, which I feel I shall be wise never to attempt to "improve on."   Let me muster assurance to confess that this comparatively recent and super- latively rich reminiscence gives me for its first train of ineffable images those of a motor-run that, beginning betimes of a splendid June day, and seeing me, with my genial companions, blissfully out of Porta San Paolo, hung over us thus its benediction till the splendour had faded in the lamplit rest of the Chiaja.   "We'll go by the mountains," my friend, of the winged chariot, had said, "and we'll come back, after three days, by the sea ; " which handsome promise flowered into such flawless performance that I could but feel it to have closed and rounded for me, beyond any further rehandling, the long-drawn rather indeed than thick-studded chaplet of my visitations of Naples—from the first, seasoned with the highest sensibility of youth, forty years ago, to this last the other day.   I find myself noting with interest—and just to be able to emphasise it is what inspires me with these remarks—that, in spite of the milder and smoother and perhaps, pictorially speaking, considerably emptier, Neapolitan face of things, things in general, of our later time, I recognised in my final impression a grateful, a beguiling serenity. The place is at the best wild and weird and sinister, and yet seemed on this occasion to be seated more at her ease in her immense natural dignity. My disposition to feel that, I hasten to add, was doubtless my own secret ; my three beautiful days, at any rate, filled themselves with the splendid harmony, several of the minor notes of which ask for a place, such as it may be, just here.

Wondrously, it was a clean and cool and, as who should say, quiet and amply interspaced Naples—in tune with itself, no harsh jangle of *forestieri* vulgarising the concert. I seemed in fact, under the blaze of summer, the only stranger—though the blaze of summer itself was, for that matter, everywhere but a higher pitch of light and colour and tradition, and a lower pitch of everything else ; even, it struck me, of sound and fury. The appeal in short was genial, and, faring out to Pompeii of a Sunday afternoon, I enjoyed there, for the only time I can recall, the sweet chance of a late hour or two, the hour of the lengthening shadows, absolutely alone. The impression remains ineffaceable—it was to supersede half-a-dozen other mixed memories, the sense that had remained with me, from far back, of a pilgrimage always here beset with traps and shocks and vulgar importunities, achieved under fatal discouragements. Even Pompeii, in fine, haunt of *all* the cockneys of creation, burned itself, in the warm still eventide, as clear as glass, or as the glow of a pale topaz, and the particular cockney who roamed without a plan and at his ease, but with his feet on Roman slabs, his hands on Roman stones, his eyes on the Roman void, his consciousness really at last of some good to him, could open himself as never before to the fond luxurious fallacy of a close communion, a direct revelation. With which there were other moments for him not less the fruit of the slow unfolding of time ; the clearest of these again being those enjoyed on the terrace of a small island-villa—the island a rock and the villa a wondrous little rock-garden, unless a better term would be perhaps rock-salon, just off the extreme point of Posilippo and where, thanks to a friendliest hospitality, he was to hang ecstatic, through another sublime afternoon, on the wave of a magical wand. Here, as happened, were charming wise, original people even down to delightful amphibious American children, enamelled by the sun of the Bay as for figures of miniature Tritons and Nereids on a Renaissance plaque ; and above all, on the part of the general prospect, a demonstration of the grand style of composition and effect that one was never to wish to see bettered. The way in which the Italian scene on such occasions as this seems to purify itself to the transcendent and perfect *idea* alone—idea of beauty, of dignity, of comprehensive grace, with all accidents merged, all defects disowned, all experience outlived, and to gather itself up into the mere mute eloquence of what has just incalculably *been*, remains forever the secret and the lesson of the subtlest daughter of History. All one could do, at the heart of the overarching crystal, and in presence of the relegated City, the far-trailing Mount, the grand Sorrentine headland, the islands incomparably stationed and related, was to wonder what may well become of the so many other elements of any poor human and social complexus, what might become of any successfully-working or only struggling and floundering civilisation at all, when high Natural Elegance proceeds to take such exclusive charge and recklessly assume, as it were, *all* the responsibilities.

VII

This indeed had been quite the thing I was asking myself all the wondrous way down from Rome, and was to ask myself afresh, on the return, largely within sight of the sea, as our earlier course had kept to the ineffably romantic inland valleys, the great decorated blue vistas in which the breasts of the mountains shine vaguely with strange high-lying city and castle and church and convent, even as shoulders of no diviner line might be hung about with dim old jewels. It was odd, at the end of time, long after those initiations, of comparative youth, that had then struck one as extending the very field itself of felt charm, as exhausting the possibilities of fond surrender, it was odd to have positively a new basis of enjoyment, a new gate of triumphant passage, thrust into one's consciousness and opening to one's use; just as I confess I have to brace myself a little to call by such fine names our latest, our ugliest and most monstrous aid to motion. It is true of the monster, as we have known him up to now, that one can neither quite praise him nor quite blame him without a blush—he reflects so the nature of the company he's condemned to keep. His splendid easy power addressed to noble aims make him assuredly on occasion a purely beneficent creature. I parenthesise at any rate that I know him in no other light—counting out of course the acquaintance that consists of a dismayed arrest in the road, with back flattened against wall or hedge, for the dusty, smoky, stenchy shock of his passage. To no end is his easy power more blest than to that of ministering to the ramifications, as it were, of curiosity, or to that, in other words, of achieving for us, among the kingdoms of the earth, the grander and more genial, the comprehensive and *complete* introduction. Much as was ever to be said for our old forms of pilgrimage—and I am convinced that they are far from wholly superseded—they left, they had to leave, dreadful gaps in our yearning, dreadful lapses in our knowledge, dreadful failures in our energy; there were always things off and beyond, goals of delight and dreams of desire, that dropped as a matter of course into the unattainable, and over to which our wonder-working agent now flings the firm straight bridge. Curiosity has lost, under this amazing extension, its salutary renouncements perhaps; contemplation has become one with action and satisfaction one with desire

—speaking always in the spirit of the inordinate lover of an enlightened use of our eyes. That may represent, for all I know, an insolence of advantage on which there will be eventual heavy charges, as yet obscure and incalculable, to pay, and I glance at the possibility only to avoid all thought of the lesson of the long run, and to insist that I utter this dithyramb but in the immediate flush and fever of the short. For such a beat of time as our fine courteous and contemplative advance upon Naples, and for such another as our retreat northward under the same fine law of observation and homage, the bribed consciousness could only decline to question its security. The sword of Damocles suspended over that presumption, the skeleton at the banquet of extravagant ease, would have been that even at our actual inordinate rate—leaving quite apart "improvements" to come—such savings of trouble begin to use up the world; some hard grain of difficulty being always a necessary part of the composition of pleasure. The hard grain in our old comparatively pedestrian mixture, before this business of our learning not so much even to fly (which might indeed involve trouble) as to be mechanically and prodigiously flown, quite another matter, was the element of uncertainty, effort and patience; the handful of silver nails which, I admit, drove many an impression home. The seated motorist misses the silver nails, I fully acknowledge, save in so far as his æsthetic (let alone his moral) conscience may supply him with some artful subjective substitute; in which case the thing becomes a precious secret of his own.

However, I wander wild—by which I mean I look too far ahead; my intention having been only to let my sense of the merciless June beauty of Naples Bay at the sunset hour and on the island terrace associate itself with the whole inexpressible taste of our two motor-days' feast of scenery. That queer question of the exquisite grand manner as the most emphasised *all* of things—of what it may, seated so predominant in nature, insidiously, through the centuries, let generations and populations "in for," hadn't in the least waited for the special emphasis I speak of to hang about me. I must have found myself more or less consciously entertaining it by the way—since how couldn't it be of the very essence of the truth, constantly and intensely before us, that Italy is really so much the most beautiful country in the world, taking all things together, that others must stand off and be hushed while she speaks? Seen thus in great comprehensive iridescent stretches, it is the incomparable wrought *fusion*, fusion of human history and mortal passion with the elements of earth and air, of colour, composition and form, that constitute her appeal and give it the supreme heroic grace. The chariot of fire favours fusion rather than promotes analysis, and leaves much of that first June picture for me, doubtless, a great accepted blur of violet and silver. The various hours and successive aspects, the different strong passages of our reverse process, on the other hand, still figure for me even as some series of sublime landscape-frescoes —if the great Claude, say, had ever used that medium—in the immense gallery of a palace; the homeward run by Capua, Terracina, Gaeta and its storied headland fortress, across the deep, strong, indescribable Pontine Marshes, white-cattled, strangely pastoral, sleeping in the afternoon glow, yet stirred by the near sea-breath. Thick somehow to the imagination as some full-bodied sweetness of syrup is thick to the palate the atmosphere of that region—thick with the sense of history and the very taste of time; as if the haunt and home (which indeed it is) of some great fair bovine aristocracy attended and guarded by halberdiers in the form of the mounted and long-lanced herdsmen, admirably congruous with the whole picture at every point, and never more so than in their manner of gaily taking up, as with bell-voices of golden bronze, the offered wayside greeting.

There had been this morning among the impressions of our

first hour an unforgettable specimen of that general type—the image of one of those human figures on which our perception of the romantic so often pounces in Italy as on the genius of the scene personified; with this advantage, that as the scene there has, at its best, an unsurpassable distinction, so the physiognomic representative, standing for it all, and with an animation, a complexion, an expression, a fineness and fulness of humanity that appear to have gathered it in and to sum it up, becomes beautiful by the same simple process, very much, that makes the heir to a great capitalist rich. Our early start, our roundabout descent from Posilippo by shining Baiae for avoidance of the city, had been an hour of enchantment beyond any notation I can here recover; all lustre and azure, yet all composition and classicism, the prospect developed and spread, till after extraordinary upper reaches of radiance and horizons of pearl we came at the turn of a descent upon a stalwart young gamekeeper, or perhaps substantial young farmer, who, well-appointed and blooming, had unslung his gun and, resting on it beside a hedge, just lived for us, in the rare felicity of his whole look, during that moment and while, in recognition, or almost, as we felt, in homage, we instinctively checked our speed. He pointed, as it were, the lesson, giving the supreme right accent or final exquisite turn to the immense magnificent phrase; which from those moments on, and on and on, resembled doubtless nothing so much as a page written, by a consummate verbal economist and master of style, in the noblest of all tongues. Our splendid human plant by the wayside had flowered thus into style—and there wasn't to be, all day, a lapse of eloquence, a wasted word or a cadence missed.

These things are personal memories, however, with the logic of certain insistences of that sort often difficult to seize. Why should I have kept so sacredly uneffaced, for instance, our small afternoon wait at tea-time or, as we made it, coffee-time, in the little brown piazzetta of Velletri, just short of the final push on through the flushed Castelli Romani and the drop and home-stretch across the darkening Campagna? We had been dropped into the very lap of the ancient civic family, after the inveterate fashion of one's sense of such stations in small Italian towns. There was a narrow raised terrace, with steps, in front of the best of the two or three local cafés, and in the soft enclosed, the warm waning light of June various benign contemplative worthies sat at disburdened tables and, while they smoked long black weeds, enjoyed us under those probable workings of subtlety with which we invest so many quite unimaginably blank (I dare say) Italian simplicities. The charm was, as always in Italy, in the tone and the air and the happy hazard of things, which made any positive pretension or claimed importance a compara-tively trifling question. We slid, in the steep little place, more or less down hill; we wished, stomachically, we had rather addressed ourselves to a tea-basket; we suffered importunity from unchidden infants who swarmed about our chairs and romped about our feet; we stayed no long time, and "went to see" nothing; yet we communicated to intensity, we lay at our ease in the bosom of the past, we practised intimacy, in short, an intimacy so much greater than the mere accidental and ostensible: the difficulty for the right and grateful expres-sion of which makes the old, the familiar tax on the luxury of loving Italy.

1900–1909.

INDEX

INDEX

THE END